CLIMBING THE SEVEN VOLCANOES

CLIMBING THE SEVEN VOLCANOES

A SEARCH FOR STRENGTH

SOPHIE CAIRNS

AMBERLEY

To the memory of my parents
To my husband Douglas
And to the people of Hong Kong, whose
Lion Rock Spirit will never die.

First published 2020

Amberley Publishing
The Hill, Stroud
Gloucestershire, GL5 4EP

www.amberley-books.com

Copyright © Sophie Cairns, 2020

The right of Sophie Cairns to be identified as
the Author of this work has been asserted in
accordance with the Copyrights, Designs and
Patents Act 1988.

ISBN 978 1 3981 0032 9 (hardback)
ISBN 978 1 3981 0033 6 (ebook)

British Library Cataloguing in Publication Data.
A catalogue record for this book is available
from the British Library.

Typesetting by Aura Technology and Software
Services, India. Printed in the UK.

CONTENTS

PROLOGUE

Most people – sane people – don't try to climb seven giant volcanoes in a row. Especially if they have lungs like stiff new balloons, straight from the packet, that don't fully inflate. And they certainly don't leave home and husband to march through jungles in Papua New Guinea with strange men holding machetes.

We had set out for Mount Giluwe that morning just after dawn. The climb to the summit had been pretty easy, despite the fact that Simpson, our hired guide, was missing a big toe. He'd climbed barefoot, clambering swiftly past me like a Cheshire-grinning spider up the wet rock face. No one had accidentally maimed me with their machete, not even once.

Now it was dark, and the six of us straggled towards the white van parked on the main road through the village. Simpson was enjoying himself the most out of all of us.

'WOO!' he hollered from the front of the group. He jabbed his arms over his head in mountain-conquering triumph. He must have been chewing betel nut again. His front teeth were blood-red.

'HO!' shouted our guide Luke from the back.

'Yay!' I shrieked, feeling jubilant. Simpson didn't speak English and I didn't know any of the local languages, so we communicated in exclamations. We reached the van. I set down my hiking poles and took my flask of water out of my backpack. I felt competent at last, like a real mountaineer. Then I raised the flask to my lips. The inside of the flask smelled like wet dog. My stomach convulsed.

I vomited so abruptly and rudely that I barely had time to brace myself against the van. The others were too busy loading their packs into the back to notice. I stooped in a semi-crouch and purged myself of days of low-level anxieties: fear of murder by cannibalistic tribes; jetlag that engulfed me like a coarse burlap sack; legs that never stopped aching.

You idiot! What made you think you could climb all these volcanoes in four months? There's no way you can pull this off, Asthma Girl.

My stomach churned in agreement. I felt this way whenever I took a step back and thought about the mountains I still had to climb – literally. Over the past two months, I'd fought my way to the top of the highest volcano in Antarctica, North America, South America and now Australasia. But I still had three more to go, and I didn't know if I had it in me to complete my mission. Still crouching, I pulled a blue inhaler out of my pocket, brought it to my lips, and pressed down on the little canister. My lungs loosened as I breathed in the vapour. It smelled like an indoor swimming pool. The smell of the medication resurrected an early memory of those high-ceilinged, antiseptic hospital wards where I spent months of my childhood. The mornings when I woke flailing and scrabbling at my throat because I couldn't breathe. My parents' distressed faces and the doctor pressing his cool stethoscope to my concave chest with my xylophone ribs, saying, 'Sophie's asthma is severe. She mustn't over-exert herself.'

Another memory. My father, dying at age sixty-four. Looking up at me from his hospital bed. The tall Englishman who had read *The Very Hungry Caterpillar* to me so many times and hoisted me onto his shoulders so we could gallop around the garden snorting like horses. The man who had lifted me out of bed with every asthma attack and raced me to hospital.

The father I had lost much too soon.

It made no sense, but my father – or the memory of him – haunted my thoughts more now than when he was alive. Despite my defective lungs and the physical dangers, I was compelled to climb. He was the reason I flogged myself up big mountains year after year. He was the reason I was now in Papua New Guinea, throwing up in the dark by a van. I needed the pain that came with the high altitudes, extreme cold and lack of oxygen. I needed physical pain, because it made my emotional pain tangible and easier to handle. Every gasp of freezing air was my punishment, every exhausting step up to 17,000, 18,000, 19,000 feet and beyond was my penance. Every time I finally emerged at the wind-scoured summit after an all-night battle and stood above the clouds, I felt redeemed.

'Hoo-OOH!!' The ridiculous yodel cut through my thoughts. Simpson was calling me. I steadied myself against the bumper of the van. The nausea had subsided, but now my throat burned. I'd trained for years to get this far. I wasn't going to give up now.

'Hee-eey!' I shouted back. I stood up, forced myself to smile and pushed away the sadness.

Maybe this is what you got for chasing impossible dreams. I splashed some wet-dog water onto my face. No, wait. This is what you got when big dreams grabbed hold of *you*. There was no choice. You just had to do it. No matter how much lunacy was involved.

I

THEN

One morning, when I was very young, my lungs tried to kill me. I had surfaced from a nightmare in which something – some furious animal – was clawing at my throat. I opened my eyes and realised the animal was me. I couldn't breathe. There was an invisible noose around my neck. I thrashed and arched my back and kicked the sunflower-yellow blanket onto the floor. My frantic sips of air wheezed like weak screams. I wanted to punch a hole through my chest, let the air in.

Can't breathe can't breathe can't breathe –

This is my earliest memory. I was three years old.

'Mom. Dad,' I croaked.

My father's smiling, expectant face appeared around the doorway. 'Yes, Soph?' His smile vanished. 'Oh no.' He strode over and lifted me out of bed.

Mom rushed into the room. 'Daughter? What's wrong?' she asked in Chinese. She only spoke to me in Cantonese. It was our language, she always said.

'Can't – breathe,' I whispered.

Mom grabbed her handbag while Dad carried me out the door of the apartment. I remember the clanking of the old elevator as we descended to street level, me still in my father's arms. I remember the sultry, grimy air of Hong Kong in August, and my crazy certainty that all the breathable air in the world had somehow disappeared. I remember Mom waving down a red taxi and the feel of the clammy plastic back seat as we raced to the nearest hospital.

'Can I help you, sir?' The young nurse behind the front desk saw my *gweilo* father – all 6 foot 3 of him – and sat up straighter, used her best English. The hospital entrance was a fluorescent hell. It reeked of linoleum and disinfectant.

'My daughter can't breathe property,' Dad said. 'She started wheezing in her sleep.'

The nurse sprang to her feet. 'Come this way please.'

A long white corridor. Rows of examination rooms with little windows in the doors. Some of the windows were shuttered from the inside to hide the unspeakable. The nurse hurried into one of the rooms. Dad heaved me on to the examination table. Mom leaned over and stroked my back.

'Don't be frightened,' she said. I couldn't speak, so I just nodded.

A young Chinese doctor came in. 'My name is Dr Lee.'

Stethoscope. Thermometer. Cold metal disk against my bony chest. Something tickled the back of my throat. I started to choke on my own mucus.

'Stop! Don't swallow it.' The nurse shoved a clear plastic bag at me. 'Spit into this. We need to run tests on it.'

She held open the plastic bag and I spat out a thick white paste that hung from my mouth like a rope and didn't break off. The more I filled the bag, the more the phlegm welled in my throat.

The nurse handed me rough tissue, pursed her lips and took the repulsive bag away.

'Bring over the oxygen,' Dr Lee said.

Another nurse wheeled a tall vertical canister into the examination room. She attached a long tube to the nozzle and muzzled me with a clammy, rubbery green mask, pulled the strap tight. She turned the valve. The needle of the little gauge jerked to life. There was a hiss as the oxygen came on and flowed into my mouth and nose, forcing open my windpipe and filling my lungs. I sucked it in. I didn't care that it smelled of rubber and chemicals. Suddenly, the room brightened. My mind sharpened. I was safe.

I stayed in hospital for a week. Every night, I drifted to sleep in the soft, soothing air of an oxygen tent. I always liked the moment when the stern overnight nurse pulled the zipper closed over my head and the warm lights came on. It felt like I was lying at the bottom of a swimming pool. My parents always came by after work to say goodnight. Their faces were distorted by the thick plastic tent, but I could see my mother holding back tears, my father masking his worry with a smile.

'Sleep well, Soph. See you tomorrow,' Dad said. The grumpy nurse watched over me all night.

On my last day, Dr Lee removed the intravenous drip and sent me to lie face down in front of cheerful, thick-armed nurses who pounded my back to loosen the phlegm. They cheered when the phlegm surged from my mouth into the plastic tub below.

Dad, Mom and I did this again and again for the next nine years. The asthma attacks struck with the regularity of the changing seasons. That was the story of my childhood: choking and suffocating. Dad scooping me into his arms. The hospital, the oxygen tent, then bronchitis or pneumonia. And antibiotics – so many antibiotics. I spent so much time strapped to an intravenous drip that the crook of my arms bore track marks, as if I were an underage junkie.

This is why no one ever expected me to climb mountains. I was the runt of the family, destined for a sheltered life. For the next thirty years, I lived the life of an indoor pet. My main sport was watching television.

It doesn't matter how safely you play it, though. Sooner or later, disaster strikes and changes you beyond recognition. A crisis always has the most mundane of beginnings, and mine began with a hangover.

~

Oh my God. My head. So much pain. I woke to the sound of a typhoon rattling the window. The hotel room was dark and stuffy; the tropical humidity had pressed its way in. The curtains blocked out the light and it felt late. Probably almost noon. I'd definitely missed the breakfast buffet.

Wincing, I dragged myself to a sitting position. Oh, this was a monster hangover. And I thought hangovers weren't meant to hurt until you turned thirty.

Had I really drunk that much last night? I took a sip of water. Blurry images surfaced. Loud music. Drunk Olympic athletes. Lots of reporters like me, celebrating the end of their reporting assignment. That's right, I was covering the 2008 Beijing Olympics for a top international newswire, and yesterday was the last day of the Games.

There was another reason for this knife-in-my-eye pain. I'd been very happy about something. Aha. Yes. I'd won Story of the Day. For my story on horse shit. Olympic horse shit.

'"How much poop can you scoop?!" That's the headline?' my colleague James shouted at me across the sticky table. The bar throbbed with Abba's *Waterloo* and the burble of the drunken crowd. I laughed and took a swig of beer.

'Yeah, well, I had a moment of inspiration. The editors changed it afterwards though. Bastards.'

'Seriously? They actually ran the story?' James shook his head, as if in despair over the state of journalism today.

'Hey, it's an important topic! I bet a lot of people wonder about this. You fly all these horses in from all over the world to compete in the Olympics. How much shit – I mean manure – do they generate? What do they do with it all?'

'How much, then?'

I took another sip of beer. 'Twenty to thirty tons of horse manure. Per day.'

James looked appalled. 'Twenty to thirty tons of horse manure.'

'Per day.'

'Per day.'

James stared at the table, doing calculations in his head. Then he leaned forward and held out his beer bottle.

'Congratulations Sophie. That is indeed a great news story.'

'Thank you. I thought so.' We clinked bottles.

James and I had been up since 4 a.m. It was well after midnight now. Our eyes were red with fatigue and we were sweaty from Hong Kong's muggy August weather. For the last three weeks, we'd been getting up before dawn to report on the Olympic equestrian sports, which were being held in Hong Kong, as Beijing lacked the facilities. It was my dream assignment. Every morning, we wolfed down a bowl of ramen in our reporters' box high up in the stands by the main arena, watching the workers prepare the grounds under the floodlights. Then we spent hours watching horses from all over the world jump, skip and gallop, followed by a triumphant victory lap after the medals were handed out. It was no surprise that our news agency had sent James and me to cover the horse sports. We both spoke Cantonese and English and knew Hong Kong well. As mixed-race Hong Kong kids, we inhabited that strange space between East and West; constantly changing languages and mentally flipping our cultural assumptions based on whom we were speaking to.

It had taken me ten years to make it home. Ever since my parents and I had left Hong Kong, all I had dreamed about was coming back to become a foreign correspondent. I wanted to witness China's development into a world power, see history in the making.

During the decade I was away I plotted my return and now, at the age of twenty-nine, I knew without reservation that I was exactly where I was supposed to be, at exactly the right time.

I loved it all: the hectic pace of newswire reporting, the palpable ambition in the streets of Hong Kong and Shanghai, the acrid tinge of coal in the air that belied China's centralised industrial might and Communist past, and the new skyscrapers that heralded a country coming into its own on the world stage. I was finally living the life I had laid out for myself long ago. That knowledge brought me relief, as if the years prior to China were just a digression from my destiny. After the Olympics, who knew what I would do next? Become chief correspondent? Bureau chief?

A drunken conga line of world-class athletes sashayed past James and me.

'Hey – are Olympic horse riders meant to drink and smoke?' I shouted.

James shrugged. 'Guess the horses must do all the work.'

I snorted with laughter and almost fell off my bar stool.

I crawled into bed at some ungodly hour, which is why it was nearly midday before I woke up to this beast of a hangover and checked my voicemail. A message from Mom.

'It's 2 a.m. your time.' Her voice was very faint. Or more like hushed, as if she didn't want anyone to overhear. 'Dad's got much worse. I've called an ambulance. We're going to a hospital in Rennes this time. Call when you can.' *Click.*

Shit. I threw off the covers. How could I have left my cell phone off? Some journalist. I called Mom's cell. No answer. They said they were in a hospital. Where again? Rennes? My parents had retired to France a few months earlier. Rennes was the nearest big city, in the north-west of the country. I'd never been to Rennes before. I didn't visit my parents as often as I should. I Googled 'hospitals Rennes' and dialled the first number listed.

'*Centre hospitalier universitaire de Rennes.*'

'*Bonjour*. I'm looking for a Monsieur Taylor? Anthony Richard Taylor?'

'*Un moment, s'il-vous plait.*'

Bingo. It was the right hospital. I fiddled with a pen as the distant ringtone rang on and on. The rain continued to hurl itself at my window.

'Hello?'

'Ma?'

'Sophie. You found us.' Her voice was low and fearful.

'What happened, Mom?'

'Dad fainted again.' I shut my eyes. Not again. Behind my eyelids I saw my father, slumped over in a chair, his face purple.

'This time he didn't come around. I couldn't move him. I had to call an ambulance.'

I pictured Mom picking up the phone with her heart in her mouth and stringing together her meagre French as her husband lay unconscious. She had always been so nervous about living in France. Her greatest fear was having an emergency and being unable to communicate. My chest clenched with worry.

'When can you get here?'

'I'm leaving right now.' I jumped out of bed, swallowed two aspirins and flung everything into a suitcase.

Twenty-four hours and no sleep later, I burst into Dad's hospital room in France.

~

Dad looked fine. A little thinner than I remembered, but awake. Smiling. Relief swelled over me.

'Soph! That was quick.' His face lit up. It always did when I entered the room. Even as a child, I'd never felt him tire of my company, unlike my friends' parents who seemed irritated by their children.

'I took the first flight out.'

I crossed the room to his bed, trundling my wheelie-suitcase behind me. My face felt grimy and my eyes scratchy from the long-haul flight. I pulled the suitcase up against the wall, where it came to a stop with an ill-tempered squeak. Everything was white. White bed, white floor, high white ceiling. That familiar smell of linoleum and disinfectant. My father looked comfortable but completely out of place. His skin was too tanned against the white sheets, his expression too vibrant for this pale room. Behind him, wall-to-wall windows let in a milky light that highlighted the summer-blond streaks in his hair. His face was slimmer than I remembered, but that only made him look younger. Dad's bed looked too short for his frame, as if it struggled to contain him.

'Hello, Dad.' I leaned over and kissed him on the cheek. He beamed at me.

'Ma.'

Mom sat in one of the blue plastic chairs facing the bed. Her leather clutch, the material supple as cloth, lay at her feet like a sleeping dog. I already knew what it contained: red lipstick, Chanel No. 5, a Chinese sandalwood fan, a long-toothed comb and bottle of hairspray to tease her permed hair, Panadol, Ricola mints and eyeliner. In her youth she was all 1980s glamour – shoulder pads and high heels, the outline of her lipstick and red nails always perfect. Next to the leather clutch was a mess of supermarket shopping bags. They contained my father's favourite foods: ham, cheese, V8 juice and Kit Kats. In one bag, her urbane sophisticated past, and in the other, her current French housewife existence.

'Hello, daughter,' she said in Cantonese. Behind her tinted, oversized glasses I could see the shadows under her eyes.

I shot her a *What's going on?* look.

I'll tell you later, her eyes said. I nodded.

'We watched the Olympics opening ceremony on television,' Dad was saying. 'Really very impressive. That's quite a coup for you, Soph, to be sent to cover the Olympics.'

That was my father's way. He was as polite as my mother and I were blunt. I did not want to talk about the Olympics. I had questions, nothing but questions crawling up my throat. What happened? Why did you faint again? What is going on? But no, chit-chat and pleasantries first.

'Yes, the opening ceremony was really impressive,' I muttered. 'The choreography was quite something. All those dancers.'

'Is it alright for you to take time off?'

'It's fine, Dad. It was the last day of the Olympics anyway, so my bureau chief gave me the week off.'

A pause.

'So. Dad. What – what did the doctors say?'

He stared into space. I could see his lawyer's mind working out how much to tell me. He was sifting through evidence, formulating an argument. He opened his mouth to answer.

'We don't know. The doctors won't give us a diagnosis,' Mom said. I turned to her.

'They don't know?'

She shook her head and let out a defeated sigh. Her head sank into her slim right hand. The three of us fell silent. We had heard this before. The last time Dad fainted, Mom took him to the rickety local hospital near their house. My father spent a month in that dump. The corridors were dark and crowded. The air was always piss-warm, which made me think of mould and infection. There was a nasty tension among the staff, as if they hated their jobs. The doctors bounced my father from cardiology to pulmonology to gastroenterology. No one had a clue what was wrong with him, not even after weeks of tests.

'It could be lupus. Probably some kind of autoimmune disease,' the pulmonologist said. I'd flown in from London, where my company had sent me for fast-track training for reporters with high potential. The pulmonologist was a short, greasy-faced man. He stank of cigarette smoke.

'All we can say is, we have ruled out cancer,' he said and walked away. He couldn't wait to get away from us, the three foreigners who spoke imperfect French.

This time, though, it felt more ominous. We were no longer in the sticks but in one of the best hospitals in the country, and still the doctors had no answers. My uneasiness grew. I walked over to the windows and stared out at the hopeless empty fields. It felt like a place that had given up on itself. An overground train clanked in the distance. I pictured the skyscrapers of Hong Kong and Shanghai. The sooner the doctors diagnosed Dad, the sooner we could fix him and the sooner I could return to my real life. I had no place here, and neither did Dad.

No, Dad did not belong to this sterile city of stricken men and women. They shuffled penitently up and down the corridors, bleached with sickness and age, tethered to chemotherapy drips on wheeled stands. The intensive care ward was filled with sinking souls, and my father was not one of them.

I spotted a medical chart tucked into a holder on the wall. I flipped through it and tried to make sense of the doctors' handwriting. Between pages, I glanced up and caught Dad raising his eyebrows at Mom. *What now?* his look said. My mother just shook her head and sighed again.

I'll fix this. Now that I'm here, everything is going to be okay. The thought was bizarre and surprising. I'd never taken care of anyone else before. Dad had always been invincible. I'd always been the sick one.

A frowning nurse bustled into the room.

'You are not meant to read the medical charts. They are for the doctors only.' She held out a bossy hand. I handed the clipboard back to her.

'When can we speak to a doctor?'

She ignored me.

'Do you have any more information on my father's illness?'

'*Non, mademoiselle.*'

The nurse clipped a plastic clothes peg onto Dad's index finger. Red angry digits flashed onto its little screen. She frowned and rushed out. A few seconds later, she wheeled a tall vertical canister into the room. 'Your oxygen level is too low. Put this on.' She handed Dad a rubbery green mask.

Dad stared at her. He didn't seem to understand. The nurse took the clammy, rubbery green mask and muzzled Dad with it, pulled the strap tight. She turned a valve and the needle of the little gauge jerked to life. There was a hiss as the oxygen came on and flowed into the tube into Dad's mask. It was all too familiar, and too, too eerie.

Dad's hand shot out and grabbed my arm. His eyes rolled and the whites grew. He goggled at me mutely as condensation formed and the green plastic turned opaque.

'Comfort your father,' Mom ordered in Chinese. 'Tell him the oxygen will help him.'

I froze in my seat. I'd never seen my father frightened before.

~

Dad did not belong here, but then again he had never really fitted in anywhere. He was English, but had spent his childhood hopping around air bases in post-war West Germany, Yemen, and Wales. My grandfather was a Wing Commander with the Royal Air Force, and my father's childhood memories are not of the green fields of England, but of skating on a frozen lake in Bueckeberg, or the sauna-like heat of Aden, or hearing Welsh whenever he and his sisters went into a store. By the time Dad went to boarding school in England at the age of nine, his allegiance to the country had withered beyond repair.

'It was hard getting used to being in England after travelling so much,' Dad said. 'England was just so boring. I had to get away. There was so much to see in the world.'

So it came as no surprise when my father fled Britain at the age of twenty-six with a borrowed suitcase, a job offer and £500 in debt. He boarded the ship travelling from Southampton to the British colony of Hong Kong, a month-long journey passing through the Indian Ocean and the Suez Canal, his childhood home of Aden and onwards to Bombay, Colombo, Penang and Singapore. He had never been to Hong Kong before, but that hardly mattered.

'I was poorer than a church mouse when I first went out to Hong Kong,' he said. 'But I just couldn't face staying in a small town in England, dealing with old ladies' legal problems.'

In 1970, Hong Kong was still a colonial city of rickshaws and low-rises. People still played cricket on the green by the harbour front in Central, well before the area was overtaken by cars and dual carriageways. Dad fell in love with Hong Kong. He loved the mountains and the water. He loved dim sum. He found the local customs fascinating and often watched the elderly men doing tai chi or taking early walks in the parks with their bird cages. He was intoxicated by the sense of freedom that Hong Kong offered after the stultifying years in Britain. Most of all, he respected the determination of the local population to start a better life than the one they had left behind, whether it had been in Communist China or pre-Thatcher Britain.

Hong Kong was a place to start over. Behind the barbed-wire fence and sentry towers, mainland China was still in the death throes of the Cultural Revolution. Hong Kong was a haven protected by the British, where refugees could start anew and foreigners build their future. Dad meant to go for only three years. He stayed for twenty-three.

Dad moved in with some colleagues from the law firm and became the self-appointed benevolent dictator of the apartment, which meant he took great pleasure in balancing buckets of water on top of half-open doors, apple-pie-ing his flatmates' beds, and generally playing schoolboy pranks. They worked hard, then hit the neon-lit streets of Wan Chai after long days in the office. Johnson, Stokes & Master became a huge law firm, as Hong Kong grew from a small town into an affluent global city.

No one expected my carefree, adventurous father to fall in love with a reverend's daughter. My mother, Penny Lee Ping, a Chinese woman of 5 foot 2, was born in the same year as Dad but had a very different upbringing. Her parents fled China when she was a child, after Japan invaded southern China in the 1940s. She still remembered the sound of Japanese bombs exploding as she hid under a bridge next to her siblings and parents. Even though my grandfather came from a wealthy family, by the time they reached Hong Kong they had lost everything, like most refugees. My mother worked three jobs to help support her family. My grandfather had to start over again too. He became the headmaster of three schools in Hong Kong. My grandmother stayed home to take care of her six children.

'Between teaching piano and studying for my English and law degrees, I never had time to think about having fun, unlike kids these days,' Mom said. 'It was always about survival. That's what it means to be poor.'

In addition to work and study, Mom apparently had to fend off an endless string of suitors. One of them was a priest who got down on his knees in her office and sang 'Born Free' at the top of his lungs.

'Wait, what? Why on earth did he do that?' I asked.

Mom looked more irritated than touched by the memory. 'Oh, you know. He wanted to renounce his priesthood for me.'

I stared at her. 'Really? What did you say?'

She frowned. 'Oh, I wasn't interested in him. I said, "Get up! Get off your knees!" Then I kicked him out.'

My parents met at the age of twenty-seven, after Mom joined my father's law firm. She was his understudy.

'I was rushing up to the entrance to the law firm, when I saw this tall, handsome, gold-haired *gweilo* leaning in the doorway. And I just fell for him. That was the day my destiny changed.'

They started dating after a few months. 'You know, it wasn't easy dating a *gweilo* in those days. Your father had to overcome a lot of resistance. Also, I was twenty-seven, and your grandfather still threw slippers at me if I came home after 10 p.m.'

'Then how did Dad win over Por Por and Gung Gung?'

'Over time, they saw that he was a good person.' She giggled. 'One time, at dinner, he picked up an ice cube, then an orange with his chopsticks. You know how difficult that is. They were very impressed after that.'

Mom fell for Dad's humour and sense of adventure. He respected her dedication to her family and her serious nature. They were married in 1976, and two years later, they had me.

'When you were first born, Dad didn't really know what to make of you,' Mom said. 'Because all new-borns just kind of lie there, like a piece of rice. But then one day he came home from work, and you smiled at him. That was the day Dad fell in love with you. From that day on, you meant more than life to him.'

~

We don't know, we don't know, was all the doctors could tell us. They carried out test after test, and yet every scan came back inconclusive, every blood test told them nothing. My father moved from the intensive care unit to the respiratory ward to the gastroenterology ward. They made him swallow barium, put him through scans and X-rays. Slowly, my tall, strong father grew thinner and thinner.

Every day, Dad peppered the doctors with questions. How long was he going to be here for? What was wrong with him? Why was the food so bad? He badgered the po-faced nurses until they invariably snapped '*Je ne sais pas, monsieur,*' and flounced out of the room.

'Those incompetent *fools*. I've been here for over a week now and they still don't know what's wrong with me,' Dad said. 'They can't just keep me here indefinitely.'

'Richard, I'm sure the doctors know what they're doing.' Mom had been raised not to question authority, whether it was her parents, the government, or the doctors. After all, they were the experts.

Dad's mind was restless. The lawyer in him demanded answers when there were none to be had. After the doctors made their morning rounds, the afternoons weighed heavily on him. He had no patience for television, so Mom and I brought him French newspapers and magazines. The staff seemed to find us odd. I had the feeling that we were the only foreigners in the hospital.

All we could do was wait, and our feeling of dread grew. Mom and I tried to stay practical. We moved into a hotel by the hospital so we wouldn't have to drive for an hour to go home every day. We tried to keep Dad's spirits up by buying his favourite foods from the supermarket. Every morning, we carried plastic bags of ham, cheese, Kit Kats and fresh fruit juice to his hospital room and arranged them nicely on his bedside table. But by this stage, Dad barely ate.

'The food here is awful,' he said at every meal. He grimaced at his tray of roast pork and gravy.

'Really?' My mother cut up a piece and tasted it. 'Seems okay to me,' she said. He shook his head and pushed the plate away. 'It tastes off. It must have gone bad.'

The third time my father complained about the food, I couldn't help myself.

'Dad, you have to eat so you can get stronger. We're trying so hard to get you out of here...' I bit my tongue. My father stared at me – I'd never shouted at him before – and looked down at his tray. Without a word he pulled it back towards him, cut up another piece of pork, and put it in his mouth. He chewed it the way someone chews a piece of paper.

The doctors started to bring medical students on their rounds. Tired, intelligent faces peered at my father as the doctor rattled off his symptoms. Then they would move on to the next patient, waddling out of the room in a huddle like so many technicians in white lab coats.

'You know it's serious when they can't figure out what's wrong with you,' Dad said as he watched them leave.

Then, the next day, they told us. Cancer. Stage four. It had spread from the oesophagus to the liver. It was incurable. They were so sorry.

~

That day, Mom forbade me to cry. 'You cannot cry in front of your father. We are strong people, and we have to keep it together. We cannot let Dad see us fall apart.'

I hid my face in my hands and nodded.

She walked back into Dad's room, leaving me in the corridor to swallow my sobs. Through the crack in the door I could make out my father's thin frame under the hospital blanket. He had a fever. He always felt too cold or too hot.

The nurses ushered Mom back out. She walked towards me, staring at the floor.

'Ma? What happened?'

Her lower lip trembled. 'Dad asked me to tell him what the doctors said. When I didn't answer, he said, 'Am I going to be dead in two weeks?"

Oh God.

'What did you tell him?'

'I didn't say anything. I didn't know what to say.'

'You never talked to Dad about his diagnosis?'

She shook her head. 'I couldn't. I just couldn't. I think the doctors have already told him. I'm pretty sure he knows what's happening.'

Mom stopped sleeping after that. She moved a cot into Dad's room. 'They can try to kick me out, but they'll never succeed,' she said. 'We need to start setting up the house for when Dad comes home. He'll have to move into the downstairs guest room. You should leave now and get some sleep. We'll make a plan in the morning.'

Mom and I lost ourselves in practicalities. Anything to avoid falling apart. Mom made lists of items to purchase and food that Dad would be able to swallow, despite the tumour in his gullet. I applied for a job transfer to France. I booked tickets back to Shanghai so I could pack up my things and give up my apartment. I forced myself to do these tasks, thinking all the while: *Only twelve months left with Dad. Every day will feel like goodbye.*

Dad only ever referred to it as a 'polyp'. Never a 'tumour'. Mom and I did the same. The doctors prescribed Dad a course of chemotherapy. Other than that, the three of us never really talked about what was happening.

~

Ten days after Dad's diagnosis, I flew back to Shanghai to pack up my life. The editors had promised to transfer me to the Paris office, so I could be closer to Dad and still work. I booked a flight for 20 September. I chose the date completely at random. That's how I made the most casual, the most thoughtless, the most destructive decision of my life.

'I'm flying back to Shanghai tomorrow, Dad. I'll be back in a week. I just need to hand in my office card, pack up my things and give back the keys to the flat. Then I'll be back for good.' I sat at his bedside, watching him stare at his lunch.

Dad looked sunken into the hospital bed, as if it was drawing him into its depths. The cancer had sucked the fullness from his face; he now looked far younger than his sixty-four years. The plate of sliced pork and gravy, and the usual tub of Jell-O, lay untouched on the over-bed table on wheels.

I looked down at the plane tickets on my lap. Then I glanced up, wondering why Dad wasn't saying anything. My stomach jerked in shock.

Dad's eyes were glowing. They were lit from within, like candles behind blue glass. It looked entirely unnatural. His eyes were not shining from tears, nor from reflected light. The grey-blue irises verged on cerulean; the dandelion-yellow rings around his pupils were burnished brass. His gaze hit me with a physical force and I had to look away.

'Is – is that okay, Dad?' I said, staring down at my tickets. 'I'll be back soon. Just a week. And Gran will be here tomorrow, so that's good.'

He said nothing. I could feel his gaze but I dared not look up. Something in the air had shifted, subtle as water evaporating off leaves. A crawling, uneasy feeling settled around my neck.

It'll be fine. The doctors said he has twelve more months. You just need to get your things in Shanghai sorted out, and then you'll come right back. After that, you can see him every day.

'Lots of love, Dad.' This was the closest we ever got to saying 'I love you.' I stood up to give him a kiss on the cheek. His eyes were normal again.

'Lots of love, Soph,' he finally said. It was an effort. Dad had been raised by the wartime generation that valued a stiff upper lip. I squeezed his hand and gave him one last smile. Then I grabbed the handle of my suitcase and slipped out of the hospital room. An hour later, I sat on the high-speed train, hurtling towards Paris'

Charles de Gaulle airport. The carriage was full of healthy parents with their healthy kids, smiling and chatting about their carefree lives. The fields of Normandy undulated past the window, but I didn't see them. I felt numb. I couldn't stop thinking about Dad's eyes. Eyes were not supposed to glow like that.

I remembered something a friend had told me about his dying grandmother.

'My grandmother was really ill by this point. She couldn't speak anymore or make any expressions. All she could do was lie in bed,' he'd said. 'But then the oddest thing happened. When I walked in the room, her eyes just... smiled.'

'It gave me such a shock. Her eyes were shining, and I could tell it was pure love.'

~

I arrived in Shanghai the next day and went into the newsroom. After a brief phone call with Human Resources in the privacy of the conference room, I walked out of the building and out of my career.

Three days later, the call came. I never switched off my phone anymore. I was wide awake in bed in my packed-up apartment. I rolled over and looked at the clock. Two a.m.

'The doctors think something is going to... happen... this weekend.' Mom's voice faltered. I booked the next flight back to France. I'd left Dad only five days ago.

For the entire 12-hour flight, I sat unmoving and could not sleep. I landed at Charles de Gaulle airport on Friday evening. There was a payphone by the luggage conveyor belt. I ran over and called Mom. I didn't have a French cell phone.

'How is he?'

'Oh. Not good. Do you want to speak to him?' Mom spoke slowly, as if she hadn't slept in weeks.

'No, not if he's resting. It can wait. I'm grabbing a train now. I'll be there in a couple hours.'

'Okay.'

I ran on to the next train to Rennes without stopping to buy a ticket. At Rennes, I ran out of the station and down into the subway. I travelled a few stops and raced out across the car park towards the hospital. The hospital buildings loomed in brooding congregation under the night sky, as if they had been expecting me. All I could hear was my panting and the scrape of suitcase wheels on tarmac.

The intensive care unit was empty and silent. Visiting hours were long over. I ran down the corridor to my father's door, my shoes smacking the linoleum, suitcase wheels buzzing. A large nurse appeared from a doorway and hissed at me to stop.

'*Mademoiselle!*'

'It's okay! They're expecting me!'

'*Mademoiselle! Stop!*'

My hand closed around the door handle.

I'm here I'm here I made it we're okay now that I'm here everything is going to be okay...

I swung open the door and saw my father. He was sleeping. I padded over to the bed, so as not to wake him. *He looks so different.* The room was so quiet. I looked more closely. My blood turned to ice. I saw my mother. She was sitting on the other side of the bed. She wasn't speaking. She had her head in her hands. 'What's going on?' I asked her in Cantonese. Our language. She looked smaller than usual.

'Dad left us two hours ago,' was all she managed to say.

~

The weeks after Dad died were a numb haze of listless, late mornings and television soaps. We lived underwater, in the murk, in a stupor. The volume of the world had been turned right down. Mom and I holed up in shock in the cold French farmhouse my parents had bought for their retirement. The tiniest tasks – going to the supermarket, even leaving the house – felt frightening, complicated, exhausting. It had all happened so suddenly, so cruelly, that it did not feel real.

Just like that, Dad was gone. Where had he gone? How could it be that, at the moment he turned from a man into a memory, I was not there to comfort him? I had failed him.

I could not get my father's eyes out of my mind. Had he known he was about to die? Was there a place where he still existed? Was he now on some invisible plane – a world behind the world – that I could not see?

Strange and unwelcome questions lodged in my brain like splinters. I lay in bed until midday most days, distracted by my thoughts. Death became a presence in my life for the first time, and now it was here, it overshadowed everything.

Mom and I no longer ate meals at the family table. We no longer bought Dad's favourite foods. We made no plans. My last boxes from Shanghai arrived and remained stacked up in the garage, unopened. Sometimes I went out to stare at the garden, which soon became covered in frost.

After Dad was cremated, I joined the ranks of the unemployed in the little town of Ernée, where my parents had planned to retire.

'What will you do?' Mom asked me a week after Dad died. 'Will you go back to China?'

I sat at the kitchen table and stared into the dried-up coffee grounds in my mug. I wanted my old life back. But there was no way I could leave my mother to fend for herself. There was no way she would move with me to Hong Kong. I could not make the same mistake twice by leaving her. When there's just two of you in a lifeboat, you don't jump ship.

I looked up at Mom. She was drying a bowl with a kitchen towel. I hadn't realised how much weight she'd lost in the past few weeks.

'I'm staying with you,' I said.

She nodded without looking at me, blinked a few times and turned away.

~

When you're unemployed, there are too many hours in the day. And yet, they pass by too quickly to get anything done. I was out in the front yard one hopeless November afternoon, staring across the endless frost-covered fields, when Mom hurried out of the house holding the white cordless phone.

'Phone call for you.' She frowned. 'I think he thought I was you.' She handed me the phone, pulled her thin cardigan more tightly around her shoulders and trudged back to the house.

'Hello?'

'Oh my God, Sophie, I am *so* sorry. I am *so* sorry. I was so rude to your mother just now. You guys totally have the same voice, so when she picked up I was like, "Where the hell you been hiding, you antisocial freak?" and then she said, "Who is this?" and I realised it wasn't you. You got to tell her again that I'm sorry.'

I laughed despite myself. It was so good to hear from a friend from my former life. 'I think she'll forgive you,' I said. 'How are things, Dolan?'

'They're okay. Work's the same, you know how it is. I've been such a bad friend. I've been meaning to call for so long. Sophie, I cannot tell you how sorry I am about your father.'

I looked out over the garden and blinked back tears.

'Thank you.'

'How've you been doing?'

'Oh. I don't know. It's quiet here. It's weird. It's weird not working,' I tried to find the right words. 'Everything is wrong.'

'I know. I really feel for you. When my father died, I kept thinking that it wasn't true, that it was just some sick joke and at any minute someone would say, "Hey, we were just playing a trick on you. It was all a joke. Your father's not dead. Here he is. He's just been hiding."'

My father had been hiding for six weeks. The trees had lost nearly all their leaves now. Talking to Dolan brought me an unexpected surge of relief. He was the first person I had talked to who could relate to the relentless sorrow and the strange thoughts that tormented me.

If I sit very, very quietly, and stare into space for hours, will I see my father again?

If I blast his favourite symphonies until the ground shakes and the speakers crack, will he hear me?

If I stand in the garden, and scream, and scream, and scream his name, will he come back?

Then Dolan said something more truthful than all the awkward condolences and well-meaning 'Time heals all wounds' platitudes I had received.

'Trust me Sophie, I've been there. You're going to be fucked up for at least two years.'

~

'Do you remember the time Dad took us to Èze village and we had lunch in that restaurant with the really rude owner?' Mom asked.

I snapped out of my thoughts and turned to her. Mom sat across the bedroom, propped up in one of the two single beds. I'd moved into her bedroom the day after Dad died. Her skin was wan in the yellow light of the bedside lamp. Outside, stormy clouds crushed the sky lower.

'No? Maybe. I'm not sure.'

'Really? But that was the time he bought you that satchel you loved so much.'

I thought some more. The truth was, I remembered nothing at all. How could that be? I had been there. Had I not been paying attention?

Mom looked down at her duvet.

'You were hardly here for the last five years of Dad's life, so his death will be less painful for you,' she said slowly. 'You'll have less to remember.'

Her comment stabbed me in the gut. I knew she wasn't trying to be hurtful. She was right. For the last five years, I had not been there.

'I know.'

I leaned back in my armchair and searched my mind for memories of Dad. Fuzzy snapshots of him walking in the garden, random snippets of the many conversations we must have had. But mostly, my mind's eye beheld only an erased blankness where memories of my father should have been.

'You're right,' I said. 'I was setting up my career in China. I wasn't here much. My memory isn't very sharp to begin with.'

Mom shook her head, then leaned back on the pillow and stared at the ceiling.

'You see, my problem is that my memory is *too* good. I remember every single night in that hospital, staying with your father. I remember every last thing.'

Behind Mom, on the dresser, was the black urn that contained Dad's ashes. The physical sum total of my father.

I had seen Dad so seldom in the last five years that in my mind, he was reduced to merely a voice on the other end of the telephone line, or the indentation of ink on paper. My chest clenched in envy. I wanted my mother's last memories of Dad. I should have been there. I should have witnessed his final days, however painful they may have been. Even that would have been better than this awful void. I wandered through the flea market of my mind. When it came to my days as a journalist in China, I had a clown-car of memories. Taxi rides down Shanghai's smoggy highways. Interviews with corporate executives. Beery karaoke evenings under neon lights. I could remember it all.

But the other moments? Those snatched holidays with my parents, when I dutifully flew halfway across the world and then counted the days until I returned to Shanghai? Not so much.

I looked at the urn again. We are no more than the sum of our memories, I realised. The flesh and bone, the physical stuff, is all incidental. Dad now lived only in memory.

Why had I always assumed there would be time to make memories later? *As soon as my career is established ... as soon as I get that promotion ... as soon as I'm bureau chief, I'll spend more time with my parents.* Why had I never realised that time was constantly running out? I had not been vigilant. I had lived as if time was my servant, when really it was the opposite.

Somewhere, buried in our minds is a land where memories live, as real and detailed as the shell of a turtle or droplets on a spiderweb. My amnesia was a gulf separating me from Dad, and memories were the bridge. If only I could find a way to remember. Bring Dad back.

'Mom... what were Dad's last words? What did he say?'

Mom looked at me, as if wondering how much to say. Everything I knew of my father's last days was from second-hand accounts, from Mom, my grandmother and my aunt. They had all been there until the end.

'Not much.'

'Oh.'

'But he asked for you. Many times. Even as he was slipping away, he kept saying, "Where's Soph? When is she coming back?"'

I tried not to imagine the scene, but it was too late. I started to cry. For once, Mom didn't stop me.

'It wasn't that Dad didn't want to wait for you, daughter,' she said as I sobbed. 'He just wasn't able to hang on.'

~

One of the oddest things about grief is realising that incredibly, time moves on. My old employer rehired me, at a much lower salary. Mom and I agreed that I would live in Paris, and come back to Normandy every second weekend to visit. I took over the household bills and became financially responsible for my mother. I did not question my new responsibilities. It was my duty as a good Chinese daughter.

Now that I was no longer in China, I no longer cared about journalism. My new bureau chief went from sympathetic to impatient to critical. I had no close friends in Paris. There was no one I could talk to about Dad. I couldn't talk to Mom. She was already overwhelmed by her own emotions. I could feel myself slipping into depression.

One grey, listless weekend in March, I took the train to Normandy to visit Mom. She wasn't doing so well. Neither was I. I curled up on the sofa and leafed idly through *Hello* magazine. The glossy photos of beautiful homes and rich celebrities mocked me.

Next to a shampoo ad, was an article on the British pop singer Cheryl Cole. She had just climbed Mount Kilimanjaro to raise money for charity. I stared at the photo of the dainty singer, looking drained, at the top of Africa's highest mountain. The photo was taken at sunrise; the sky behind her was a startling blood-orange. I considered the photo for a few minutes.

'Ma.'

She was at the other end of the room, ironing.

'Yes.'

'I think I'm going to plan a trip.'

Pause.

'A trip.'

'I think I want to climb Mount Kilimanjaro. In Africa.'

She was quiet for a second as she steered the iron across another napkin, folded it in half, and added it to the stack. I already knew what she would say.

'You want to go to Africa?'

I nodded.

'You want to climb Mount Kilimanjaro? With your asthma?'

I nodded.

'Are you crazy? It's too risky.'

I stared down at the magazine. The evening gloom darkened the room.

'What about taking care of things here? You need to handle the bills. The car needs a new battery. You have responsibilities now, Sophie.'

I stopped listening. I had never climbed a mountain before. I wasn't fit or strong. But I knew I had to do something – something big, something difficult, to wake myself up.

'You really can't risk your health like this, Sophie. It's not safe.'

To hell with it all. All these new responsibilities that I never asked for. To hell with asthma. I just wanted to get away.

'I'm going anyway.' I felt a rush of guilty relief. There was something liberating about knowing all the reasons not to do something, and doing it anyway. I knew I had only two choices. I could let grief destroy me. Or I could fight.

2

SEE YOU AT THE SUMMIT

Boy, did I hate mountain climbing. I could no longer remember a time or place before this dark night. The banshee wind screeched at me to turn around and head back down. The freezing gusts scoured my cheeks and tightened my throat. Every part of my body was in pain. The cold bit through my too-thin trousers and stung the skin around my eyes, easily finding their way past my ill-fitting goggles. I had long ago lost the feeling in my fingertips and smaller toes.

Our summit push had started at 11 p.m. I was operating on less than two hours' sleep and the altitude made my head spin. For seven long hours, I fought the cold and the dark and the pain as I struggled towards the summit of Kilimanjaro. The summit was invisible in these dark hours before dawn. All I could make out was the shuffling line of exhausted climbers above me who were as ill-prepared and unfit as I was. If I raised my head, I could see pinpricks of light on the switchback trails high above. Sometimes, I thought I was looking at head torches, but when I blinked I realised they were stars.

I had eaten nothing for the past several hours, except for a bite of frozen Snickers that nearly cracked my teeth. During our short hourly breaks, I was able to take only one gulp from my water bottle before the oxygen drained from my system and I had to snatch the bottle away, gasping.

Our group of climbers had long ago stopped talking, but now, the mountain guides began to sing. They sang in Swahili. It sounded like a hymn, lyrical and tender. 'Kilimanjaro,' they murmured. 'Kilimanjaro.' As they sang, I inwardly chanted the same words with every swing of my climbing poles.

Don't stop. Don't stop. Don't stop.

I hated every painful step of summit night. It felt like purgatory. But what I felt at the summit changed everything.

At the top of Kilimanjaro, the warmth of the rising sun seeped into my bones, and below us lay a dreaming layer of cloud. Snow draped the slopes and tucked itself around rocky outcrops. The summit didn't seem like the top of a great mountain so much as a jumping-off point to the sky. At that moment I wished with all my heart that I could make a perfect swan dive into the heavens, shedding everything I no longer needed.

I wasn't a spiritual person. Never had been. But in that transcendent moment at the top of Kilimanjaro, I felt something. It was a feeling I recognised. I had felt it in that shocked instant I looked into Dad's eyes and saw they were glowing; I had felt it in those ghostly moments by Dad's bedside in the cold hospital room, hours after he had departed. I felt it now. I felt my father thinking about me. Something indefinable, something beyond. Soul, spirit, I didn't know.

I had climbed through my pain and the noise of the world to a place where Dad still existed. I felt beaten up and exhausted, culpable and forgiven all at the same time. It was too much. My legs shook and all at once I felt close to falling to my knees and sobbing for everything I had lost, and everything never to be.

'Dad, Dad, I'm so sorry.' No one heard me above the shrieking wind. Tears leaked from the corners of my eyes and froze to my face. 'I'm so sorry I didn't say goodbye.'

The wind turned warm and the mauve-brown summit vanished and the clouds became a harbour and all of a sudden I was no longer in Africa but in the New Territories of Hong Kong. I could see the hills, I could smell the harbour air.

My father stood by the edge of the path with his back to me, looking out over Hong Kong harbour and I was nine years old again and waiting for him to finish his cigarette so we could hike back down the hill. He turned and saw me. He smiled. 'You have to look up and out, Soph. Up and out.' He always told me that when I was frightened.

I blinked. The vision was gone. I was back on Kilimanjaro, watching the sunrise.

'Come, we stay fifteen minutes, take photos, then go back to lower altitude,' the mountain guide shouted over the wind. We turned and started the long descent to reality.

3

ENDS OF THE EARTH

Mountain climbing became my release. For the next five years, I threw myself at peak after peak. Mount Elbrus in Russia. Aconcagua in Argentina. Mont Blanc. Every painful summit night, I sweated out my guilt and regret. I didn't care about the physical dangers, or the risk of an asthma attack. Climbing Kilimanjaro had lit a fire in me and all I wanted was to experience that surreal moment again at the top of the mountain and feel that somehow, Dad's spirit was nearby.

I chased that feeling across the world, until one day I found myself in Punta Arenas, a humid little town at the southern tip of Chile, waiting to board a flight for the coldest, most hostile continent on the planet. Antarctica.

The men in the departures hall had the lean, clear-eyed look of greyhounds at the starting gate. They looked nothing like my typical climbing partners of the past five years, those floppy-haired, amiable weekend warriors with day jobs and hidden whiskey flasks. Some of these men had sponsor's logos stitched to their jackets. Others wore their national colours. I had sponsorship too, but I sensed it was nothing like the backing these guys had. I pulled

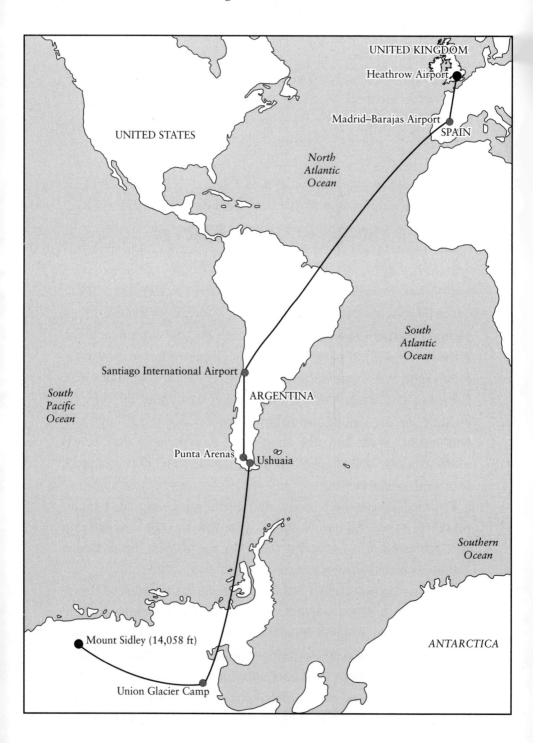

up the collar of my fleece, tried to act as if I belonged. They barely glanced at me as I weaved through the crowd.

About thirty climbers milled around the departure gate, wearing brightly coloured climbing gear and large boots. They looked like lost astronauts among the tanned locals dressed in T-shirts and shorts. The floor-to-ceiling airport windows revealed a cloud bank brooding over the unsettled water between us and Antarctica. I shivered, even though it wasn't cold. Nerves, probably.

'Yes, I ran five marathons last year. I did the Iron Man too,' said an extremely thin man with a French accent. He lifted his lip, as if trying to smile at the other men. Instead, he just kind of bared his teeth at them.

'This year, I come to climb the Vinson Massif in Antarctica.' The Vinson Massif was the highest mountain in Antarctica.

I drifted closer to listen.

'And you? Why are you all going to Antarctica?' the French man asked.

'I am going to climb Mount Vinson too,' said a tanned, stocky man. 'I am doing it for my country.' He smiled a slow, camera-ready smile.

'Ah! You are professional climber?'

'No,' the other man said. 'I am a professional adventurer.'

A pause.

'You are a what?'

'A professional adventurer. You know, I climb mountains, I paraglide, do base jumping. I am on television a lot.' That smile again. 'Just Google me.'

I swallowed. What had I got myself into? These people weren't just here to climb mountains. They were here to set records. They would laugh at me if they knew what I was planning. My right hand closed around the asthma inhaler in my pocket.

By all accounts, I looked like I belonged. I was no longer that fragile girl weeping at the summit of Kilimanjaro. I was strong now. My quads were as thick and dense as hams. As part of my training, I'd carried 25 kilogrammes of water on my back up Ben Nevis in Scotland and Pen y Fan in Wales. I'd gained 4 kilograms of fat and muscle in preparation for this expedition. Temperatures in Antarctica often reached minus 30 degrees Celsius, and a climber could easily burn 6,000 calories a day. Even my asthma had subsided, as if I'd bullied it into submission.

'And you? Why are you going to Antarctica?'

'What?' My thoughts scattered like dandelion seeds. The French man was now looking at me.

'Who, me? I'm – I'm going to climb Mount Sidley.'

Silence.

'Mount Sidley? I do not know this mountain.' He frowned, as if he thought I was making it up.

'It's not climbed very often. Mount Sidley is the highest volcano in Antarctica. It's only slightly lower than the Vinson Massif.'

'Ah. And why do you choose this mountain?'

I started to answer, but he was staring over my shoulder. I'd lost him already. What I should have said was, 'I'm climbing Mount Sidley because I want to set a new world record. I'm going to climb the highest volcano on each continent in the fastest time, from Antarctica to Iran to Papua New Guinea.' But the French man had already turned away to talk to someone more interesting. I was alone in a sea of synthetic jackets and backpacks. Where were my teammates? Where was my mountain guide? There were meant to be five of us, including the guide.

Climbers sat in little groups on the floor of the departures hall and compared their expensive cameras. Everyone seemed so confident, so ready for the challenge.

I walked over to the café that doubled as a souvenir shop. One of the tables was encrusted with climbers. Maybe my teammates were there.

'Hi,' I said. A blonde woman with bright pink lip gloss was taking a selfie. 'Are you guys on the Mount Sidley expedition?'

She squinted at me, as if wondering why I was talking to her.

'No?' She looked back at her phone. I was back in the high school cafeteria, asking to sit with the cool kids.

'So... which expedition are you all on?'

'I'm climbing the Vinson Massif. We all are,' she said without looking up. The man on her left – she was surrounded mostly by men – let out a loud whoop and high-fived the guy sitting opposite. Most of the group wore sunglasses, even though the departures hall wasn't that bright. Their clothes looked so new I half-expected to see the price tags still attached.

'Oh, okay. I'm going to Sidley but I still haven't found my teammates. I'm beginning to wonder if it'll be just me on the expedition,' I smiled. Nobody responded. The blonde woman frowned.

Then it hit me. *They all saw what happened this morning. They think I'm an idiot.*

A few hours earlier, I'd embarrassed myself in front of nearly everyone at my hotel, including a lot of climbers. I'd got a little over-excited, and when that happens I tend to act before thinking things through. I'd just received the call giving the green light to fly out to Antarctica. We had been waiting three days for the weather over the Drake Passage to clear.

'Sophie?' It was someone from Adventure Network International, the company organising the expedition.

'Yes?'

'We've got a weather window. The winds are calmer over the Drake Passage. You packed?'

I looked across the dingy hotel room at the giant red duffel bag on my bed. I'd been packed for days.

'Yes. I'm ready.'

'Okay. Wait for us downstairs.'

Moments later I was in the hotel lobby. Outside the large window, the sultry ocean breeze flapped the Chilean flag. The cable clanked against the flagpole and the waves broke against the embankment. Everyone in the lobby was dressed in light clothing: T-shirts and hiking pants.

I resembled the alarming bastard child of the Michelin man and a giant grape.

I was smothered in a purple goose down onesie as thick as a duvet. Under the plush expedition suit, I wore two pairs of climbing pants, a soft shell jacket, a fleece top, a pair of inner gloves, a pair of outer gloves, and plastic boots. Not to mention thermal underwear. My plastic climbing boots barely closed around my ankles, which were adorned with three layers of socks. I'd put on my entire climbing wardrobe, because we were heading to Antarctica, and Antarctica was a very cold place. In short, I looked like a lunatic wrapped in protective padding on her day out of the asylum.

I sat on the sofa next to some tourists in shorts and T-shirts. They stared at me. I checked my phone and wondered when the bus would arrive.

'You don't need to wear all your climbing gear,' an East European-sounding voice shouted across the lobby.

I looked up to see a tall, blonde mountain guide staring at me. She looked as if she had caught me drinking from the toilet bowl. She was dressed in light clothing, like everyone else.

'What?'

'You do not need to wear your Antarctica clothes yet. Everyone changes on the plane.'

More people turned to stare at me. I did my best to appear thoroughly normal.

'Oh this? No, I just get cold really easily.'

She did not smile.

'I – I was told we needed to put on warm clothes for the flight?'

She just shook her head, turned away and resumed talking to her friend.

Sweat and shame trickled down my temples as I slunk down the hall to the washroom. I felt the stares of the other climbers on my back. The expedition hadn't even begun, and I'd already embarrassed myself. That was the thing about being an amateur climber. An attack of the Stupids is never far away. Amateur climbers are the eager, clumsy puppies of the mountaineering world. We try to climb Everest before we can put on crampons. We create traffic jams beneath the Hillary Step. But everyone has to start somewhere, and the mountaineering package brochures – snowy peaks! A world of adventure! Change your life! – are hard to resist.

Maybe that's why these cool kids in the airport were ignoring me. They'd been in the hotel lobby that morning and seen what happened. I was still trying to work out what to say next when one of the organisers clapped her hands.

'Okay, folks! Weather's clearing. Everyone line up here to board!'

The climbers threw away their soda cans, pulled on their jackets and headed to the gate. The blonde woman strode past me without another glace, so I shrugged and followed the crowd to the boarding gate. I'd probably meet my teammates as soon as I landed in Antarctica. My stomach started churning.

You've put in the training. You can do this. I clenched my calf muscles, unclenched them. They felt like coiled springs, eager for the mountain.

I can do this. My throat tightened. *Can't I?*

The gate opened, and we boarded the monstrous plane to Antarctica.

~

Climbing a mountain is rarely just about climbing. People don't just climb a mountain 'because it's there,' to quote Sir Edmund Hillary.

Like a lot of people, I used to assume that people who climbed high-altitude mountains were self-indulgent adventure junkies. I was wrong. People climb for deeper reasons. Heartbreak is one. A need to prove others wrong is another. For me, it was a bit of both.

The blonde woman and her group sat in the row behind me during the 4-hour flight, looking like a bored J-Crew catalogue. Next to her, the mountain guide who'd shouted at me in the hotel lobby leaned back in her chair and closed her eyes, as if she were commuting to work, which I supposed she was. How could they look so calm? What were their reasons for travelling to Antarctica? I was so excited that I couldn't stop drumming my feet. Antarctica! Literally the end of the Earth! My mission was finally starting and I could barely sit still.

The plane to Antarctica felt massive, reinforced, industrial. A flying tank. The 200-ton Ilyushin-76 was an ex-Soviet aircraft designed to transport heavy machinery to remote corners of the USSR. Now, it ferried mountain climbers over the Drake Passage to Antarctica. Our route took us from Punta Arenas across the Strait of Magellan to refuel in Ushuaia, and over the infamous Drake Passage to the interior of the icy continent.

The high-domed hull resembled the stomach of a whale that had swallowed up a gaggle of climbers and a grumpy Russian crew. It had only a few rows of seats for passengers. Otherwise, it carried mostly equipment, including a big yellow truck strapped down behind the rows of seats. It trembled with the plane's vibrations, threatening to break loose at any moment. I shifted in my seat and pushed my ear plugs further in. Our only window onto reality was a small LED screen mounted at the front. Underneath the screen sat a dour, heavyset man, the Load Master, in a military jumpsuit. He sat on an odd little platform at right angles to us and muttered into his headset. The skin around my eyes tingled with the increasing cold. I pulled the zip of my fleece up over my chin and shoved my hands into my armpits.

The LED screen blinked and the vague green landscapes gave way to an eerie grey. We were over the Drake Passage. I imagined the brutal winds and 100-foot waves below us, now reduced to a two-dimensional rectangle of colour. Grey gave way to white, and everyone cheered and clapped. We had crossed over.

There was a jolt and a lurch and our engines screamed as we hurtled down the blue-ice runway. The only way the plane could stop was by reversing its engines, like hairdryers against the wind. My knuckles turned white as we skated and screamed to a halt under the fierce 2 a.m. sunshine of Antarctica.

The Load Master jumped to his feet and cranked open the hatch. It gave way with a clank, letting in bright daylight and icy air.

'All right!' someone shouted. People gave each other high fives. The French man leaped up in the row behind me, clapped his hands together and grinned. Everyone was standing up, gathering their mittens and woollen hats, filming and taking photos with their cell phones. I put on my puffy purple onesie again, and this time no one thought I was crazy. The outside temperature must have been around minus 20 degrees Celsius. One by one, we climbed down the metal ladder onto the ice runway.

At first glance, it looked like we had landed in a binary world of blue and white. The deep blue sky was enormous. It felt not so much like the bottom of the planet than the bottom of the ocean – the untouched snow was our seabed, everything else was sky. Then I turned slightly to the right and saw the white-and-charcoal Ellsworth Mountains, which looked triangular, like sections of Toblerone. Their gritty slopes peeked out from under a blanket of snow. The sun flashed off the ice runway and blinded me. The beauty of it all was overwhelming. I was so overcome with the beauty around me that I nearly fell off the metal ladder onto my backside.

'Okay everyone, welcome to Antarctica! These snowcats will take you to Union Glacier Camp.' The woman with the clipboard waved at three large orange jeeps with oversized tyres. I scuttled across the ice and climbed in.

Union Glacier Camp is the only privately run concession in Antarctica. It is located in west Antarctica near the Heritage Range, not far from the Ellsworth Mountains. During the Antarctic winter, when temperatures fall to minus 50 degrees Celsius, Union Glacier Camp does not exist. At the end of every season, the tents, snowcats, bulldozers and scaffolds are buried beneath the snow. They slumber unseen beneath the icy white desert until the next season, when they are resurrected and once more filled with life. I had read so much about Antarctica's gnarly conditions that I was shocked by the luxury and comfort of Union Glacier Camp.

Our snow jeeps trundled towards neat lines of clamshell tents. Each tent stood next to a happy little sign bearing its name: Nansen, Shackleton, Amundsen. Next to the clamshell tents were two large parallel tents that served as the cafeteria and the staff tent. Not far away were the solar-powered hot showers.

'Everyone come into the cafeteria tent for debriefing!' the organiser shouted. 'I know it's 2 a.m. Chilean time now, but it won't take long. You can all go to your tents soon to rest up.'

This was it. I was about to step into the elite mountaineers' headquarters, where the best and the fittest hung out before heading out to the South Pole or conquered unclimbed peaks. I was about to meet the real athletes. The hardcore. I squared my shoulders and walked into the tent.

The first person I saw was a Chinese man in linen pyjamas. His bedraggled hair fell halfway down his back. So much for being among elite climbers.

He was poring over a map on one of the cafeteria tables. Everyone around him wore thermals, fleeces and down jackets. He was listening intently to another man (his personal assistant?) who jabbed the map and said in Mandarin: 'The toilets are over here. That's your tent there.'

Pyjama Man nodded.

What the – ? It was bizarre beyond words. Then it dawned on me.

Mr Li, we meet at last. I'd heard of this guy. His reputation had reached me before I'd even left Chile.

Three days earlier, I was trying on the purple goose down suit at a clothing rental store in Punta Arenas.

'So, you're from Hong Kong? Have you heard of this famous Chinese actor who just left for Antarctica? Mr Li?' the shop assistant said.

'No?' I pulled the hood over my head.

'Well, he came into our store wearing just... pyjamas. Didn't bring any cold weather clothes. Nothing.' She helped me zip up the suit and checked the fit.

'Wait, really?'

'When we told him he couldn't just wear pyjamas at the South Pole, his assistant said, "Mr Li does not mind the cold".' She laughed.

'So what did you do?'

She shrugged. 'There wasn't much we could do. We just gave him the clothes he needed to prevent hypothermia. That way, he couldn't sue us if he got frostbite.'

Antarctica was turning out to be a much stranger place than I'd expected. The mess tent was a long white semi-cylinder that resembled the inside of a space station. Climbers huddled at the rows of plastic tables, some reading, some nursing cups of coffee.

I walked over to a map of Antarctica hanging on the wall. A very tall man strode up.

'What are you looking for?' He looked tense. His waves of greying hair were combed into a greasy mane.

I stepped back and smiled. 'I've been reading a book about an expedition that's retracing Shackleton's journey to the South Pole. I was just checking their route.'

He shot me a wild-eyed look, the kind that told me he had no idea what I was talking about.

Maybe he hadn't understood me. 'You know, Ernest Shackleton, who tried to –'

The man exploded.

'Oh yes, by all means lecture *me* on Ernest Shackleton and his accomplishments!' He vibrated with disdain.

What the –? His blast radius was impressive. For the second time that day, people were turning to stare at me. My mind went blank.

'Have you heard of the James Caird Society? Do you even know who Sir James Key Caird *was*?'

No. I'd never heard of the James Key Caird Club. Why was this strange man was so upset?

'Well, James Caird was the name of one of Shackleton's boats,' – at this point he began waving his hands – 'and is also the name of a club that meets once a week in London *and I am a member of that club!*'

Oh. I understood now. This man knew I was an amateur climber and wanted to put me in my place. He exhaled slowly, relieved to have restored the pecking order. 'Anyhow. You were saying you read a *book* –' he said indulgently.

I wasn't going to let him rattle me.

'Yes, I did. I did read a book.' I looked him right in the eye. 'And what I was going to say was, I was impressed by how *modest* the author was. He was a highly trained former soldier. But even he was surprised at how exhausting the Antarctic expedition was, and he was humble about it.'

The man didn't say anything.

'*He* was not arrogant.' I continued to stare at him. 'Not arrogant at all.'

The man started to give me the wild-eyed look again, so I turned and walked away.

~

That was the first time someone had treated me with such open contempt for being an amateur climber. I had a feeling it would not be the last. It was clear that Antarctica was the domain of a whole other calibre of climber: aggressive, driven and seriously Type A. I was out of my depth.

I pushed open the door of the cafeteria and walked out into the sunshine towards my tent. The camp staff had delivered my duffel bag to the door of my tent, and for a silly second I was relieved to see a familiar sight, even if it was just an item of luggage.

Shouting Man clearly saw me as a wide-eyed upstart who had listed 'Climb Big Cold Mountain in Antarctica' under 'Swim with Dolphins' on my bucket list. He was right. I was an upstart. I couldn't climb without a guide. But I also wasn't a total beginner. I liked to think that I was a lot more responsible than the idiots who set off for the mountain with nothing more than power bars and a smile and ended up calling for rescue. Over the years, I'd signed up for several mountain safety courses. I knew how to self-arrest, tie the right climbing knots and winch someone out of a crevasse. I had not come to Antarctica to make a fool of myself.

What a relief I hadn't told anyone about my mission, the Seven Volcanoes Project. How that man in the cafeteria would have laughed if I'd told him I planned set a world record in mountain climbing. I climbed into my tent and pulled off my plastic boots.

Mount Sidley was only my first stop. For the next few months, I planned to climb the highest volcano on each continent. The line-up:

Mount Sidley, Antarctica (Antarctica): 14,058 feet (4,285 metres)
Pico de Orizaba, Mexico (North America): 18,491 feet (5,636 metres)
Ojos del Salado, Chile (South America): 22,615 feet (6,893 metres)
Giluwe, Papua New Guinea (Australasia): 14,327 feet (4,367 metres)

Mount Kilimanjaro, Tanzania (Africa): 19,341 feet (5,895 metres)
Mount Damavand, Iran (Asia): 18,403 feet (5,610 metres)
Mount Elbrus, Russia (Europe): 18,510 feet (5,642 metres)

Only a few people in the world had completed the Seven Volcanic Summits. So far, the fastest time was eighteen months. I planned to climb them in just four months. If I lined up the climbing season on each hemisphere correctly, and minimised downtime between expeditions, there was a chance I could make it. The climbing season in Chile and Mexico lasted from January to March. Russia's climbing season began in June. Tanzania and Papua New Guinea were open year-round. Antarctica had the smallest window: December to early January.

I wasn't surprised that the Frenchman at the airport hadn't heard of Mount Sidley, the highest volcano in Antarctica. Most people had not even heard of the Seven Volcanic Summits. That was because everyone was much too obsessed by most fashionable record of the day: the Seven Summits. The Seven Summits challenge – 'bagging' the highest mountain on each continent – attracted more record attempts than flies to a horse turd.

First person to climb the Seven Summits.
First woman to climb the Seven Summits.
First American woman to climb the Seven Summits.
First to ski down the Seven Summits.
First American to climb and ski down the Seven Summits.
Oldest person to climb the Seven Summits. Youngest person to
    climb the Seven Summits.
Fastest to climb the Seven Summits.
Longest time to climb the Seven Summits.

A pattern of tiny variations on the same theme.
First married couple to climb the Seven Summits.

First twins to climb the Seven Summits.
First openly gay man to climb the Seven Summits.

I'd once toyed with climbing the Seven Summits, before I realised that there was no way I was physically capable of climbing Mount Everest. I had zero desire to freeze to death in the world's highest traffic jam. My asthma had receded, but I lived with the constant fear that it would return.

But the Seven Volcanoes? Maybe I could manage that.

Volcanoes are mountains that were born in violence, an explosion of magma. They come in all shapes, from ice cream cone to a sprawling pile of rock. The Seven Volcanoes were lower, less expensive, and most importantly, much less hyped than the Seven Summits.

And why did I need to chase a world record by climbing big volcanoes?

Because the pain of loss never goes away. The only thing worse than losing Dad was losing my memories of him. I needed to find a way to keep Dad's memory alive. If I could do that, he would never really be gone.

To my mind, a world record was the most indelible of gestures. It didn't matter if someone later beat my record. The Guinness Record books would forever log my attempt to climb the volcanoes in Dad's memory. It would be a testimony more permanent than a headstone that would eventually crumble, or a photo that would one day rot.

Everyone has personal reasons for climbing mountains. Of course, had Shouting Man asked me my reason, I would probably have said, 'Because they're there.'

~

The next morning, I was eating breakfast alone when a 7-foot-tall man strode into the mess tent. The frost on his shiny jacket seemed to chill the air around him.

'Hi, are you Sophie?' he pulled out the chair opposite and sat down. The metal joists of the long cylindrical mess tent clanked over the chatter of the groups of climbers.

'Hi. Yes. I arrived last night.'

'I'm Peter. I'll be your guide on Mount Sidley.' He adjusting his green ski hat. Peter looked exactly how you expected a mountain guide to look. He was tanned and bearded and towered over everyone in the cafeteria.

'How was your first evening in Antarctica?'

I thought of Pyjama Man and Shouting Man. 'It was fine. I met a man wearing pyjamas in the cafeteria.'

Peter grinned.

'Ah yes. Mr Li. He's an actor back home. He always wears pyjamas.'

'Seriously?'

'Yeah. I saw him a few days ago at the South Pole. I looked out of my window and saw this Chinese dude outside, practically naked. I looked away and rubbed my eyes, but he was really there. I just thought I'd been in Antarctica too long.'

His eyes flicked around the cafeteria, as if to reassure himself. Everyone knew Peter. Like a lot of guides, he chased the climbing season year-round from Antarctica to Nepal to Chamonix. I trusted him immediately.

'All kinds of people come to Antarctica. You've got your tourists who want to see the penguins, take photos and whatnot. Then you've got your crazy ambitious climbers and athletes who want to set Antarctic records. And a whole bunch of people come here to climb the Vinson Massif because they're trying to complete the Seven Summits.'

'Yeah, I've met a few of those.' I glanced at the blonde woman from the airport, sitting a few rows behind Peter. She sat in the middle of a group of young, photogenic climbers, looking like a North Face advert.

'Your teammates are already here.' Peter turned and pointed towards the back of the cafeteria. 'Two of them just got back from the South Pole.'

My eyes slid from Peter's face to two dishevelled men and a woman approaching our table. They were dressed in black and their hair was spiky with dried sweat. At last, my teammates. I started to stand up, a relieved smile on my face.

'Hi! Peter,' one of the men drawled in a Russian accent. He clapped Peter on the shoulder.

'Hey guys! Congratulations! How was the South Pole?'

'Tiring,' said the other man. He raised his eyebrows at me.

I'd seen these guys earlier that morning. They were sitting with a group of heavyset, unsmiling men in matching red jackets, looking like bouncers. They were the famous Russian 7 Summits Club, known for being so hardcore that they were known to climb through lightning storms to reach the summit. They were also known for their drinking, often while climbing to said summit.

'This is Pavel, Vladimir and Olga,' Peter said.

'Hi! I'm Sophie.' I held out my hand.

'Pavel,' said the second man. He bowed slightly as we shook hands.

Vladimir held up a lazy hand in greeting. He glanced at me, then looked away without saying anything.

'I think I saw you earlier this morning?' I said. Funny, he didn't seem that happy to see me. 'I thought you were mountain guides.' I meant this as a compliment.

Vladimir stared at me with distaste. He looked so dour that I felt my own smile slacken to match his expression.

~

At our first lunch together, Vladimir, the bastard, could barely contain his laughter as he described how his teammate had died.

Years ago, his expedition team had been trudging down the lower flanks of Mount Everest – drunk – when they turned around and saw their teammate get sucked into a crevasse, the way someone falls through a manhole. He couldn't remember whether they had been roped up, but he knew that when he turned around the man was gone. Apparently, this was hilarious.

'Wait, weren't you guys roped up?' I asked.

Vladimir continued talking, so Pavel answered by shaking his head. He made a drinking motion with his right hand, that double flick of the wrist towards his mouth.

'No,' Pavel said. 'They drink too much.'

Vladimir's sinewy hands did most of the talking. They jabbed and sliced the air as he chortled his way through the story, the rest of us stirring our mugs of lukewarm tea. Flaccid used tea bags wrapped around cheap camping spoons lay scattered across the cafeteria table, and through the window behind his head I could see the salt-and-pepper slopes of the Antarctic mountains.

'So, were you able to rescue him from the crevasse?' I asked Vladimir as he took a sip from his mug. He started, as if he'd forgotten I was there.

'No,' Vladimir said, as if I'd missed the entire point of the story. He waggled his hand at me. 'He was … not experienced climber. He did not take care.' Then he shrugged – *What do you expect of amateur climbers* – and said something in Russian to Olga and Pavel. They laughed. Pavel didn't translate this time.

Vladimir was from Siberia and clearly felt he could climb as well as any mountain guide. Pavel was a soft-spoken real estate investor from Moscow. Olga was a twenty-something economist from the Caucasus region of Russia with climbing in her blood. She was also my tent mate. Olga didn't speak any English, so our communication was limited to smiles and gestures.

Vladimir, Pavel and Olga got along famously. Pavel and Vladimir spoke some English, but didn't bother speaking it. Pavel, sitting to my right, translated a few phrases into English every so often. But for the most part I spent every conversation going by my teammates' expressions: the dumb pet searching their faces for scraps of meaning. I spent the entire meal chewing mutely on the canteen food, exasperated at being ignored but obliged to eat with the team. Glances from the other climbers in the cafeteria told me we were a curious unit – three raucous Russians, with me as some sort of awkward token non-Russian.

I gulped down the last of my tea and stood up. 'See you later,' and nodded to my teammates. Olga smiled. The other two ignored me.

Vladimir clearly didn't think much of amateur climbers like me, and he was letting me know it. Fine. I'd just have to prove him wrong once we got to Mount Sidley.

I walked past the rows of crowded tables. What right did he have to be so arrogant? Was it because I wasn't in the 7 Summits Club? Or was it just the high-testosterone nature of Antarctic expeditions? From what I'd gathered so far, they seemed to attract a whole other league of aggressive Type A people with unlimited funds.

As I approached the exit, the door opened and Shouting Man burst in with a gaggle of mountain guides. I tried to meet his gaze, but he didn't see me. For some reason, I swung from irritation to worry.

What if Vladimir was right? What if I turned out to be the weakest climber in the team? What if I let them all down on summit night?

I needed to get some air. I shoved open the cafeteria door with both arms, as if pushing away my concerns.

~

Nothing about Antarctica felt real. We lived under a vast turquoise sky. Every day I woke up in a world of deadly beauty where nothing lived, and the veil between life and eternity felt thinner. Our little camp huddled at the foot of great mountains, and during those austral summer months we lived an immortal day.

Union Glacier Camp is located in the Antarctica Chilean zone of the continent, 1,000 kilometres from the South Pole. Union Glacier Camp is run on Chilean time, which was important as night didn't exist. When I went to bed in my clamshell tent the sun was in the left corner of the sky, and when I woke up it was in the right corner. It never actually set. For the first few days I felt discombobulated, as if I had jet lag. I wore two sleeping masks every night, but they never fully blocked out the light and I had to be content with a kind of constant glowing orange behind my eyelids. The few times I burrowed deep into my down-filled sleeping bag, I erupted minutes later like a salmon, gasping for air.

Antarctic Logistics Expedition (ALE) started flying tourists out to Antarctica in 1985, after Canadian mountain climbers Pat Morrow and Martyn Williams set out to climb Mount Vinson so they could become the first to complete the Seven Summits. Until then, Antarctica was mainly the realm of actual explorers like Ernest Shackleton, and scientific researchers like the British Antarctic Survey (BAS). ALE soon realised that modern-day adventure-seekers, tired of the well-worn paths of Kilimanjaro and Machu Picchu, would gladly pay for guided adventures in the remotest continent of the planet so that they, too, could achieve Seven Summit fame. We were no longer in the age of exploration, but the age of commercial adventure.

Union Glacier Camp felt a lot like summer camp. Between the day hikes, cross-country skiing and quad bikes, there was a lot you could do without venturing out of camp. Our tents were warmer and more comfortable than most youth hostels. We ate poached salmon with roasted almonds, Cointreau-flavoured chocolate biscuit pudding. We took hot showers in the solar-powered bathroom opposite the mess tent. If I ignored the bulldozers parked at the edge of Union Glacier Camp, I could almost forget that I was on the most hostile continent on Earth.

'Okay guys, here's the deal.' Peter walked over to our table after lunch and swung his huge frame into an empty seat. 'There's going to be a delay getting out to Mount Sidley. The weather's not lining up.'

Vladimir and Pavel stopped talking in Russian. Olga and I looked up. Peter produced a map of Antarctica and unfolded it on the table.

'We're here.' He pointed at Union Glacier in the northwest corner of the map. We nodded.

'Mount Sidley is down here.' His arm moved across to the Marie Byrd Land region.

'The plane can't get there on one tank of fuel. We need to re-fuel halfway between Union Glacier and Mount Sidley. Right around here.' His finger circled a spot on the map. It was blank.
We nodded again.

Mount Sidley is one of the remotest mountains on Earth. While the Vinson Massif Base Camp is only 150 kilometres away from Union Glacier Camp, Mount Sidley is approximately 975 kilometres from Union Glacier.

'The problem is, each spot has a different weather system. We can't land at any of these spots unless they all have good enough weather. Right now, it's fine here, but over at the refuelling area the wind is too strong for the Twin Otter to land.'

'So... we're just going to have to wait? What are the odds that there'll be three pockets of good weather at the same time?' I asked.

Peter shrugged. 'We'll see. You know, about 90 per cent of mountain climbing is just waiting around.'

Over the next few days, we waited for the weather to line up. It was maddening, like a slot machine where the pictures never matched up. In the meantime, we watched all of the other climbers at Union Glacier head out to the Vinson Massif. We were the only expedition heading to Mount Sidley that month.

So Vladimir, Pavel, Olga and I waited, and watched everyone else start their adventures.

'Alright, Antarctica baby!' shouted a female voice behind me. I turned around. It was the blonde woman I'd spoken to at Punta Arenas airport. Another group was leaving for Vinson Massif. They clustered around the cafeteria tables, exchanged high fives.

'Have fun,' I said.

'You're not going to Vinson?' She gathered up her gloves and climbing poles.

I shook my head. 'Nope. We're heading to Mount Sidley.'

'Where?'

'Mount Sidley. We were meant to fly there today, but the weather hasn't cleared yet.'

'Oh wow! Good for you!' She paused. 'But why Sidley?'

I paused for a second.

'Oh, you know. I wanted to try something different. It's the highest volcano in Antarctica.'

She shot me a brief, uncomprehending look.

'Oh, okay. Have fun!' She flashed me a perky smile from under her Ray Bans and headed out.

Most of the people I met at Union Glacier Camp seemed to want to climb the Seven Summits, but there were other people chasing much more difficult records as well. While we waited in the safety of camp for the weather to clear, others were experiencing raw survival for real. Out in the hostile Arctic wilderness, the lunatic fringe of world-class athletes pursued their lonely journeys across the continent.

One expedition was trying to retrace Captain Robert Scott's Terra Nova expedition from 1912. Their journey was 1,800 miles long – roughly the distance from Paris to Moscow – and expected to take four months as they hauled 200-kilogramme sleds from Scott's Hut on Ross Island, across the Ross Ice Shelf, up the Beardmore Glacier to the South Pole, and all the way back again. They sent back bulletins via satellite, which we read in the cafeteria with awe.

In fact, a lot of the climbers at Union Glacier seemed to model themselves after the explorers of previous centuries, like Ernest Shackleton. This included Shouting Man. I learned his story over lunch the next day. Shouting Man only ever sat with mountain guides at lunchtimes, even though he was a paying tourist like the rest of us. At that moment he was telling – shouting – a story, his hands flying around like exploding popcorn.

I jerked my head in his direction. 'What's his story?' I asked the man eating opposite me. I'd ditched Vladimir, Olga and Pavel to have lunch with the jet engineers and pilots. I got along with them more easily than with my own team.

'Him? He's a regular. Been coming here every year. He does first ascents.'

'First ascents?'

'Yeah. There are still a ton of unclimbed peaks in Antarctica. If you want to make history, you basically pick one and ask the guides to take you up. Then you get to become the first person in history to reach the top of that mountain.'

I felt a sneaky little seed of admiration begin to form. So that's why that man shouted at me on my first night here. He must be under a lot of stress.

'Wow. He must be a pretty experienced climber,' I said.

'I don't know about that. I mean, you go up with two guides. They map out the route for you and lead the way. All you need to do is follow them up.'

'So what you're saying is, you don't need to be an expert climber?'

He grinned. 'Not really. Anyway, that guy only began climbing five years ago.'

Shouting Man and I had started mountain climbing at the exact same time. It sounded like we'd both taken up mountain climbing after going through difficult times. Turns out, we had more in common than I thought.

~

Eight days after arriving in Antarctica, we finally got the go-ahead to fly to Mount Sidley. Vladimir, Olga, Pavel and I sat in the empty cafeteria. The wind was about to tear the place apart. The metal joists of the empty cafeteria tunnel tent clinked under the wind's blustery warning not to test our limits. The sun hovered in the left-hand corner of the sky, which meant it was around 7 a.m.

I tore into a pile of toast, biscuits, potatoes and bacon. Olga and Vladimir slouched opposite me as if they were waiting to see the dentist.

'Do you think it's safe to fly in this wind?' I asked Vladimir.

He didn't look up. 'Is no problem.'

'You're not eating anything?'

'No.' He sat back and pulled his ski hat over his eyes.

The metal door crashed open and Peter strode in. 'Okay, guys. You ready? Time to go.' He looked lit up, ready to do battle against the weather gods.

I shoved one last Christmas cookie in my mouth and jumped up. The Russians pulled themselves to a standing position and we made our way to the canteen's vestibule to put on our outer layers. I was so excited that pulling on the bulky down jacket and gloves felt like an annoyance – just one more thing keeping me from starting my mission. The sugary cookies fizzed in my stomach. I pushed open the cafeteria door. The wind seemed to catch my mood and almost knocked me over, kicked snow in my face. I leaned into the wind as I walked to the plane. Its turbine engine screamed above the sound of the wind and tendrils of aviation gas laced the air. Our expedition had finally started.

Our pilot, Troy, sat in the cockpit with his sunglasses and mike on. He had his game face on. 'Mornin' folks!' he shouted over the thrumming of the engine and propellers. I heaved my backpack onto the back of the plane and myself after it. I sat down and put in earplugs. Through my window, the snow glowed like a danger sign in the harsh, bleak morning.

Olga gave me a thumbs up. I grinned back. Vladimir and Pavel, sitting in the seats behind us, fiddled wearily with their headphones.

I felt a pang as I looked back at the two men. I had always had the urge – irritating even to me – to make the best of things, be nice to everyone, make things work. Maybe it was naïve, but on mountain climbs I saw it as a matter of survival. Maybe the expedition would turn us into friends by the time we returned.

The Twin Otter took a run-up and flung itself onto the wind. We rocked and lurched like a canoe on invisible rapids as we clawed our way upwards. Minutes later, we burst through the cloud layer into the sunlight. The plane calmed down. Pavel and Vladimir shouted at each other over the thrum of the engine, telling each other to look below. Olga fell asleep.

I could not tear myself away from the window. The beauty of Antarctica's white plains and dark chocolate peaks drifted below us. Through the thin clouds, the sunlight danced like golden threads on the snow, like rays on the bottom of a swimming pool. Surreal and haunting. I lost myself in the other-worldly view and forgot about time. Suddenly, the plane started to descend. One second we were above it all, and the next, the thin clouds had risen back over our heads and our plane was skidding through thick unmarked snow in the middle of a white desert.

We clicked off our seat belts and climbed down. The cold made me gasp. It must have been 30 degrees below. We had landed on an endless, blank page that stretched to every horizon. I shuffled through the foot-high snow and did a 180-degree turn.

From horizon to horizon, vast white emptiness. There were no mountains, no snowdrifts, no features. The landscape – snowscape? – looked exactly the same from every direction, and if it hadn't been for the plane and the fresh tracks I would have lost all sense of direction. Olga and Pavel ran around taking photos of the nothingness, while Vladimir also stared at the view, finally impressed into silence.

We waited for the refuelling plane.

There was a buzzing in the distance. We turned to look. Out in the deep distant blue was a dot, which slowly morphed into a plane. It was another Twin Otter aircraft, carrying eight heavy barrels of aviation fuel. We watched as the plane careened straight at us. The engine roared as the pilots landed the magnificent metal beast. It raced past us, snorting and churning up the snow, made a U-turn and pulled up alongside our Twin Otter. The pilots opened their door. They looked round in their thick layers of clothing.

'Howdy,' one of them said. One by one, the two men rolled eight green fuel barrels down a makeshift ramp out of the belly of the plane and over to our Twin Otter. Troy jammed a pump into four of the barrels, and the other end of a hose into the Twin Otter's fuselage, started the pump's engine and refuelled our plane. The Russians and I watched and shivered. The refuelling completed, the other pilots climbed back into their plane. They wished us luck. Then they took off, leaving us completely alone.

I walked a short distance from the plane for a last look around before we took off. There's no easy way to describe nothingness, except that it looks like eternity. Or amnesia.

Having a bad memory feels a lot like living in a fog. What is a person but his or her memories?

...I wish I could remember more... I wish I HAD more to remember – Dad's eyes were glowing before he died – they were blue – no grey – I'm not sure anymore. Did all that really happen?

Was any of it real, why can't I recall properly –? The more I tried, the more the memories eluded me, grew vaguer. They taunted me like disappearing tendrils of smoke.

You were hardly there, you'll have less to remember –

What is a person without memories? A person who has died and is not remembered, disappears. A person who loses their memories loses part of herself.

'Okay! We're good to go!' Troy shouted. I snapped out of my thoughts. We re-boarded the plane.

~

The Twin Otter wouldn't take off. There was too much snow, or too many passengers. Three boisterous Russians, two Canadian pilots, a 7-foot-tall mountain guide and me, packed in a tiny plane in the middle of Antarctica.

Our plane had already skipped three times across the immense white nothingness like an ineffectual gnat. Each time, the cotton-wool snow had folded us back into its embrace. The pilots, Russ and Troy, slowed down again. We made a U-turn and taxied back to the strip of flattened snow called a runway.

The plane swung around, engines churning, until we faced south once more. Behind me Peter murmured into his headset to the pilots. I glanced back, but couldn't see Peter's expression behind his sunglasses. He didn't seem overly concerned. Russ and Troy, were all business. Headphones and mics on, they made last checks, flipped a few switches.

There was a second of anticipation and suddenly the plane lurched forward. Russ eased the throttle forward, Troy's hand clasped over his to steady it as we picked up speed. The engine's thrumming sharpened to a mechanical howl. We stormed down the runway, snow spewing to either side, still not taking off. What happens if we get stuck here?

I glanced across the aisle. Vladimir was bundled up in layers of down and fleece, his weathered face grim. Suddenly, there was a cheer from the pilots. The wings bit into the air and winched us off the snow. We were up.

In the vastness of the Antarctic, we left little evidence that we had ever been there. Had we not witnessed it, it might never have taken place.

Two hours later, we were circling over Mount Sidley. It looked like a volcano that had toppled onto its side. One side of the crater rim had sunk and merged with the plains around the mountain. This meant the volcano's summit was the top of the other side of the rim, which pointed skywards. Mount Sidley is a shell volcano that exploded 4.7 million years ago. It is part of Antarctica's Executive Committee mountain range, which ended with Mount Waesche immediately south-west of Mount Sidley.

The pilots circled low over the crater, looking out for crevasses. And each time they lifted the plane higher and flew out into another wide arc, my heart leapt. The steep walls of the crater flashed by our windows, then the snow plains, then the crater again. Previous expeditions had not landed in Mount Sidley's crater. They usually set up base camp somewhere further out, on the plain. Hanging above us was a bizarrely huge lenticular cloud. It almost looked as if it had been painted on to the sky. Blue ice glinted near the crater.

If we crashed here, we would never get out. Another expedition would need to rescue us.

We landed, and my heart tried to escape through my throat. We shrieked towards the crater wall, the plane ploughing through the deep snow. Just as we were about to collide with the crater wall, we slowed down and made a sharp turn right. As we taxied across the 5-kilometre wide crater it struck me how bizarre the situation was. A plane taxiing inside a volcano.

The Twin Otter came to a stop. We had become the first climbing expedition to land a plane in the crater of Mount Sidley.

'Alright!' Peter opened the hatch and climbed down out of the plane. The Russians followed, and I climbed down last. Apart from our cheers echoing off the walls of the massive frozen volcano, there was absolutely no sound. It was heart-wrenchingly beautiful. In a terrifying kind of way.

~

We camped that night in the crater of Mount Sidley. The next day, the weather closed in. We were marooned in our freezing little settlement of orange tents with the plane anchored close by. The cloud muffled the rest of the volcano from sight and enveloped us in white. Snowdrifts piled higher and higher around our tents.

The kitchen tent became our clubhouse while gales hurled the snow around outside. I liked the kitchen more than the small orange tent I shared with Olga. For a start, it had a barbecue grill 4 feet tall and 5 feet across. Under the grill were stacks of plastic tubs filled with frozen eggs, real bacon, brownies, sweet and sour chicken, pasta, chocolate, red wine, beer, and lots of fiery *aji* sauce. The seven of us huddled in the Quaker-style kitchen, the three Russians at one end conferring among themselves, the rest of us listening to the wind outside and filtering good coffee through cheap paper napkins. Every so often, Vladimir complained, 'If it was 7 Summits Club,' – the Russian climbing team with their matching red jackets – 'we do not care about weather. We go anyway.'

The floor was covered in loose snow, and every time someone fought their way to the zipped-up door they let in a blast of wind and ice. Peter had lit one of the burners of the grill, but its meagre flame didn't make much of a difference. Outside, the plane sat anchored to the frozen ground. Troy and Russ started up the engines once a day to keep them from freezing.

We had nothing else to do but wait.

'Why is it that there are so few female action heroes?' I asked. 'I mean, there was Sigourney Weaver in *Aliens*, Linda Hamilton in *Terminator*, and maybe you can count Hilary Swank in *Million Dollar Baby*. But why aren't there more?'

All the guys jumped in: 'Angelina Jolie in *Tomb Raider*!'

'Nah! She's more of a cartoon figure than a real character.'

They looked crestfallen. We spent the next hour in heated debate.

Another evening, Peter managed to single-handedly re-enact the entire Hollywood movie *Gravity*. A geologist by training, he was incensed by the crimes committed against science in the supposedly 'true to life' production. In between acting out how Sandra Bullock *would* have continued to spin in zero gravity forever instead of reuniting with George Clooney's ghost back at the space station, Peter distracted himself into acting out all the main scenes, complete with voices and expressions. It was quite good. When he was finished the tent was silent.

'Now we do not need to see movie,' Vladimir said.

~

We set out for the summit Mount Sidley on the third day. I had been dwelling on summit day for so long that it was a relief to finally get going. The weather had cleared, and at 10 a.m. Vladimir, Pavel, Olga and I clipped our carabiners onto the rope. I was third in line. Each of us dragged a sled packed with food and camping equipment. Peter quickly walked around checking that we had tied our ropes correctly, then took his place at the front of the rope.

'Alright! Let's climb this thing,' Peter shouted.

We set off. Peter walked slowly, the rope unspooling from the pile behind him. As it lifted off the ground Olga moved off, not letting the rope stretch too taut, not letting it drag on the snow. The sleds scraped audibly as we trudged across the snowy amphitheatre of Mount Sidley's crater, carrying tents, gas stoves, food supplies. In front of us the crater wall reared up, dark rock showing through the ice and snow. We made our way out of the crater and around the side of the volcano. We plodded in unison like a chain of donkeys.

I stared out at the immense expanse of white icy desert stretching away from the volcano crater to the horizon. It looked like the most forbidding, or forbidden, place on Earth. The volcano seemed to watch us as we moved, ant-like, across the crater. My stomach clenched in nervousness as we crossed the virgin snow, as if we were trespassing.

Peter kept shouting out encouragement, Scout-leader-style.

'It's all about systems, guys,' Peter said. 'You should keep your sunscreen, your energy bars and your mittens all in the same place. That way you don't need to think too hard when the altitude starts playing tricks on your brain.'

The cool air brushed my face where my skin peeked out from under the fabric buff. We started up the side of the mountain. The punishing sun made my hands sweat inside my gloves and my legs burned. Peter set a slow but relentless pace – there was no resting as we were all on the same rope, crisscrossing the giant mountainside.

The exertion burned through my energy stores. I'd need to eat some sugar soon, or risk burning out. We panted, losing huge amounts of water. The mountain side was not yet very steep, and at just over 6,500 feet we were not very high up.

'Sophie!' Vladimir suddenly shouted. I looked up.

'Yeah?'

'Do not point toes down mountain! Point up the mountain!'

I looked down at my boots. Was my footwork wrong? It seemed fine to me. I wanted to shout back at Vladimir, but instead I just looked at Peter, eyebrows raised.

Peter glanced at my feet. He shrugged and yelled, 'Don't worry about Sophie's feet! It's perfectly okay to point your boots downhill! Just focus on what you're doing!' Vladimir grimaced and muttered something. I felt like I was constantly under Vladimir's scrutiny. He couldn't wait for me to screw up. I would need to be careful. We resumed climbing.

'Drag your sleds onto these rocks,' Peter said. One by one, we reeled each other in on the rope. My heart hammered the inside of my chest, deep beneath all the layers of clothing. We stood on a smattering of rocks at the side of the slope, near the lip of the yawning, sheer-walled Weiss Amphitheatre within the crater.

All around us lay the eerie beauty of the frozen continent. Above us was a huge white wall glittering in the sun. There were few rocky outcrops, but mostly the slope was one big snowfield, which meant few breaks on the way up. I chewed on some energy gels and drank some water. I sweated so much my top felt wet, but at the same time my mouth was so dry my tongue stuck to my bottom teeth. A few hours later, we heaved our stubborn orange sleds over the last of the rocks and across the snowfield to high camp at around 9,100 feet.

Shortly after that, Peter started shouting at Vladimir.

'There's nothing wrong with taking a break,' Peter bellowed. Vladimir flung his arm in the direction of the summit, then pointed up at the clouds. He clearly didn't want to stop to set up camp. He wanted to head to the summit immediately.

'Look, my job is to make sure we get up safely,' Peter said. 'I've seen people who seem to be doing fine, then they climb higher without a break and they just – *urgh*!' He clutched his chest and pretended to collapse.

Vladimir turned and walked off, muttering to himself.

The snowy slope fell away gently beneath us, and above us the rim of the volcano arched out of sight, like the long neck of a swan. A few hundred feet beyond the 'safe zone' Peter had marked out, the soft napkin of snow gave way to rocky cliffs that plummeted into the crater.

We were only hours away from our push to the summit. I should have felt ready. Instead, my stomach fluttered with fear and I prayed my lungs wouldn't close up. In a few hours, I would find out whether I was a strong enough climber to be part of this team, or whether my asthma would sabotage the expedition. I took my inhaler out of my pocket and took a quick puff.

'How're you getting on? The cold air getting to you?' Peter shouted. He stopped and turned towards me, hands on hips.

I nodded, holding the drug in my lungs for as long as possible. When you have asthma, your air passages are chronically inflamed. This narrows the airways, which means less oxygen gets into the lungs. Cold air tends to make it worse.

I exhaled. 'Nope. Just a precaution,' I shouted.

Peter smiled. 'Gotta have that salbutamol.' He gave me the thumbs-up and turned back toward the mountain.

~

When I was young, my asthma overwhelmed my mother. She gave up her part-time job as an investment adviser – she had long ago given up law – and now my illness became her new full-time occupation. In between week-long hospitalisations every three months, I woke up to the sound of my mother pouring bottled water into the humidifier next to my bed and hanging up damp towels on the back of the chair, to keep the air in my room humid. Every day, she tried to cajole me into eating a full meal. She presented me with dishes loaded with carbohydrates: Chinese congee, spaghetti, shepherd's pie. She didn't let me take in anything that Chinese custom describes as 'hot', like orange juice, fried foods, as they made me produce more phlegm. Whenever my Chinese cousins came over, my mother waved a red HK$100 note in front of them.

'I'll pay you HK$100 if you can make Sophie finish this plate of rice,' said to my cousins, Dawn and May, who sat next to me at the dinner table.

'I'll have a try this time,' Dawn said, glancing at me.

It never worked. I had long ago lost interest in food. It wasn't that I wasn't hungry. I was. Everything just tasted like cardboard. The illness took away my interest in the outside world, and left me a scrawny little girl. Most days I just wanted to stay indoors and watch television.

Mom said I wasn't allowed to lie down on the carpet (dust!), run around or breathe in the vicinity of Hong Kong's many construction sites (paint fumes and dust!). Nor was I allowed to eat greasy food, flick the bed sheet or play with the curtains. I wasn't allowed to do much at all.

Dad took the opposite approach. I was his only child, and I would have to learn to survive. The more frightened I was of something, the more he pushed me to do it until I lost my fear. While my mother fretted about losing her only daughter and wanted to minimise any kind of risk, my father seemed to see this as a reason to double down. Mom and Dad would argue about this often, usually at the dinner table.

'I don't want our daughter growing up under a mushroom!' he snapped at my mother. That was his way of saying he didn't want me to grow up too sheltered. I looked across at Mom, who had turned pale.

'You can't prevent her from doing new things,' Dad said.

'But Richard, you can't take risks with her asthma.' A crease appeared between Mom's eyebrows.

'No. I don't want Sophie to grow up weedy.' As usual, Dad's word had absolute authority.

Dad threw me into the pool on weekends. He tossed his watch into the deep end again and again, and ordered me to dive in and fetch it. He invented a game where he clung to the edge of one side of the pool, I to the opposite side. Then we'd both take a deep breath, and swim underwater to the other side, waving to each other or high-fiving as we crossed in the middle.

Dad took me cycling and paid for tennis lessons, but what I loved most of all were our hikes in the New Territories, the northern region of Hong Kong that bordered China.

The breeze cooled my sweaty neck as I stared down the slopes of Tai Mo Shan. My father and I were standing half-way up Hong Kong's highest mountain, which at 3,140 feet is really not all that high. The one year the top of Tai Mo Shan briefly turned white, people queued for hours just to get their first glimpse of snow.

The plateau we stood on was littered with dark grey boulders. I sat down panting on a boulder and plucked at a few fat waxy blades of grass hidden among the dried-out grass.

My father looked out at the water.

'When I first came here, all those buildings weren't there,' he gestured at the white high-rise residential towers below. 'In the 1970s, you could still see paddy fields out in the New Territories.'

I laughed. 'No way! Paddy fields? In Hong Kong?' It sounded absurd. But then again I was only nine years old, and had no sense of history.

'Oh yes. You could go for a walk around Kam Tin and still see farmers with oxen pulling ploughs through the rice fields, and it was all lovely farmland. It was a completely different place back then.' He sounded wistful. 'Hong Kong has changed so much.'

'Why did you come to Hong Kong, Dad?'

He took a cigarette out of the packet, tapped it against the box.

'Oh, I couldn't stay in England.'

I fiddled with a blade of grass. 'Why not?'

Dad thought for a second as he watched the boats in the harbour. Then he turned and grinned at me.

'I wanted to travel,' he said simply. 'There was so much more of the world to see.' He took a drag on his cigarette. 'You have to look up and out, Soph.'

So I did. I looked up at the light grey-blue sky, the white wisps of clouds sailing the high winds far above us. I felt the breeze on my face that carried the dry scent of baked earth. Below us the dusty white path ribboned its way towards the harbour and the tower blocks of Tsuen Wan district clustered near the coastline. Further down, the paths descended into bottle-green jungle that resembled a quilt of foliage, the individual trees canopied with creepers. Residential tower blocks clustered in the crooks of the hills; even further out was the harbour, where ships, yachts, ferries and the odd sampan drifted between the dreaming islands.

Dad turned back to the view and stretched. He put his hands on his hips and stood tall, as if taking the measure of the city below, his adopted home. I followed his gaze. The streets of Hong Kong had long surrendered to the skyscrapers, the traffic, the noise, the wet markets, the neon signs, the godowns, the flotsam of Cantonese chatter and smog mixed with salty air off the harbour.

But these hills?

These hills belonged to us.

~

Until I climbed Kilimanjaro, those hikes with Dad were my only experience of mountain climbing. I'd never imagined actually camping on a mountain, much less in Antarctica. It didn't matter how much I'd climbed since Kilimanjaro. I still found it bizarre to sleep in a tent, and I never lost my nervousness before the push to the summit.

At 5 a.m., Peter, Vladimir, Olga, Pavel and I set out for the summit of Mount Sidley. There was a breeze, but the light cloud cover cocooned us and it felt no colder than it had at Union Glacier

Camp, around minus 20 degrees Celsius. We set off along the east ridge. I relished the feel of my crampons crushing the soft snow as we climbed through mist that danced and parted, revealing rocks here, sky there. No one spoke; even the Russians had stopped their usual banter.

As we climbed the cloud grew thicker and the air much colder. At times I could barely see 2 feet in front of me and I started to worry. Peter kept stopping and checking his GPS. The wind was getting stronger and the sky darker: a warning that our weather window was shutting. Peter started stopping every few feet.

'Think it's this one,' Peter shouted. We stared up, shivering wordlessly on the rope behind him.

The summit stretch of Mount Sidley, though, was the strangest I'd ever seen.

No one told me there would be ice mushrooms as big as bungalows. I had no idea how you climbed one. What confronted us looked like a cross between the bulgy top of a giant cupcake and an albino Yorkshire pudding. The three Russians and I had spent the last 4 hours climbing into a growing snowstorm. We had almost reached the top of the highest volcano in Antarctica. What I hadn't counted on were the frozen blobs three storeys tall.

We weaved through the eerie maze of rime ice formations on the summit ridge. Only Peter's GPS knew the precise location of the highest point of the mountain. Like some kind of polar perennial, these frozen plumes shrank and grew with the seasons. We found ourselves in the odd situation of checking whether the summit this year was still in the same place as last year.

Everything was white upon white. The squat form in front of Peter was no more than a lumpy silhouette pasted bleakly against a rice-paper sky.

'It *is* this one!' Peter yelled. This blob was merely the size of a garden shed. We closed the remaining few feet between us as he reeled us in, the rope pooling neatly in the flurries of snow by his knee-high boots. The wind was getting stronger, and he was keen to ship us back down the mountain before conditions got worse.

One by one we unclipped from the rope and put down our ice axes. Peter scrabbled up the frozen side of the mushroom with ease. As he reached down to help me up, I realised that my double-shell boots and steel crampons – not to mention the extra 4 kilos of fat and muscle I'd purposely gained as part of my training for the expedition – were heavier than I expected. I stood there, one leg raised and flailing to find a toehold in the obstinate icy wall, like a dog trying to avoid pissing into the wind.

I grunted as several pairs of mittens slapped my backside and gave me a shove. I hauled myself over the top, laughing and swearing at the same time.

We had done it. We were 14,058 feet high, at the top of a frigid cloudy volcano in the boondocks of Antarctica. 'Nice job,' Peter said, hugging us in turn. I did a little jig, turned to Olga and gave her a hug. She smiled and said something that was whipped away by the wind. I didn't feel the cold. I felt cocooned in my muscles, as if nothing could touch me.

Vladimir and Pavel struck Superman poses, then started picking at their clothing.

'No! Don't take your shirt off! We don't have time,' Peter yelled over the wind. He shook his head and shepherded them back across the promontory.

Vladimir shrugged in disappointment.

I took a deep breath as the snowy gusts cooled my sweat-soaked back and watched Olga pose with a Russian banner. Vladimir and Pavel finished taking pictures and ambled towards me.

'Well done, Sophie.' Vladimir clapped me on the back. He smiled, and for once his eyes smiled too.

'Thanks.' I smiled back, and felt my animosity towards him fade away.

Above us, the sun was framed by a halo of light. It was a parhelion – an optical illusion caused by refraction of the sun's image by ice crystals. It was beautiful. It gazed upon us like a benevolent, all-seeing eye.

~

The next morning, Olga and I sat behind a pile of equipment haphazardly strapped down behind the pilots. We took off smoothly, and as we headed north I felt a mixture of sadness and relief to be heading back, and away from the approaching bad weather. As we climbed away, my eyes were drawn to the sickly yellow stain of our pee hole, the indelible sign that we had camped there. In these temperatures, it would probably never vanish.

'Come! Drink!' Vladimir shouted over the noise of the engine. He held out a bottle of Scotch. Now that we'd made it up Mount Sidley without incident, he was suddenly relaxed, even friendly. He'd taken off his woollen hat and his sweat-caked hair stood up in spikes.

I nodded and took the bottle. I poured some Scotch into the lid and knocked it back. It felt good. Pavel handed me a packet of dark chocolate.

'You try. It goes good with whiskey,' he said. It certainly did. The smoky bitter chocolate took the edge off the whiskey, and before long all four of us were drunk.

A few hours later, we looped over the scattered assembly of tents and snow machinery that made up Union Glacier Camp. As we drew closer, tiny people came out to the runway to welcome us, summoned by the buzz of our plane. We touched down.

'Hey, welcome back,' someone shouted. 'Well done, guys,' said another. It felt like we had returned from another planet.

~

Once I'd climbed Mount Sidley, I couldn't wait to leave Antarctica to get on with the volcanoes project. But as always, the weather got in the way. We had now been here nearly three weeks. We were meant to head back right after returning from Mount Sidley, but our usual foe, the weather, prevented the Ilyushin from flying over from Punta Arenas to pick us up. I was starting to think I would never get out of Antarctica. It felt as if we were marooned on a giant ice floe.

'Ah, we are not leaving today,' Vladimir said as he sat down at our usual cafeteria table. He pointed at the beer can on the table. Beer on the cafeteria tables meant we would not leave that night. On a day an Ilyushin is scheduled to land at Union Glacier, no alcohol is allowed for safety reasons. No drunk climbers (or pilots) were allowed on the plane. We got used to glancing at the cafeteria tables as soon as we entered at dinner time.

It was almost the end of the Antarctic climbing season, and Union Glacier Camp had grown quiet. The mess tent was nearly empty most days. Olga had already left for the Vinson Massif with a different expedition, leaving me the tent to myself. I spent the long lonely hours walking around camp and looking at the mountains. My mind had already left Antarctica and was waiting for my physical body to catch up.

On 4 January, I was reading in the cafeteria when Peter walked in. Vladimir and Pavel were watching Russian videos on a laptop, sharing a pair of earphones and giggling at jokes only they could hear.

'Hey guys. You're getting out today. An Ilyushin finally made it across the Drake Passage.'

Pavel looked up, took the earphone out of his ear.

'We are leaving?'

'You're leaving. Time to pack your bags.'

At 3 o'clock in the morning, in eye-stabbing sunshine, a large group of climbers slithered across the blue ice runway towards the giant aircraft. The wind froze my cheeks as I tried not to fall on the slick ice. The noise of the aircraft's engines rumbled through me and as I drew near it looked like a giant metal bird of prey, with its high-shouldered wings and top windshield like the hooded eyes of a predator. I reached the metal ladder and clung onto it as the line of climbers shuffled up into the plane. I took one last look at Antarctica. I would miss these mountains, the 24-hour daylight and peaceful isolation.

An hour into the flight, the white LED screen give way to the grey-blue of the Drake Passage, then turned green as we flew over southern Chile. Trees, grass, leaves – we had almost forgotten what vegetation looked like after weeks in monochromatic Antarctica. Now we welcomed it back like an old friend. A few people started to cheer, and soon we were all hollering in celebration, wild at the idea of returning to warmth and safety.

I changed out of the purple goose down suit for the last time and lay it across my lap. It looked like a spent chrysalis. The Seven Volcanoes Project – my bid for a world record – was a go. I needed to climb another six volcanoes in the next three months. I clenched my hands to control my nerves. Time was going to be tight, but that was understood. If there was anything I'd learned, it was that time is always running out.

4

CLIMBING WITH ALLIES

I checked the clock for the tenth time. When was Douglas coming home? I'd returned hours ago, unpacked my Antarctica clothes and shoved them into the washing machine. Now I sat at the kitchen counter, drumming my fingers. Every time I looked at the clock, I was convinced it was running slower.

I'd always believed that time ran forwards, like a movie reel. I was wrong. I learned that after Dad died. Time is not linear; it stretches and splits like melted plastic. I could be sitting at my laptop, or walking down the street, and a rogue memory would appear and shove me through a trapdoor straight back into Dad's hospital room. It was as if space-time had forked the moment he'd died, and I now existed simultaneously on two timelines. Most of me lived in the present, but the rest of me re-lived Dad's last weeks on a loop.

After Dad died, it was hard to believe that life went on for the rest of the world. I was forced to move forward, too. I recovered, the way a tree grows around the car that crashed into it, all the while resenting the passage of time for dragging me further from the last time I saw my father. So I unpacked my boxes from

Shanghai and helped Mom sort out the household bills. I went back to work for my former employer, this time in the Paris bureau. I attended a press conference and got into an argument with my future husband.

~

Who the hell does he think he is?!

I folded my arms and glared at the man opposite. Douglas wore a business suit and looked respectable enough, but he had just royally pissed me off.

'So... Again. What is your outlook for the stock market?' I snapped. 'Our readers would really like to know.' Douglas was an investment specialist based in London. He had come to Paris to give a media presentation on emerging markets. I was one of Paris newsroom's few reporters with knowledge of China, so I went. More fool me. So far, the man hadn't given me a single straight answer.

Douglas leaned forward and clasped his hands together.

'As I said earlier,' he said slowly, 'I *cannot* comment on this.' His Scottish accent made him sound polite, but his eyes narrowed with irritation.

We sounded like a weird slapstick routine. Every time I asked a question, Douglas told me he couldn't tell me anything. The tension grew. The public relations man, who'd set up the interview, hovered in the corner of the conference room and wiped his hand across his forehead.

I sat back and slapped my pen down on my notepad. To hell with this. I'd come here to interview a fund manager but it looked like I'd be returning to the office with no story. It was March 2009. The markets were in meltdown. Our readers were desperate for any kind of market outlook.

I couldn't believe I'd lost my temper during an interview. I'd never behaved so unprofessionally before. There was something infuriating about this stubborn, very handsome man. Six months earlier I would have been interested, but I was an emotional wreck after Dad died. The old me had thrived on complexity and excitement, but the grieving me just wanted to be left alone.

I shrugged. 'Okay, I don't have any further questions. Thanks for your time.' I gathered up my notepad and pen and stuffed them into my satchel.

The PR person came forward with a relieved smile. 'Thank you for coming today. Email me if you need anything.' I nodded.

'So, what do you do when you're not doing interviews?' Douglas' shoulders relaxed now that the grilling was over.

I shrugged.

'Oh, you know. Nothing special. I walk around Paris, or read.' A few more minutes of chit-chat and I'd be able to leave.

'I'm also going to climb Kilimanjaro in August. I'm trying to raise money for cancer research.'

Douglas smiled. He still looked a little irritated.

'That sounds fantastic. Have a good time.'

'Thanks. I have to get back to the newsroom. Bye.'

Thank God I'll never see him again. I walked briskly through the cold spring breeze towards the Paris metro.

Two weeks later, Douglas sent me an email. 'I will be in Paris in three months' time,' it said. 'Would you like to have dinner with me?'

Three months' time? What the hell? My eyes slid to the calendar next to my computer screen. Each day had a big fat cross through it. I was constantly counting down to the weekend.

How do you turn down an invitation to a date… in three months' time? Could I tell him I was washing my hair that evening?

I met Douglas anyway. Turned out, it wasn't even a date. We had dinner in a café, and after that I went home even more confused.

A few months later, Douglas asked me on a real date. In America. In his twin-propeller airplane.

'Have you ever flown in a small plane?' he emailed.

I was standing in line for coffee during my lunch break.

'No?' I tapped out on my Blackberry.

After a few minutes, the reply. 'Would you like to?'

Two weeks later, I met Douglas at Omaha airport. We drove out to Council Bluffs, where his Beech Baron airplane was parked close to the terminal. It was a pretty plane, white with a red trim, and covered with decals from sponsors.

Douglas was a Royal Air Force flying instructor in the 1980s. His RAF career ended after only four years, when he was diagnosed with Type 1 diabetes. Devastated, he left the RAF and joined the financial industry. He thought he would never fly again, until he found out in 1999 that the United States had started allowing people with diabetes to fly privately. Douglas immediately went to the USA, bought the Baron and resumed flying. Flying was part of Douglas' soul, and being grounded had been torture. He had a lot of lost time to make up for.

I climbed into the passenger seat. We taxied down the runway and took off. The fields of Nebraska drifted beneath us as we climbed into the sky.

'Would you like to do some wing-overs?' Douglas's voice buzzed in my headset.

What the hell are wing-overs I started to think when Douglas hurled the plane into a nosedive. The engines roared. I watched in horror as the ground surged up to meet our plane, then dropped away as Douglas pulled the plane up in an arc with stomach-crushing G-force. We soared upwards, then went into a nosedive again. Just before we hit the ground, he pulled us up again. Douglas laughed. I grabbed a sick bag and dry heaved.

'You okay?!' he shouted over the mike. We were flying level again.

I clasped the sick bag to my face, mortified. This was disgusting behaviour for a first date.

'I'm fine.'

Douglas grinned and leaned over. 'Don't worry, I still fancy you,' he said, and kissed me.

Three years later, we were married in the Highlands of Scotland.

'It was when you mentioned Kilimanjaro after our interview that I realised that you might not be so bad,' he said.

~

I was replying to one of hundreds of emails when the front door opened and Douglas walked in.

'Congratulations on Mount Sidley!' he shouted. He held his arms over his head in excitement. 'That's the big one done and dusted.'

'Thank you!' I ran over and hugged him. It was so good to be home. It felt bittersweet, knowing that in a few short days I would be away again, on and off, for the next three months. Luckily, Douglas had carried out so many long-distance flying projects that he understood my need to climb the volcanoes. When it came to the Seven Volcanoes Project, he was my biggest supporter.

A few days later, I landed at Mexico City airport. About an hour after that, I found myself staring into the face of an alarmed security guard and praying he wouldn't Taser me.

He'd been eyeing me like a wary bull since I staggered through the arrivals gate. Not that I could blame him. My bags looked like they contained enough TNT to blow up Mexico City airport.

'*Como?*' the security guard barked.

The straps of my duffel bag dug into my shoulders. It was much too big for me. Reasonable people dragged huge bags behind them. They did not strap it to their backs and sling another large backpack onto their chests like a walking hot dog.

'*Donde... donde esta... el...*' This wasn't going well. 'Is – is this the only arrivals hall?'

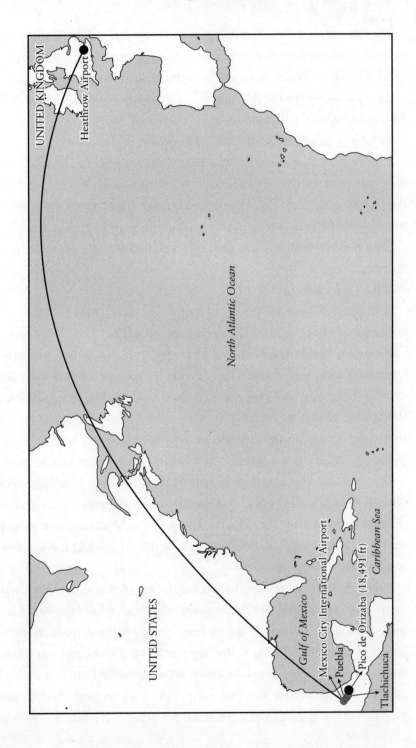

He shook his head without understanding. His dark grey uniform bristled with weapons: a gun, a truncheon, and other unidentifiable objects designed to subdue unruly tourists.

My jet-lagged brain felt around for another word. '*Llegadas?*' I blurted. '*Aquí? Solamente?*'

Finally, a grudging smile. '*Sí.*' He nodded and walked off.

I must have just missed Tina. Last time we talked, all we'd said was 'see you in the arrivals hall' of Benito Juárez International Airport, in Mexico City. But my 13-hour flight from Heathrow airport had arrived late, and she was nowhere to be found. I'd tried calling her but couldn't get through. I pulled out my phone again. At last, a signal.

'Hi,' Tina said.

'I'm here! Where are you?'

'Just round the corner. By the bus ticket office.'

I made a lumbering U-turn and sweated my way back past the families eating early breakfasts, voluble groups of women just starting their day, and rows of fast-food outlets. The smell of fresh bread and coffee wafted through the air. Every so often I saw a miniature Santa Maria figurine in a glass case, arms held wide as she supplicated me not to carry my duffel on my back like an idiot.

Was I really in Antarctica only a week ago? The memories were already fading. The cold, the ice and my Russian team mates seemed distant now, like characters in a movie I'd once watched. My new reality was so vivid and rowdy that it pushed the last few weeks into the fog of the past.

I rounded the corner and saw a small-boned woman in her early sixties sitting on the bench opposite the bus ticket counter. Like me, she had an oversized duffel bag, lying on the ground next to her like an obedient dog. I already knew what the bag contained: ice axe, carabiners, harnesses, double-shell plastic boots. It looked as if it weighed more than she did. Tina was so absorbed in her novel that she didn't notice me until I loomed over her.

'Made it,' I gasped.

Tina looked up, as if remembering where she was, and smiled her slow smile. 'Hi. I'm not really awake.'

I last saw Tina two years ago, after we'd destroyed our feet coming down from Mount Denali in Alaska. Now, however, Tina looked perfectly recovered and content.

'Want to get some food? The ticket office doesn't open for an hour,' she said.

'Sure.'

Tina grabbed the strap of her duffel and started dragging it behind her. It scraped out a synthetic hissing sound. We made a ridiculous pair as we ambled in the direction of the cafés. We tottered through the airy main hall. A few people stared at us. I guessed we made for an unlikely pair of mountain climbers.

Tina is in her sixties, which meant we had a thirty-year age gap. The people watching us probably thought we were mother and daughter, and berating me for not helping Tina carry her bags. They had no idea who they were dealing with. Tina was a climbing machine. A veteran of the California Sierra Club, Tina had a resting pulse of 50 and was one of the few climbers to have climbed all 248 peaks in the Sierra Nevada, all 99 peaks in the desert southwest and all 275 peaks above 5,000 feet in Southern California. Twice.

Tina was made of steel, but she was so modest that most people didn't realise her strength until they were on the mountain, about to collapse from exhaustion and watching Tina leave them in the dust. I learned this on Denali, where we first met and shared a tent for three gruelling weeks. She had made the brutal 18-hour descent of North America's tallest peak without a whimper, while I nearly fainted from exhaustion.

The only sign that Tina was not a climbing machine was the alarming apparatus she attached to her leg.

'So... Did you bring your leg brace this time?' I tried to keep a straight face.

She shot me a knowing glance out of the corner of her eye. 'Yes.' She knew what was coming next.

'Good for *you*,' I made sure to sound as condescending as possible. Tina laughed.

Tina's leg brace could star in *Aliens*. Not as one of the big monsters, but as one of those spidery bastards who try to impregnate humans through the mouth. It consisted of two murderous tourniquets strapped together, fringed by gangly plastic tentacles that lashed themselves fiercely around the knee. It looked horrific.

This was our comedic bit. Once, at the end of a hike, Tina had crossed paths with a random woman who made the mistake of cooing, 'Oh, good for *you*.' Which Tina interpreted as, 'That's sweet that they let a leg brace-wearing old dear like you leave the house.'

This is not something you say to Tina, mountain climber and elite track athlete. It made the very Californian Tina almost homicidal.

I glanced at Tina. She looked contented, as if imagining the wonderful days of mountain climbing ahead of us. Our roles hadn't changed. We had slipped right back into them as if no time had passed since Alaska. I was the ambitious amateur; she was the steady veteran. She was my rock. Everything was better with an ally.

~

Tina and I were heading to Pico de Orizaba, the highest volcano on the North American continent. To get there, we needed to hop on a bus heading East to Puebla, then take a local bus to a Tlachichuca, a small town about 200 miles south-east of Mexico City.

Aside from Mount Sidley in Antarctica, most of the Seven Volcanic Summits lie on the Ring of Fire, a garland of tectonic fault lines that rings the Pacific Ocean. After Mexico, I would head to Ojos del Salado in Chile and, on the opposite side of the world, Mount Giluwe in Papua New Guinea, which also lies on the Ring of Fire.

I loved the idea of the Ring of Fire. I found it fascinating that all these volcanoes, from Mexico to Asia, were related in some way. It seemed almost like some kind of fiery community, a much stronger commonality and so much more interesting than the Seven Summits, which just happened to be a club of tallest mountains.

Pico de Orizaba itself lies at the southern end of a string of more than twenty volcanoes that cinches the waist of central Mexico, stretching from the Pacific coast to the Caribbean coast. The Trans-Mexican Volcanic Belt was produced by magma oozing up as the Cocos plate sinks under the North American plate and into the Earth's mantle.

Tina and I boarded the sleek cross-country bus to Puebla. The bus was filled with city types. It purred out of Mexico City airport and threaded its way through stop-start traffic on various motorways. The buildings and noise soon gave way to farmland soaking up the sun, stretches of light brown scrubland, and dusty low-walled villages. I sank into one of those Zen frames of mind, happy to just watch and absorb the scenery and eat from a bag of crisps. Next to me Tina wrote quietly in her journal, pausing every so often to gaze out the window. We had never felt the need for forced conversation. Neither of us saw the point in chit-chat, and in any case our bond had been forged on a mountain expedition where on most days, it is perfectly alright to conserve energy and shut up.

I remained Zen for a surprisingly long time. After all, Pico de Orizaba was not the highest volcano on the list. It was not a technical climb. I felt pretty confident that Tina and I would get to the top, enjoy our few days in Mexico, and afterwards she would return to California and I would move on to Chile, where the real monster – Ojos de Salado – awaited.

That is, I remained Zen until I saw a large shadowy shape on the horizon.

'Is that what I think it is?'

Tina turned to squint out of the window.

We stared in growing horror. The blurry form shimmered in and out of sight as the bus wound through curving roads. Then the mirage coalesced into a roughly triangular shape. Then we saw it properly: Pico de Orizaba.

It was gigantic. It could have been the relative flatness of the surrounding landscape, or the fact that there were few neighbouring landmarks. The volcano dwarfed everything around it. It looked like a giant traffic cone in a sandbox. My chest clenched in excitement and trepidation.

'Wait, we have to climb *that*?' I said.

~

Pico de Orizaba loomed over the town like a snow-capped octopus head, surveying all before it. It towered over the little town of Tlachichuca, and when we arrived at the large metal gate of our guesthouse, the volcano seemed to stare straight down the street at us. The mountain was once known as *Poyautécatl*, or 'the ground that reaches the clouds'. On a clear day, you can see the Gulf of Mexico from the summit.

I knocked on the gate of the climbing agency and looked up at Pico de Orizaba. I felt awed by its beauty. It was a perfect single cone, like a cartoon volcano – but there was something else. A feeling of brooding. It felt almost as if the volcano was assessing us as well, deliberating whether we were worthy of climbing it.

The gate clanked open and a woman appeared. She looked at Tina and me, pushed her wavy short brown hair off her face and stuck her hand out with a warm smile. 'Welcome,' she said. 'I am Maribel.' Maribel was the manager of the agency.

'Hi!' I said. 'We're here to climb that huge mountain over there.'

She held the door wide and ushered us in. We left the dusty, quiet street and entered a symphony of birdsong. Birdcages and plants festooned one wall of the courtyard. The late afternoon air was soft with the smell of flowers. On the left, was a long squat building, and on the other side was the three-storey dormitory. Piles of backpacks and camping equipment dotted the courtyard, and a couple of climbers sat in the lazy sunlight, reading or writing in notebooks. Even though it was warm, the air turned chilly when the sun ducked behind clouds – a reminder that we were at an elevation above 6,500 feet.

There were fewer climbers than I'd expected, probably because Pico de Orizaba was not one of the Seven Summits, and so not as interesting to the kinds of adventure tourists I'd met in Antarctica.

I felt as if I'd been invited to stay at someone's home. Summit Orizaba was a small mountaineering agency run by the Cancholas family. Generations of Cancholas had climbed and guided on Pico de Orizaba. There was self-assurance and pride in Maribel's smile as she showed us around the courtyard. This was her home, and we were her welcome guests, not just clients. I could see the kitchen through one of the large windows. Two women were chopping vegetables at the table, while three or four children milled about or watched TV. The scene was so intimate, so cosy that I felt my eyes grow hot. I'd forgotten how it felt to live in a complete family. Without Dad, my mother and I had settled into something of a partnership. I took care of her household bills, and she let me know when things needed to be fixed around the house.

'We are very full,' Maribel was saying to Tina. Maribel had lively, naughty eyes, as if she were constantly on the verge of telling a dirty joke. 'You have three beds in your room. Is it okay if I put a man in your room too? He is travelling alone.'

Tina said nothing. She remained expressionless, except for a slight pursing of the mouth.

'Or – or you can choose!' Maribel said, seeing our hesitation. You can choose someone else! You know, blond, tall, handsome ...'

I had visions of Maribel throwing a Blond Climbing Ken into our room in the middle of the night.

'No,' Tina said. The word fell like a judge's gavel. There was a pause, then Maribel nodded.

'Maybe he can sleep in the truck,' Maribel muttered to herself. 'Okay, you come to the dining room in a few minutes for snacks.' She hurried off.

The Cancholas' living room walls were covered with framed photos of mountains. I noticed that a lot of them featured the same well-built, older man at the summit.

'Is that the summit of Everest?' I asked Maribel as she walked into the room.

She set down a plate of quesadillas on the dining table, glanced up at the photos and smiled.

'Yes,' Maribel beamed. 'That is my father.'

'Nice,' Tina said, walking over. 'So your whole family climbs?'

'Yes. All of us. My father is right now on Pico de Orizaba, but he is back tomorrow. I used to climb a lot too, but now I run the agency down here,' Maribel said. Climbing mountains was part of who the Cancholas were.

She turned and strolled back to the kitchen, pausing briefly to lean over and tousle the hair of one of the kids at the table before joining the two other women – I guessed they were her mother and sister – at the kitchen table.

Children's laughter tumbled in from the adjoining kitchen. The tables were covered in magazines, toys, and food being prepared for the climbers' dinner. The kitchen glowed with affection and the whole house felt warm and safe. It was almost too much: the noisy kitchen, the children, the palpable closeness of the Cancholas. The family was so clearly part of this region. They belonged here.

Maribel came out from the kitchen holding a basket of bread. 'Come, we eat.'

Tina and I sat down at a little round table in the Cancholas' living room. Other climbers drifted into the room. There was a team of about a dozen climbers who had just come down from Pico de Orizaba. They made straight for the fridge and took out bottles of beer to celebrate.

'Mind if I sit here?'

I looked up to see a tall, earnest-looking man. He had the expression of a man who had just escaped house arrest and could barely believe his luck.

'Sure,' I said.

'I'm David. I'm from Canada.' He reached out to shake our hands. 'Looks like I'll be joining you on your climb.'

'Nice to meet you,' I said. There was a sudden cheer from the long table of climbers next to us. Someone was giving a toast. They clinked their beer bottles in victory. I turned to glance at their exhausted, sunburned faces. I couldn't wait to bag the next summit.

'That'll be us in a few days,' David said, following my glance. He nodded and rubbed his hands together as Maribel set down a plate of beans.

Tina was giving David one of her calm, steady looks. She was a private person who chose her climbing company carefully. What did she make of David? I loved climbing with Tina, and it wasn't just because I felt reassured by her mountaineering experience. I always pushed myself harder, watched my technique more carefully, when climbing with Tina, because I didn't want to let her down. I bit into my bread roll.

'Have you climbed in Mexico before?' Tina passed him the bowl of beans.

He shook his head. 'When I was in my twenties I was a really good climber. But then I got a nasty concussion, and I met the woman who was to become my life partner and everything kinda stopped after that.' He emphasised the word 'woman' more than 'concussion'.

'So I haven't been climbing in a long time, but I've always had this dream of climbing Everest one day,' he said. 'I'm treating Pico de Orizaba as sort of a test run.'

Tina just raised her eyebrows in response. That's because climbing Pico de Orizaba as a test run for Everest is a little like taking a ride on Space Mountain as a test run for the Apollo mission.

I tried to bridge the awkward silence. 'So – David. You're planning on climbing Everest?'

'Yeah, if I can get the free time. How about you guys? Why Pico de Orizaba?' David asked through a mouthful of guacamole.

'Sophie and I shared a tent on Denali. We wanted something a little less tough this year,' Tina said.

David nodded, his gaze already drawn to something else. The climbers at the large table scraped back their chairs and picked up their beers to leave. As they headed outside, one of the female climbers strode past David.

David jumped up and stretched out his hand to her. 'Hey! Congratulations on your summit!'

She brushed right by him. She was probably too exhausted to hear him. David stared after her.

'Well, I guess every group has to have an unfriendly bitch,' he said, just loud enough for her to hear.

~

The next morning, my spine did a jig as the battered red truck rattled over the pitted earth road on the way to La Piedra Grande, or base camp on Pico de Orizaba. Some of the crevasses looked big enough to swallow a small cow. Tina and I were squished into the back seats next to a bearded American in his thirties. Our climbing gear clanked in the trunk.

'Hi, I'm Simon,' he shouted over the noise of the truck.

'I'm Sophie,' I screamed back. 'You climbing Pico de Orizaba too?'

The truck plunged into another pothole and I slammed my head into the ceiling.

'Yeah,' Simon yelled. 'My brother and I drove here all the way from Seattle and we're planning to go on down to Patagonia. I actually went up to Piedra Grande but I got altitude sickness, so I went down again. I'm trying again today. My brother's already up at the hut.'

'Yeah, it's a big jump in altitude from Tlachichuca to Piedra Grande,' Tina said.

I nodded and smiled, but I could already feel the dull ache of the altitude behind my temples.

Altitude is an unpredictable beast. It affects people in different ways. Some climbers function perfectly well at an altitude of 16,000 feet, while others immediately get ataxia and lose control over their bodily movements.

I was worried. *What if I'm not ready for the climb tomorrow? And with five more volcanoes to go. What if my asthma flares up and I can't breathe?*

In general, once you're above an altitude of around 10,000 feet, the usual advice is not to increase your sleeping elevation by more than 1,000 to 1,600 feet per night. Last night, we'd slept at 8,530 feet. Tonight we'd be bedding down at 14,000 feet at La Piedra Grande. I swallowed. That was a serious altitude gain in a short space of time.

I held more tightly to the door handle. If I already had a headache now, would I also have to head back down to Tlachichuca this evening, like Simon? I usually adapted quite quickly to high altitudes, but with such a large jump, I wasn't sure I could cope.

Our truck crested the top of the muddy road. We passed waving farmers, skinny cows, and ramshackle farmhouses before we plunged into the forest, the track weaving in and out of deciduous trees. There was more crunching of gears as the truck groaned in four-wheel drive, the driver not saying a word, eyes glued to the next gashes in the road.

As we climbed, the vegetation morphed from alpine forest into scrubby highland, and eventually became bare earth and rock. We lurched to a halt. I leaned forward to stare through the smeared window. I couldn't see a thing; everything was blotted out by white fog. Next to me Tina was sitting back with her eyes closed. Did she feel as bad as I did?

Our driver switched off the engine, gave a satisfied laugh and got out of the truck. He walked a few paces and was swallowed up by the mist until all I could see were his disembodied boots moving over the earth. Then, the smoke-like mist parted and a three-storey stone building suddenly appeared. We had arrived at La Piedra Grande, also known as high camp.

'I guess this is it.' I opened my door. My head felt light as I stepped out and slung on my rucksack.

The building's rusty metal door squealed as I pushed it open. La Piedra Grande felt colder inside than out. The right side was dominated by three storeys of wooden bunks reaching up to the ceiling and stretching from one end of the building to another. On the left, a row of thin-paned windows let in the sickly white light and the walls around them were covered in flaking red paint. It reminded me of one of those dank cellars for curing meat, lined with shelves of preserved carcass.

At first, my eyes were drawn to the local guides tinkering with stove pots at the far end of the room, but then someone shifted above my head and I realised that the wooden bunks were full of people. Rows and rows of climbers lay swaddled horizontally in sleeping bags, staring down at us.

'Hi.' I waved. A few of them nodded back. They looked hunched and drawn, as if shrunken into themselves in response to the altitude. Some played cards; others stared into space.

Tina and I exchanged a glance, eyebrows raised.

'Want to go here?' I nodded at the bottom bunk. No way was I going to sleep any higher up. I didn't really care for heights. The second-storey bunk was taken, and the open ledge of the top deck was at least 10 feet off the ground.

We heaved our rucksacks onto the bottom bunk and started to unpack our gear, saying little as we unrolled our sleeping bags. One of the guides started brewing tea, and amid the clang of pots against the stove I could hear David trying to make friends with the other climbers.

'I'm really seeing this as a test run for Everest.' David leaned against the wall, clutching a mug of tea. The climbers on the bunk beds listened silently.

'You see, really early on I met a woman, and she came with a couple of kids, and I spent the next twenty years being a family man and working as an editor. That's basically why I never tried climbing Everest.'

I was beginning to sense a pattern with David. I had the feeling that he was desperate to make up for lost time, lost opportunities, as if the time spent with his partner had held him back from his true calling. He had a curious way of referring to his 'woman' with an edge to his voice, as if he were referring to his manager. David obviously saw Everest as the only real mountain worth conquering. All the other climbs were just practice.

Nobody said anything to David's announcement. I took a mug of tea from one of the guides and ambled over to my bunk.

'David, if you're keen on climbing Everest, why don't you go for the Seven Summits? I've seen a lot of people climb them for charity.' I sat down on my bunk.

David looked at me as if I'd farted in his elevator.

'Oh God,' he spat. 'When I was an editor, we kept getting press releases saying "I'm doing this or that mountain climb in the fastest time for *charity*." We just tossed them in the trash.' He smiled a caustic little smile.

I blew on my steaming mug of tea. 'Um. Okay. But what's wrong with climbing for charity?'

David bristled at me.

'Well, I mean, so *what*?' he said. 'So what if you're trying to climb a mountain in the fastest time, or whatever? So many amateur climbers get in over their heads trying to do things for charity.' He said the word 'charity' with the same edge he reserved for his 'woman'.

'Well,' I said. This was obviously a bad time to mention that I was climbing Pico de Orizaba partly to raise money for cancer research. 'I always thought charity climbs were good. At least they help get people moving, and not just sit on their backsides all day.'

David shrugged.

'And – and – a lot of them have personal meaning. For the climbers. You know, like when they climb in someone's memory,' I stuttered.

David took a sip from his mug and glared into mid-air. He wasn't interested. Shrugging, I stood up and carried my mug of tea outside.

The bright sunshine burned off the chill of the stone hut as I walked over to a boulder and sat down. Pico de Orizaba brooded above me, the summit wreathed in spindrift that merged with the plumes of cloud carried on the high winds. It looked almost like Pico de Orizaba was giving off smoke, and all of the white plumes turned black and I was no longer at high camp staring up at a volcano in Mexico but in our backyard in Hong Kong watching the hill that had gone up in flames behind our house. I was six years old in this memory. The fire had started early that afternoon and laced the air with a vicious black smoke that drifted down and settled on our garden. I was crying, because my parents were among the flames, beating at them with sticks and sackcloth and trying to put the fire out.

I was only six, so I didn't really understand when they told me that a fire broke out on the hill behind our house in the New Territories, and that it was too dangerous to take me. Thick black smoke spewed out of the burning undergrowth and it looked like nothing was being done to put it out.

They had been gone for half-an-hour when I finally spotted them. I could only just make out my parents – tiny figures at the base of the huge plume of dark-grey smoke halfway up the hillside. They were standing among the Chinese family graves with their ceramic pots of bones and offerings of tangerines and incense. My father whacked at the fire with a branch while my mother waved madly to me. I waved back, sobbing. 'Don't cry,' Ha Jie said and dried my tears. 'They'll be alright. Don't cry.'

I was terrified they were going to die. My parents had left for the hill an hour earlier. The flames had sprung up among the Chinese family graves and was spreading fast. Soon it would spread to the nearby villages. The fire service couldn't reach it – the hills were laced with footpaths, but it was impossible to drive a fire truck up them.

My father decided to take action. 'If we don't put it out, no one else will,' he said. My mother could never be described as outdoorsy, but that day she put aside her high heels and pulled on a pair of old jeans and sneakers.

A few hours later, my parents returned. The fire was out. Their hair was grey with ash and they had greasy black marks on their faces. They walked slowly up to me. My father slumped down on a bench in the garden while my mother walked up to me, smiling through eyes half-closed with exhaustion. She knelt down and hugged me.

'I knew you were crying, even though I could hardly see you,' she said.

I snuffled into her smoky T-shirt. 'How did you know?'

Mom stroked my cheek. 'Of course I knew. You're my baby,' she said softly. 'I knew it in my heart.'

The black plume of the hill fire morphed back into clean white spindrift, and suddenly I was no longer a child but three decades older and back at high camp on Pico de Orizaba.

I'd almost forgotten that memory. It wasn't a very clear one – was the sky clear that day? Overcast? I blinked, confused. I dashed away a tear because I had regained a piece of my past, fuzzy as it was. Behind the picture, the message. Dad taught me to attack my challenges, no matter how overwhelming. Like saving a hillside and nearby villages from a fire.

If here were here, he'd have told me to swallow my fears and attack Pico de Orizaba. To hell with my fears about the altitude and my asthma. 'You should just go for it,' he would have said. Just – go.

The sun was starting to set and a chill settled over camp. It was time to head inside – I'd spent enough time with the ghosts of the past today. In my mind's eye I still saw them in the distance: my father attacking the hill fire, my mother waving down to me. I felt phantom eyes on my shoulder blades as I pushed open the door to La Piedra Grande.

I don't know why, but as soon as I walked back into La Piedra Grande I felt relieved. As if the reassuring din and bustle of humanity would block out the ghosts outside.

~

The next morning, I was drinking coffee outside La Piedra Grande when David shambled up to me.

'Listen,' he said. 'I… didn't really mean what I said yesterday about charity climbing.' He squinted up at Pico de Orizaba and shuffled his boots in the loose earth.

I glanced over at him. 'Mm?'

'I mean, look at me,' he grimace-smiled. 'I spent all those years as a desk editor who only talks about climbing Everest. But really, I'm just an armchair climber.' He'd lost his sheen of bravado. It made me like him a lot more.

'Don't worry about it.' I took my hand out of my glove and rubbed my temples. He nodded, and headed to the outhouse.

I watched him go. Why was it always so hard to talk to other climbers about why they climbed? Maybe it was just too personal. I guessed that for David, climbing probably represented freedom – from domesticity, from an armchair existence, maybe something else. And I couldn't begin to explain to him why I was climbing the volcanoes. If I'd met someone who told me they were attempting to climb volcanoes to bring back memories of their dead father, I'd have thought they were nuts.

Maybe it was just easier to go with ego and bravado and adventure. Not everything had to be an intense soul quest. Maybe David really just wanted to climb Everest because it was there.

It was our second morning at La Piedra Grande below Pico de Orizaba, and I was wrung out and uneasy. The altitude was wreaking its havoc but that wasn't surprising, given how fast we'd climbed. Also, La Piedra Grande was loud. Everything echoed, the metal door banged every time a climber opened it. At night, I could hear every single creak, mutter or thump from people shifting or heading out to the toilet huts. Tina and I only slept about two to three hours at a stretch. Every time, I would lie staring into the darkness and listen to the scratching of mice, as I waited an hour to fall back asleep. David's words, 'So many amateur climbers get in over their heads' came to haunt me.

~

The mist hid everything above and below, so that Piedra Grande felt like an island lost in nothingness. There was no above or below, and no sun. Tina, David and I set out for our acclimatisation hike by tracking the crumbling aqueduct leading up out of camp. After a few hundred feet the weatherworn concrete gave way to a rocky trail and Tina took the lead. David followed and I brought up the rear so I could take my time. At times the mist seemed to retreat and reveal glimpses of the side of Pico de Orizaba, only to close in again like a lace curtain covering a widow.

Half-an-hour later, we had climbed to an altitude of 14,800 feet. My head throbbed. We stopped and turned. We could hear nothing from the La Piedra Grande, and only barely make out the moving flecks of people before more mist blotted them out, walking in and out of the stone building. Beyond the layer of mist, we could now see the road we had driven up out of Tlachichuca, and above the treeline the scrubby fields were covered in faint parallel stripes.

The three of us turned back to the track and continued climbing. All we could hear was the scrape of our boots against the earth and the regular *pik* of our walking poles against the rock. As we climbed, a wall of abrupt sepia boulders – some as big as houses – grew steadily to our left.

'Hey, there's the Labyrinth,' I shouted.

The Labyrinth is a section of rock that stretches from 14,500 to 16,000 feet on Pico de Orizaba. It was notorious for luring inexperienced climbers into its disorienting trap of false turns, ice and steep snow gullies winding among the rocks that sprained ankles and snapped bones.

'Hey – wasn't someone killed here a while ago?' I asked.

David turned slightly. 'Actually, it was just last week.'

'Wait, really?'

'Yeah. Apparently he was messing about in the Labyrinth and he fell and killed himself. One of the guides told me was playing hide and seek with his girlfriend or something.'

I shuddered, imagining the scene. As we climbed I stole uneasy glances at the hushed rocks. We climbed the rest of the way in silence.

When you have a guide, it's easy to get lulled into a false sense of security and forget that you're in a hostile environment. Take away the guide, and it's just a bunch of people wandering the mountains. I never let myself forget it.

By the time we reached the stretch of moraine just below 16,400 feet, my head throbbed and I felt dizzy. The three of us stood still, craning our necks at the line where the Ruta Normal met the stark whiteness of Jamapa Glacier. We would need crampons on summit day for sure. I reached round for my water bottle and took a swig.

The sky darkened. We started to pick our way back down. Suddenly David, tired of the gradual pace, snorted past us in bovine fury and charged full-pelt all the way down. Tina and I couldn't keep up, and we didn't even try. Before long, David had become no more than a mad red speck far down the trail, leaping off boulders and possibly destroying his knees.

'I wondered whether he would do that,' Tina murmured.

'I guess he showed us.' I laughed. We were back to showing off again.

It's easy to get impatient during mountain climbs. Everything has to go slowly on the way up, to ensure acclimatisation. There are no shortcuts to the top. Of course, a lot of amateur climbers still tried to find one.

That evening, the newest arrival at La Piedra Grande had discovered a shortcut to the summit, and he couldn't wait to share it with us.

'So I bought this hyperbaric tent and I've been sleeping in it at home to prepare for the altitude.' The diminutive man poured himself a glass of red wine. We watched from our bunk beds, wrapped up against the chill, as he unpacked boxes of pasta and all manner of condiments to cook on his shiny camping stove.

'I don't think it's cheating. Last time when we got to 14,000 feet on Aconcagua, everybody else was in their tents recovering. We just headed straight out for a jog around camp.' He chuckled.

The man – Neil – had arrived at La Piedra Grande that morning. As he talked, he threw freshly-chopped tomatoes and spices into the large pot of fragrant simmering broth. I admired the way he thought suffering was optional on a mountain climb. Naïve but funny.

He paused to sip his wine. 'I don't believe that mountain climbing needs to be difficult. If you can shortcut some things, it's worth it.'

'So how do you use a hyperbaric tent when you're at home?' I asked. Before leaving London, I'd considered paying for a session at one of those expensive high-altitude training centres, to shorten the acclimatisation process. I'd never heard of anyone privately owning a hyperbaric tent.

'I moved it into the bedroom,' he replied.

'Wait, you sleep in the tent at home?' David asked. Then, as if he couldn't help it, he blurted, 'What does your wife think?'

The next morning, Neil was gone. He'd driven back down to Tlachichuca before breakfast.

'What happened?' I asked David. 'Altitude sickness?'

'No. Diarrhoea.'

That was the thing about mountain climbing: there are no shortcuts. If you hadn't put in the training, if you didn't acclimatise properly, the mountain let you know it. It was an unforgiving sport, but it was also honest.

It's not just the training, either. When it came to climbing, I was cardio-fit, but I was also built like a shrimp. In the eight months running up to the climb of Mount Sidley in Antarctica, I deliberately added 10 per cent to my body weight in eight months. Mom was proud. She had spent most of my childhood trying to make me eat more.

One day of high-altitude climbing can burn more than 4,000 calories. That's because a typical day of climbing feels like climbing stairs for 7 hours straight. Add to that a 20-pound backpack, extreme altitude, bitter minus 25 degrees Celsius cold and only hourly 5-minute breaks with minimal food, and it's very easy to run out of reserves and stamina before reaching the summit.

'You have to eat and drink your way to the top,' was a comment I heard often, and I took that advice to heart.

My gluttony began eight months before I set out for Antarctica. I took out a calculator, some graph paper and calendar, and set out monthly body weight targets. Those eight months were a glorious chain of calorie-counting and twice-daily protein shakes. The more I trained, the more I ate: wholegrain spaghetti, pizza, canned tuna, garlic bread, pop tarts, avocados, brown rice, lemonade, Philadelphia cheese, Nutella, stacks of meat and as much fruit and vegetables as I could stand. My favourite part was 'fat loading'. Sports nutritionists say it is a way to make the body burn fat so it can conserve glycogen, which is essential for endurance. This was my cue to keep a jumbo bag of peanut M&Ms, those delicious chocolate-covered fat pellets, on hand at all times.

What I gained in fat, I compensated for with extra muscle. It was a shock to realise what I could accomplish if I put my mind to it. I needed to be able to carry heavy backpacks for hours for some expeditions, like Denali in Alaska. So I started by putting water in my backpack. One litre of water weighs a kilogramme, which made my load easy to calculate. Every week, I added another litre or two. I didn't limit myself to the treadmill, either. I hiked the chalky stretch of Britain's southern coastline known as the Seven Sisters; up and down Ben Nevis in Scotland, and along the sides of several motorways near our home in Buckinghamshire. In short, wherever there was the slightest slope among the pancake-like contours of Britain.

I drove to the Brecon Beacons in Wales and checked into a cheap dowdy hotel close to the trails. That weekend, I hiked up Pen y Fan, the highest mountain in southern Britain at 2,907 feet where the Special Air Service (SAS) train, with 5-litre bottles of water stuffed in my backpack (and smaller bottles stuffed into the outer pockets). The weather was not good. I spent hours battling howling, chilly wind that tried to blow me off the path, my hair pasted to my forehead and the drizzle rolling under my collar and down my back. I ended up crouching on all fours to avoid being blown over the cliff, my rucksack pushing my boots deeper into the mud as the mist rolled in.

When the weather was bad, which was often, I measured the distance between one mountain camp and the next, and worked out its equivalent in steps. Then I took the train into central London and climbed the 175-step emergency spiral staircase in the Russell Square tube station. None of the tourists I passed ever asked me why I was climbing the staircase with a tank on my back, catching the lift down again, only to climb back up again, thirty times in a row.

My crazy training regimen paid off. By the time I started the Denali expedition, where I first met Tina, I was able to carry 26 kilogrammes without flinching.

The body adapts in numerous ways to intense physical training, not all of them appealing. After months of hard work, my weight had increased from 53 kilogrammes to 58 kilogrammes. I had quads like tree trunks and a generous roll of fat around my middle. My husband Douglas was not so impressed. 'You're obviously fit, but you don't look it,' Douglas said one evening, a week before I left for Antarctica. I raised an eyebrow, stood up from the sofa and walked across the living room to Douglas, who is not particularly dainty. Then I picked him up clear off the floor.

'No – no – NOOOOO!!!' he shouted in horror. He wriggled like a fly in a spiderweb. I carried him across the living room like a Viking with a tree trunk. Sensing the futility, Douglas stopped kicking. I laughed evilly. Douglas was mute with terror. What had become of his skinny wife? Had this blubbery monster eaten her?

'There.' I set him down in the corner. 'I can now literally put you in your place.'

Later that evening, I sat down on the edge of our bed before going to sleep. The fat beneath my sports tank top rolled itself elegantly into doughy layers, like blubber. I looked down and counted. I had five spare tyres. Douglas just sat in the bed and stared. Even in the dark, I could see the appalled whites of his eyes.

'Bloody hell,' he said, with a hint of awe.

The transformation was complete. I had become the Hulk version of myself. My thighs were like buildings. My footsteps made holes in the pavement. People scattered when I thumped into the supermarket, my meaty arms stretched out towards the nearest shelf of fat and complex carbohydrates. I was ready.

~

The next morning, by the time Tina's alarm tinkled softly at 12.30 a.m. I had only just fallen back asleep. For once the hut was not creaking or echoing. My heart sank when I realised how little rest we'd had. This was going to be some summit day. We lay there for a while in neighbouring sleeping bags, not speaking yet very aware of how reluctant the other person was to get up. Tina later said she saw a dead mouse next to her upon waking, but I didn't spot it. She must have squashed it in her sleep.

In the darkness the guides eventually stirred, then started the business of heating water and preparing breakfast. Tina and I silently sat up and started pulling on the usual —headlamps bobbing about in the dark: more layers of clothing, thick socks, boots, harness. I staggered out to the toilet hut and realised that, unusually, my stomach was in knots. I felt queasy. It might have been the early hour or the altitude, but I think it was more to do with nerves. After dry heaving, I walked back to the hut under the beautiful full moon. At least it wasn't cold. There was the odd gust of wind, nothing serious.

Back in the hut, I swallowed two packs of hot ready-mix oatmeal and drank some coffee, hoping the caffeine would settle my system. Then, water bottles filled and packs ready, we started off into the night. The snowy top of Pico de Orizaba glowed beautifully above us in the moonlight, behind great arching slopes of dark rock interlaced with snow and ice. As we started walking, I did an internal audit. I really didn't know if I had it in me to climb to the summit.

Within half-an-hour the altitude had hit all of us hard. I had to stop a few times to retch unproductively while Tina and David, who had joined us, looked as miserable as I felt. We weren't getting enough oxygen and felt shattered before we'd properly begun.

'Is there any way we could go a bit slower?' I asked our guide Juan. He nodded – 'No hurry' – as he assessed us, and we started off again, painfully slowly, over the rocks.

Within minutes we all felt miles better. My nausea disappeared, and Tina and David told me later how much better they'd felt after the change of pace. The next few hours passed without mishap. We climbed by the light of our headlamps, and while I concentrated on my footwork and keeping a steady pace, every so often I would glance up to look at the beautiful cliffs and rocks known as the Labyrinth around us, bathed in moonlight.

At around 15,000 feet we strapped on our crampons and took out our ice axes, and eventually reached the edge of the snowfield leading to the Jamapa Glacier. Tina, Juan and I took a break. David and his guide carried on separately.

'What altitude is this?' I asked Juan.

'About 16,400 feet.'

We had now cleared the rocky terrain. I looked up at Pico de Orizaba rearing up directly in front of us. I couldn't believe we had at least another 2,000 feet to climb. That was more like the kind of altitude gain on a usual summit day, and we still hadn't started on it yet. The sun began to rise, and lit up the valley with a beautiful warm glow.

We set off across the glacier. On our right we passed a rock formation called the Sarcophagi and as we did the wind started up. That whistling and roaring wind would not let up until we'd been to the top and headed down again to the same spot. We think it might have been around 35 kilometres per hour, speeding up to around 50 as we got higher and it turned our faces into cold masks. It was probably minus 15–20 degrees Celsius.

We started switchbacking across the glacier as we worked our way up. Heading on the west-facing zig was so much worse than the opposite zag of our zigzags. We tried marching straight up the slope for a bit, but that was tough too. So we shortened our zigzags and plodded on.

The going got steeper. We walked like elephants. We took one step about every two seconds – any faster meant having to pause, drained. We tried to minimise effort by raising each foot by the bare minimum needed to take a step and swinging the leg forward. We panted rhythmically, as it was the only way to get enough oxygen. I didn't have the energy to do more than play the same mindless, random pop tune in my head. It helped to blot out the faint knife-edge of panic with the knowledge that my reserves of energy were depleting rapidly with the huge elevation gain, and the whispers that I was not physically prepared for this challenge, not that night.

It was bizarre, but as low as my morale could sink and as shattering as it felt, I still loved this aspect of climbing. The way exhaustion forced out everything except immediate reality. The future and the past fall away. It didn't just cleanse the mind, it purged and polished it.

But this time was different. Something was wrong.

I began to hyperventilate. Huge inhale, quick exhale. I wasn't getting enough air. What was worse, the intense cold air was forcing my throat to tighten and the emergency puff I'd taken before we left was losing its effect. I forced myself to hyperventilate – inhale-exhale-inhale-exhale every second. It didn't really help. I'd only ever felt this awful once before, on Mont Blanc, for similar reasons. I couldn't breathe, so I couldn't focus.

The sun turned the sky warm and golden as it rose. It cast a dramatic shadow across the valley. While our snowy slope was in shade, the sun's rays lit up the Sarcophagi and turned it the colour of baked clay. The sky was turning progressively turquoise and flanked by a bank of light clouds. I didn't notice the beauty around us though. I was too busy gasping for air.

We lurched forward for three paces, stopped, leaned on the poles and panted, then walked another three paces, stopped and gasped. *I'm going to pass out.* The last time I felt like this was on Denali, in Alaska. It was the same wind, the same dancing golden snow, the same my-insides-have-been-sucked-out feeling. I stopped again and turned to face Tina.

'What do you think?' I shouted against freezing wind.

'Not much further.'

I looked up again. The summit may as well have been on Mars.

'It's too hard.' Tears leaked from the corners of my eyes and froze on my face.

A pause. Tina called back, 'Not much further. Slow and steady steps.'

I turned back to the path. I put one foot in front of the other. The burnished glow of sunrise grew into daylight. We worked like dogs for every few feet of ground gained, and by the time we got to the top I was desperately wrung out.

This is exactly what had happened on Denali. Maybe I'm not ready for this. I don't understand, all that training and I'm still so weak.

As soon as we sat on the snow by the crater, I collapsed and started sobbing. My whole body started shuddering from the effort. I could not hold my hands still. Tina limped a few feet away from me and sat down. A little further away, David threw up in some rocks, then slumped down against them onto the snow. We sat in a pool of still air and drank in the sunshine. I kept well away from the edge of the crater, which dropped away with horrifying abruptness. I felt so weak that just by staring, I felt in danger of falling into the huge, hungry abyss to my death. I wasn't just exhausted, I was worried.

Something is wrong. I should not be this tired. I can't get enough air. Don't tell me the asthma's back.

More than half-an-hour passed before I stopped shaking.

~

A few hours later I limped back into La Piedra Grande, feeling and looking like a sweaty, dehydrated wreck. Tina and David had overtaken me about an hour earlier. I staggered into the building. A couple looked up from their card game on the second bunk. I raised my hand in greeting.

'Thank you.' I bowed, then collapsed onto my bunk bed. 'That was... gruesome.'

The girl smiled, shuffling her cards.

'I was so slow,' I said with a weak smile.

She smiled gently.

'But you got up, didn't you?'

5

EYES OF THE SALT PLAIN

The mountain climbs were coming closer and closer, like waves whipped up by storm winds. The next volcano was the most intimidating of the Volcanic Seven. Ojos del Salado in Chile is not only the highest volcano in Latin America, but the highest volcano on the planet at nearly 23,000 feet.

'Good luck,' said Douglas as I kissed him goodbye at our front door. Behind me, the taxi waited to take me to Heathrow airport. I hugged him tightly. The few days we had spent together since I returned from Mexico hadn't been enough. I was only six weeks into the project, and still months from the end. So much time apart. This was harder than I expected.

'I'll miss you.' Tears blurred my vision.

'Me too. But you have a mission to accomplish. Go for it. I'll be thinking of you.'

~

'Sunscreen City,' said Matt as we stared out the windows at the sandy haze rising to meet our plane. My new team mate and I squinted to see Desierto de Atacama airport lounging below us like a metal armadillo in the sun. There was nothing much around it, save desert and nothingness and a long, straight tarmac road. Our plane touched down and the other passengers, mostly Chileans, burst into applause, as if surprised we had landed in one piece. We trundled to a halt. The airplane door opened, and as I stepped out onto the flimsy mobile stairs I received a face full of hot air, like the burst of heat when you open the oven door.

'Definitely summertime in the southern hemisphere.' I pulled my cheap plastic sunglasses down over my eyes.

'Uh-huh. Nothing wrong with that.'

We had landed just outside Copiapó in northern Chile, an hour's flight from Santiago. The sunlight flashed off the airport terminal's massive windows and the warm wind ruffled my hair as we climbed down the stairs to the warm tarmac. Matt ambled beside me, his lean and long-limbed frame towering over the noisy passengers. We were total strangers until only a few hours ago, and now would be spending the next three weeks camping together. We'd met that morning at my hotel in Santiago, where I'd spent the previous day on the patio glancing nervously at every grey-haired American who could be a mountaineer. I liked Matt right away.

The sun's glare winked out as we entered the airport terminal building. I blinked away the spots in my eyes that obscured the baggage reclaim area and joined the crowd around the conveyor belt. It clanked into motion. After a few minutes, it spat out my red duffel bag.

'Here, let me take that.' Matt leaned over and helped me drag it off by the strap.

'Nah, it's okay,' I said. I hoisted the red duffel onto my back, trying to look elegant. I didn't. 'If I can't lift 20 kilogrammes I have no business being on the mountain,' I said. The bag felt lighter than it had in Mexico. Maybe I was getting stronger.

The crowd clustered around the exit of the baggage reclaim, elbowing each other in their eagerness to offer taxis to the tourists and hugs to returning family. Our mountain guide was meeting us here. Matt and I drifted through the exit. I spotted a sheet of paper with our names on it. It was held by a particularly suntanned man in shorts, heavy metal T-shirt and a baseball cap. A long, greasy ponytail snaked down his back. The man stepped forward.

'Matt, Sophie, hello.' A lazy smile appeared above his goatee. 'My name is Fabio. I am your guide.'

Matt grabbed Fabio's hand. 'Good to meet you.' I nodded my hello.

Something felt off about this guy, but I couldn't say what. He seemed friendly enough. But there was something behind his expression that made me uneasy. He was smiling, but only with his mouth, not his eyes. I watched Fabio's face as he spoke to Matt. Maybe I was just tired from the journey over. *Shut up, Sophie. Nothing's wrong. You're just tired.*

We followed Fabio through the thicket of people and out into the desert sun. All around us was the blankness of the desert, the sky above suspended between baby blue and grey.

'My truck is not far.' Fabio loped off towards the car park. We followed him to a dusty, navy truck with an orange tarp covering the trunk. Fabio started untying the tarp and I peered in through the back window. There was litter everywhere. Empty plastic water bottles on the seats, while gym shoes, loose bits of paper and old food packaging were strewn on the floor. Meanwhile, Matt pinged enthusiastic questions at Fabio – 'How are the climbing conditions right now? How's the weather forecast look? Have you had a busy season?' – followed by slower, indistinct murmurs from Fabio.

'Come. Let's go.' Fabio threw our backpacks into the trunk and jerked a thumb towards the mountains.

Matt folded himself into the front seat. I swatted away an empty plastic water bottle and pulled myself up into the back. Fabio hopped behind the wheel, wound down the windows and gunned the engine. We roared out of the parking lot and down the dusty tarmac road east towards Copiapó. The breeze cooled the truck, and as the breeze brushed my face I closed my eyes and wished Douglas were with us. Maybe then I wouldn't feel so uneasy, and so alone.

'Have you climbed much outside Chile?' Matt shouted to make himself heard over the engine. 'I went to Bolivia a few years and then Ecuador, but I've heard Chile is fantastic.'

'If you love climbing, Chile is like a paradise,' said Fabio. I listened for a while, but it was too noisy to make myself heard from the back. I pushed my sunglasses up my nose and watched the desert landscape flash past. We zipped past vast dun-coloured expanses. On the horizon the mountains loomed, looking like little more than dust blown into giant plushy heaps.

An hour later, we arrived in Copiapó. The city was a gritty, hardscrabble regional town where the wealth had been wrung through hard labour from mines scattered across the Atacama Desert. In the dusty air, the squat run-down buildings hinted at a town built around mining rather than tourism. The plan was to stay in Copiapó tonight, then set out for Ojos del Salado in the morning.

Ojos del Salado was a game-changer at 22,615 feet, or nearly 7,000 metres. I'd never been higher than the summit of Kilimanjaro at 19,341 feet. Twenty thousand feet was a scary number. Everything changes above that level, because that's when the altitude really starts to hit, and there's no way of knowing beforehand how it would affect me. Once you're above it, all bets are off.

We checked into a motel, which was made up of several little cabins arranged in a semicircle. The place was deserted.

'You unpack, then meet in the restaurant in half-an-hour.' Fabio gave us that lazy smile again and slouched back to his room.

An hour later, the three of us sat down at a table in the middle of the empty restaurant patio. The waiters were dressed in ironed white shirts and black trousers. We were dressed in crumpled climbing clothes and dusty boots.

'I have an idea. Let me show you.' Fabio leaned over and grabbed his backpack. He took out a large notepad, flipped it open to a blank page and slowly drew a calendar and numbered the days. Fourteen days in total.

Matt and I closed our menus and leaned closer to look.

'With the programme from the agency, we have acclimatisation hiking on these days, yes?' He ticked off three of the days.

'That's right. We're meant to reach the summit on Day 11 and have two back-up days for the summit,' Matt said.

'Yes. Instead, I have a different idea,' Fabio ticked off three different days. 'We do acclimatisation climbs on these days instead. This way, the process of acclimatisation is more even.'

Matt and I stared at the new itinerary. It did seem to make sense. Fabio's plan looked more balanced than the one the agency had suggested. Instead of spending most of our acclimatisation time at lower altitudes, Fabio's plan provided better spacing. We would spend three days acclimatising at 10,000 to 13,000 feet, three days at 13,000 to 16,000 feet, and finally three days at 16,000 to 20,000 feet. After that, if the conditions were right: summit day.

'Looks okay to me,' I said. Fabio certainly seemed to know what he was doing. Maybe my first impression of him was wrong. I often misjudged people and wanted to give him the benefit of the doubt.

'That looks good,' Matt said. We clinked Coke cans to the coming adventure. A waiter brought over our starters, and as Matt and Fabio chatted I watched the evening sun warm the dusty red mountain behind the villas, which were draped with bright bunches of bougainvillea.

I smiled. The magenta flowers and I were old friends. Lush waterfalls of bougainvillea hung over the walls of our weekend house in Hong Kong. Every Friday evening, my parents and I drove out to the New Territories to spend lazy afternoons by the pool and hike the nearby hills. My father especially loved his garden, with its fat waxy grass and tropical plants. Sometimes my Chinese grandparents and cousins visited, and the whole family spent a happy afternoon picking lychees and longans off the trees, packed them in newspaper to take home.

I loved the evenings in the New Territories most of all. When the humid darkness fell and the lights in the pool shimmered on, I drifted to sleep to the sounds of the grownups talking as they played backgammon outside, the air tinged with barbecue charcoal. I never felt cold in Hong Kong, and I never felt alone. It was home.

My memory is not the best, but whenever I think of my childhood the same images resurface. Dad and I, hiking in the New Territories. The two of us looking down the windy mountain slopes at the boats in the harbour far below. Walking among the fields of Kam Tin, the brown hills hazy in the heat, talking to the Chinese farmers.

The day I found out that we were leaving Hong Kong was the day I learned what dread was. It was one of those warm, close days when I broke into a sweat just crossing the playground. Primary school had ended, and my classmate Sabine and I were dawdling by the gates waiting for our Chinese nannies, our *amahs*, to pick us up. The sun filtered blearily through the tall banyan trees.

'So when are you leaving Hong Kong?' Sabine asked.

I rummaged through my school bag for a juice box. 'What do you mean?'

'*Everyone* has to leave,' she said, pleased to know something I didn't. 'Before the Chinese take over.'

I stared at her and sipped the juice through a straw, not sure whether to believe her. The soupy air glued my shirt to my back.

'I'm going to stay here forever.' Even as I said that, I felt a creeping anxiety as I recalled snippets of conversations between my parents when they thought I wasn't listening. Something about schools, and properties.

Sabine shrugged. She waved at her *amah*, who had just arrived, and walked off to meet her.

Hong Kong was returning to Chinese rule in 1997, and the deadline hung heavy over the city. Like most of Hong Kong's population, my Chinese grandparents had fled the war, famine and revolution in communist China to seek a new life in Hong Kong, which was under British rule. Fear of what would happen to Hong Kong after the handover led to an exodus in the 1980s. Every morning, queues formed by 5 a.m. outside the US, British and Canadian consulates. People were desperate for foreign passports. They wanted to get out any way they could.

'Dad, are we leaving Hong Kong?' I asked that weekend as we drove out to the New Territories.

Dad paused before answering. I was sitting in the back seat and saw the sides of his cheeks tighten. He was calculating how much to tell me, gauging how much a nine-year-old could comprehend.

'Yes, I think so.'

A hollowness formed in my chest. I hadn't really taken the prospect seriously, but now it was horribly real. 'But why?'

He paused, flicked the indicator, made a turn. 'Because it's time we went back to England.'

Back? I had no idea what he meant. The way I saw it, we were not one of those expatriate families who stayed in Hong Kong a few years and then returned to their cold European countries, as if the city had meant nothing to them. I had seen plenty of those families at my international school. Hong Kong was home. We were a Hong Kong family – my mother and I were Chinese – and I just happened to have a foreign father. It felt so wrong that Dad could just uproot the three of us to go 'back' to a strange place. I'd only been to England a few times. Each time, I was bewildered by the odd mannerisms and the cold weather.

'I think, if we didn't go back, one day when you're older you'll wish you had a better education,' Dad said.

'But I like my school here,' I mumbled. It was as close as I dared to contradict him.

Another silence. 'It's time we went back to England,' he repeated. That was the end of the conversation.

From that day on, a countdown ticked in the background, in tandem with the garish billboard on the Shenzhen–Hong Kong boundary ticking down the minutes until the handover. I could not understand how my father could bear to leave. Everyone has two homes in life: the one you are born into, and the one you later adopt. I'd assumed my father had given Hong Kong a place in his heart.

We left in 1992. I was fourteen years old. The day we left, I vowed to return as soon as possible. Nothing else mattered, except returning to Hong Kong. I needed to recover what I had lost.

I hadn't realised that Dad was also searching for a long-lost home of his own: England. He'd been away for so long that his past had become as distant as Dad's memory felt to me now. I'd been too young to understand that Dad was also trying to piece together his past.

Suddenly, I heard someone calling me.

'What do you think, Sophie? Do you want to buy fresh fruit for the trip or are you okay with just the dried stuff?' Matt was asking.

I snapped back to reality, and to the happy task of planning for a mountain expedition.

~

The next morning, Matt, Fabio and I roared out to the Atacama Desert.

The morning was scorching. I wound down my dusty window as we sped out of Copiapó and towards the *Ruta de los Seismiles* that snaked east out of Copiapó, right up to the Chile–Argentina border where the highest mountains were clustered. The back of our truck rattled with a half-dozen extra canisters of fuel and a dozen plastic bags of steak, fresh tomatoes and bread that we had bought at the supermarket.

An hour after leaving the congested streets of Copiapó, we cruised through deep warm valleys between the tan-khaki mountainsides. The vegetation slowly petered out, leaving only arid rock baking in the sun.

My apprehension of Fabio had vanished overnight. I'm the kind of person whose outlook on reality changes vastly, depending on the amount of sleep and caffeine I've had. I was happy to lose myself in the scenery as we wound through the desert roads. In the bright mid-morning sun, the arid Atacama Desert shimmered its welcome; long-haired Fabio and sinewy Matt were my fellow adventurers. This was how a mountain climbing expedition should feel. *Bring on the mountain.*

After a minute, Fabio reached down and turned up the volume on his heavy metal music, as if to blast away the beauty around us. Ozzy Osborne, Iron Maiden, Skid Row, Motley Crüe. All classics, all angry songs. Matt and I started to sing along whenever we knew the lyrics. Fabio turned up the volume.

We drove past hilltops with zigzag tracks, like huge cat scratches. 'That is a minery,' Fabio shouted over the music. The top of the mountain looked like it had been lopped off, blasted away. The mountains in the Atacama Desert are full of gold, iron, and copper, and have been mined since the late 1800s.

Things were fine until we drew up at a toll booth. Fabio smiled and chatted with the young woman in the booth as he paid the fare. Everything seemed fine. She handed him the change. Fabio beamed.

'*Gracias,*' he said. His pleasant tone made me smile as well. We pulled out of the toll booth.

'POR NADA,' Fabio shouted at no one in particular.

What the hell? Fabio's scathing tone made me look up. He wasn't smiling any more. His lip curled in a sneer and his eyes glared at the road. He looked inexplicably, undeniably, angry. I blinked and his expression was gone. I wasn't sure what I'd just witnessed. But now I was sure. Something was eating at this guy. Anger? Frustration? I couldn't be sure.

We arrived at Valle Chico by late afternoon. It was a grassy little oasis wedged between steep slopes of dark brown scree. Fabio pulled the truck off the gravel road and parked it on the scrubby grass, and as I hopped down out of the vehicle the earth smelled baked and fragrant. I breathed in deeply, trying to shake off the stale air of the truck. Matt joined me, stretching his arms and grinning as he took in our campsite for the next two nights.

Valle Chico stands at an altitude of 10,500 feet, and beyond the towering scree slopes, rainbow hills ranged from khaki to terracotta. We were ensconced in a medley of slopes, ridges, boulders and cliffs. The dry, still air lulled me into a strange contentment, as if the mountains were protecting us on our pilgrimage to Ojos del Salado.

'It's all so pretty.' I gestured at the brook that wound its way along the edge of the site.

'Yes,' Fabio said, suddenly appearing behind us. 'Perfect for cold beer.' He strode over to the river, clutching a rustling plastic supermarket bag containing a six-pack of beer. Fabio lowered the plastic bag into the chilly water, bending over awkwardly as he wound its handle around some rocks.

'Like it,' Matt chuckled. We started unloading our bags and fanned out to look for places to pitch our tents.

Beyond the creek was a larger field that stretched about 200 feet down the valley and was fringed by tall bushes of crabgrass.

'Lots of landmines here.' Matt pointed at the little piles of horse manure that pockmarked the field. I smiled and kicked aside a few tufty turds as we unpacked our tents. In the background I could hear the clang of Fabio pulling out camping stools and a foldaway table from our truck. He threw a steak about an inch thick onto the barbecue, then took out Tupperware boxes of chopped tomatoes in olive oil, cans of beer, bottles of condiments.

'Matt, you want a beer?' Fabio called as he squatted to fish a can out of the river.

'No. I don't drink,' Matt said with a smile.

Fabio frowned for a second, then shrugged.

'So, why do you want to climb Ojos del Salado?' Fabio asked me as he turned the steak over on the barbecue. I perched on a little camping stool, watching the fire.

I gave my usual bland answer. 'I'm climbing the highest volcano on each continent to raise money for cancer research.' I never told anyone about Dad.

'The highest volcanoes? You don't want to do the Seven Summits?' Matt asked.

I shook my head. 'Not really. I did try to climb Aconcagua a few years ago, but we got turned around by the wind.'

Fabio grimaced. 'I climbed Aconcagua also. But I don't like.'

'No?' I asked.

Fabio shook his head. 'Too many people. The camps were dirty, there is so much rubbish. Also, I feel very sorry for the *mulas*. All the time they are hitting them, making them work too hard. It is only about money. Ojos del Salado is better, more natural.'

I nodded. Above us, so small it was just a speck, a hawk circled lazily. It was probably drawn to our barbecue smoke. Day turned to evening, and in my naïveté I felt that we belonged in that sheltered spot. As if we were truly part of it all.

'One time, I see a *puma* here,' Fabio said. 'I think he was hungry, because usually they never come down here. I hide under the truck, and I only see his eyes in the dark, jumping here – here – here,' he said, tracing his finger through the air. 'I was never so scared before in my life.'

The mountain puma is so rarely seen in Chile that it's known as the ghost cat. There were signs of it everywhere – like cleanly picked bone fragments, white vicuna skulls on the mountain – but like phantoms, no one seemed to have any evidence, just stories to prove they were real. We were being watched by unseen ghost cats.

As darkness fell we tore into the tender steak and fresh tomato salad, telling stories and swapping jokes. The stars started to wink into sight. By the time I headed back to my tent, our campsite lay under an awesome sky of diamonds.

~

'Today we climb the Goat-Devil Mountain,' Fabio said the next morning.

'Goat what now?' Matt looked up from his breakfast of toast and peanut butter.

'I call it Goat-Devil. Because… the mountain make me think of him,' Fabio said.

Matt and I exchanged glances.

'Who the hell is he?' I said.

'*El Chupa Cabra*,' he said. 'Like, half man, half goat.'

It was morning, and the three of us were sitting at the foldable camping table by the truck, drinking coffee and eating toast cooked on the barbecue. Fabio chuckled, jumped up from his camping chair and rummaged in his backpack. He pulled out his large notepad.

'I don't know what you call this in English,' he said, flipping through the pages. He stopped at a page and showed it to us. Sure enough, Fabio had drawn a half-dozen alarming creatures with the head of a man (with horns) and the physique of a goat. Goat-Man.

'I see,' I said, not seeing at all. Matt stared at the drawings as if he couldn't work out whether he was looking at porn. Fabio frowned.

An hour later, we headed off up the mud track leading out of Valle Chico and came to the foot of a mountainside covered in scree. Goat-Devil Mountain. It looked simple enough. The path was well-worn by previous climbers and possibly a few animals, and as we started up the track the sun burned the exposed skin on our necks, ears, the backs of our hands. The stifling air grew increasingly warm and I started to sweat. Fabio led at an easy pace. The only sound was the satisfying crunch of our boots on the scree.

For 40 minutes we zigzagged across the face of Goat-Devil Mountain. Our campsite had dwindled to a green streak of grass many feet below between the massive rocky slopes. We reached the top of the slope and hauled ourselves up onto a high plateau. The wind whipped my hair out of my collar and across my face.

We sat down on the loose rock on top of the ridge and unpacked our lunches. Our waterproof jackets rustled with the wind. Now that we were at the top of Goat-Devil Mountain, the landscape opened out into a massive high plateau that stretched for miles, leading to other peaks and ridges well over 13,000 feet high. The sweeps of mountain slopes, high plateaus and sky were immense, alien to human scale.

'Wow. What a view.' Matt opened a packet of wafer biscuits.

I peeled a banana. 'Mm-hm. How're you feeling so far?'

'Good. But then I guess we're not so high up yet.'

I looked over at Fabio. He sat cross-legged, staring into space.

'How far are we going today?' I asked.

Fabio looked up and pointed at a distant peak. 'Over there. We cross big plateau, then up to the peak at 13,000 feet.'

I smacked my lips. 'Matt, you got any of that powdered energy drink? What's it called? Zuko?'

'Sure do.' He tossed over the packet of Zuko.

I ripped open the little packet, unscrewed the top of my water bottle and tipped in half the packet. 'Thanks.'

'I might have some of that too.' Matt poured the rest of the powder into his bottle, closed the lid and shook it.

I glanced at Fabio. Something felt off. He wasn't smiling or talking as much today. Maybe he was hungover from all the beer. After a few minutes he stood up and dusted off the back of his trousers.

'Come. Let's go.' He set off for the plateau. Matt and I swallowed our lunches, took another swig of energy drink, and followed.

We walked. Actually, Matt and I marched. We chattered away as we took in the high plateau which led us past abrupt jutting rocks which the wind had eroded into weird, Dali-esque shapes.

'How're your feet?' I asked.

'Good,' Matt said.

'Nothing worse than sore toes.'

'Tell me about it.'

We were talking faster and faster. We sounded like we were on speed.

'On Denali, I got two black big toenails. Took a while to grow out.'

'Oh man. Nothing worse than that.'

'One time, I got a black toenail,' Matt said.

'Really?'

'It fell off.'

'Yeah?'

Matt and I drew up alongside Fabio, who walked slowly with his head down, staring at the ground just in front of him. We passed him, like motorcyclists passing a worn-out old bus. Fabio ignored us.

'And guess what,' Matt said.

'What?'

'The next one that grew in was black as well,' Matt said.

'Wow. Hideous,' I laughed. I felt fabulous, more full of energy than ever.

Matt and I marched up the hill like hyperactive energiser bunnies. We only stopped when we reached the ridge at 12,000 feet.

'We're here?' I said.

'Yeah. This is it.'

'This is the spot Fabio said?'

'Yep.'

'Where's Fabio?'

'Oh yeah. Where'd he go?'

'Dunno.'

'Huh.'

We turned and looked back the way we came. Fabio was now a good few hundred feet down the slope. His greasy curls fluttered in the wind from under his navy baseball cap, and even from where we sat I could make out his gaping mouth as he panted from the hot sun and the baking sand. The sweat shone on his face.

Matt and I sat down in the shade of a giant rock and faced down the mountain. We exhaled and dug our heels into the light sand.

'Want more Zuko?' I said. I dug out the empty packet of Zuko, our orange-flavoured energy drink powder.

'Nah, I got more.'

'This is good stuff,' I flapped the packet at him.

'Yeah,' he said, 'I feel great.'

'Totally. I feel fantastic.' We were talking at warp speed.

I took a closer look at the label. Oh. This explained everything. I started giggling to myself like a crazy person.

'What's up?' Matt asked.

'You know what? It says, "Add two litres of water."'

'Wait, what?'

'Two litres.'

'But we only added one.'

I paused.

'Yeah. Our Zuko was way too strong. We've been drinking pure sugar.' I started giggling. Matt looked at the packet and started laughing. We'd chugged the equivalent of mountain crack. We may as well have just snorted the stuff.

While Matt and I sat laughing under our rock, Fabio continued to plod towards us. If he were a cartoon he would have had a little black cloud over his head. When Fabio reached us the atmosphere seemed to darken, as if infected by his bad mood. He unfastened his backpack and flung it to the ground in revenge for some unspoken travesty.

'I hate when I have hot feet,' Fabio spat. He bared his teeth in something almost, but not quite like a smile. He sat down in the shade of a neighbouring rock and unlaced his boots, flinging them off in disgust. Matt and I glanced at him.

'Hey Fabio, what's up?' I started to say, but stopped myself. I had the feeling it would only annoy him more. I was beginning to feel like I was walking – climbing – on eggshells with this guy.

By evening, I was starting to feel downright tense around Fabio. Something felt really off. A propos of nothing, Fabio announced: 'I want to see Matt drink beer.' He smiled leeringly at Matt. 'I imagine when you drink, you are crazy, yes?' It was a strange moment.

Matt's eyes widened in the dim evening light. He half-grimaced and waved Fabio off.

'No, thanks.'

Having got nowhere with Matt, Fabio now half-heartedly turned to me.

'And you? You drink?' he asked me without much interest. I shook my head and headed back to my tent. Fabio shrugged and cracked open another can.

That night, I was woken by the dismayed yipping of a desert coyote on the mountain high above our valley. The coyote sounded wary, as if in fear of the humans invading its territory. I lay awake for a while and listened, then fell back asleep.

~

After two nights in Valle Chico we dismantled our tents, packed up the truck and continued along the desert road to our next stop, Laguna Santa Rosa at 12,500 feet. Chile's Nevado Tres Cruces National Park is home to several lakes and lagoons surrounded by the foothills of the Andes. We followed the dusty mountain road past gullies harbouring vivid sprouts of vegetation and climbed to the pass at 13,100 feet. All around the earth was dry and baked earth, dramatic mountains coloured in layers of light chocolate to brick red to mustard. After the pass, the road dropped in the direction of the massive Salar de Maricunga salt plain and the Cerro Tres Cruces, a monumental massif of three snowy peaks – Tres Cruces Sur, Tres Cruces Central, Tres Cruces Norte – that dominated the landscape. We turned off the road, and that's when I saw the lake.

Nothing I had read had prepared me for our first sight of Laguna Santa Rosa. The water possessed a preternatural beauty that was compelling and familiar. I had never seen so many shades of blue in one place. The sight stunned me. Laguna Santa Rosa was a moody, fluid mosaic which seemed to shift with emotions swelling beneath the surface. The water was light grey-blue here, cerulean there and turquoise elsewhere. Dozens of Andean flamingos dotted the lagoon like pink confetti. Behind the lake, the Tres Cruces reared up like tidal waves transformed into rock.

'This is other-worldly,' breathed Matt. I nodded and walked closer to stare at the water.

Our home for the night was a wooden shelter by the lake. That evening, as we headed off to bed, Fabio said, 'At night, we keep the door locked. Because of the fox.'

Matt and I nodded as we leaned over the railing watching the sun set behind the Tres Cruces. Suddenly, a scrawny, grey-brown creature ran out of nowhere and circled our cabin. Its malicious eyes fixed on us as it sniffed the food inside the shelter.

'There's the fox,' Fabio said.

I stared. This thing was no fox. In Britain, foxes are sleek, auburn-coloured animals, graceful as a cat and not that much bigger. The thing glowering at us now was grey, shaggy and as big as a calf. *That's not a fox mate, that's a coyote.* My skin started to crawl.

An hour later, I lay down on a mattress on the floor and tried to fall asleep. The cabin was pitch dark, with the odd head torch flickering on as a climber searched for a toothbrush or a last drink of water before settling down for the night. I lay in the darkness, enjoying the soft mattress. All was quiet. Suddenly, the back of my neck went cold. *The coyote was in the room.* I wasn't sure how I knew, but I could feel its presence in the expectant silence, like the pause between lightning and thunder. I slowly felt for my walking pole lying on the floor next to the mattress.

A step. A rustle. It was definitely in the room. I steeled myself and got out of bed. I stalked through the dark to the kitchen. The moonlight streamed through the open door. I flipped on my head torch and stepped out onto the porch. There was trash everywhere – on the kitchen floor, in the doorway, all over the steps leading out to the desert. It was a big smelly mess. Cursing, I cleaned everything up and jammed the door shut with a chair.

It occurred to me as I returned to my mattress that I had no reason to feel angry. The coyote wasn't invading our space. We were the ones invading its space, with our trucks and our noise and our shit pit. We were the intruders, not they.

~

The next morning, we struck out across the desert, past mysterious little power stations on the right and the Salar de Maricunga on the left. We reached a T-junction; a left turn led to the 15,400-feet-high San Francisco Pass to Argentina; a right turn led around the Tres Cruces, past several mining stations and further into the land of high-altitude desert lakes. In the distance, we saw Incahuasi ('Inca House'), which has several Inca ruins on the summit at 21,700 feet.

I continued to sit in the back seat, wedged between climbing boots and bags of food. The mountains of the Atacama were so beautiful that the sight of them soothed the odd tension in our little group. Natural beauty like this was vast and eternal. We humans were here only a short while with our petty problems and would soon be gone. That was exactly as it should be.

After hours of driving through the greys, tans and slate of the Atacama Desert, the neon turquoise of Laguna Verde jolted my eyes like a splash of water in the face. The blueness of the mineral lake actually glowed, as if lit up from below. It was even more vivid than Laguna Santa Rosa. Its shores were leached bone-white from the salt, and above it towered massive, brooding volcanoes, like silent protectors.

Laguna Verde is a salt lake at 14,100 feet, next to Camp Murray at the start of the trail to Ojos del Salado. The altitude was increasing, but we still hadn't seen Ojos del Salado, hidden as it was behind the Tres Cruces. The gravel crunched under our tyres as we juddered down towards the lake's edge. Fine dust brushed my face through my open window. I lost myself in the beauty of the lake.

The dead cow was a startling sight. At first I thought it was a white rock that had morphed into a disturbing shape. But as we approached, I realised that it was the bleached, desiccated carcass of a cow. It must have died weeks ago. There was no smell. The cow looked oddly peaceful as it knelt penitent by the side of the road, still crouched in the shape of its death.

A tattered squat building by the lake shore was the only sign that the place had once been a tourist concession. The big welcome sign now lay rusting by the side of the building. Someone had spray-painted something about keeping the place clean. The refuge seemed old and faded, as if it held only memories of what once was.

Inside the refuge, previous climbers had attempted to fix up the flimsier patches of the clapboard walls with random bits of debris. The power was long gone; the electric cables ended in frayed naked wires.

Something stank. I walked around to the back of the cabin and almost stepped into a sea of trash. The back of the building was open to the sky and piled high with garbage. The ripe smell of rotting orange peel, bad eggs, urine and faeces invaded my throat. I gagged. This was the legacy of the refuge's past inhabitants. Flies buzzed among the stained plastic bags, the broken poles, the shattered bottles. My throat started to convulse and I staggered away to the edge of the emerald lake. I stared at the white-blond crags, wondering how many of them also hid festering human shit pits.

~

Despite the tension, Matt, Fabio and I had become an odd little team. Matt and I got along well, though Fabio seemed to prefer his own company. Sometimes, as Matt and I read or chatted in the shade of the refuge, Fabio went out to sit alone in the front seat of the truck. We assumed he was taking a nap on the cushioned seats. But he wasn't. He was just sitting there, staring into space and frowning.

I was reading in the shelter the next day when Matt returned from his search for a place to defecate. His lanky frame blocked out the sunlight as he entered the shelter.

'I had to walk way out there to find a spot to go.' Matt waved a toilet roll at me.

I smiled over the top of my book. There were no strangers here. 'Found a good spot, did you?' I asked. Matt nodded, looking pleased with himself. He came and sat next to me at the rickety table and took out his book.

Fabio was at the counter making seafood rice on his little camp stove. The warmed-up herbs in the rice smelled delicious. He handed me a plate.

'How old are you? You have children?' Fabio asked as he turned back to the hissing stove. He seemed eager to chat for once.

'I'm thirty-five. No children.' This was encouraging. Maybe we could defuse some of the tension. 'And you said earlier that you're twenty-six, right?'

Fabio turned around again. He considered me for a second, then shot over a smile. It didn't match the hostile expression in his eyes.

'No. I am *thirty*-six, not twenty-six.' He turned back to the stove.

Oh dear. 'Sorry, I must have misheard you last time.'

Fabio shrugged. He came over and sat at the wooden table. He stared at me.

'So... You are thirty-five?'

I nodded.

'Ah. You are just about to –.' He made a downwards sliding motion with his hand, to illustrate the swift decline of my youth. His eyes scanned my face for wrinkles.

Silence. From the corner of my eye I saw Matt look up from his book, raise his eyebrows, and wordlessly lower his gaze again. The awkwardness settled over us like drizzle.

~

I'd lived through plenty of stilted dinnertime conversations, thanks to those awkward years after Dad moved us from Hong Kong to England.

'Would you like some more peas?' someone asked at dinner.

'Oh no, would YOU like some more peas?' Dad replied.

'Oh no, after you.'

'Please, you have some first.'

They pushed the bowl of peas back and forth.

Will someone just take the goddamn peas?

I was fourteen and had just started boarding school in England. Life there was bizarre from day one.

'So Dad, when someone wants something, they have to ask someone else if *they* want it first?' I asked from the back of the car as we drove home.

He glanced over his shoulder at me. I could tell he was about to get annoyed. 'Yes. It's good manners.' His tone forbade further questions.

During a Chinese meal, there is no to-and-fro over who takes the peas first. Everyone sits down, the host says, 'Everybody eat,' and then we eat.

In England, there was a social code I just couldn't crack; a club that I could never belong to. For one thing, everyone thought I was Canadian. Or Irish. Anything but English. After years of feeling accepted and secure in Hong Kong, life became a series of mini-confrontations. Everyone demanded an explanation for accent, my ethnicity, my looks. People told me I didn't look Asian enough to be from Hong Kong, or that I didn't sound English enough to be from England. I should have just let it slide. But I was young, and insecure and belligerent in the way of most adolescents.

My father seemed to slip effortlessly back into life in England, but Mom and I found it harder to adapt. I learned that Brits, or at least the Brits I met, never said what they really meant. Over the years I tried, but my understanding of British mannerisms never really improved. I came away from most conversations confused as to what had actually been said. Everything was implied, nothing stated outright. I yearned for the self-deprecating, down-to-earth directness of Cantonese.

Mom and I, on the other hand, were blunt to the point of rudeness. 'Why waste time beating around the bush? Just say what you mean,' she always said to me in private.

What bothered me most about English mannerisms were the multiple 'pleases' and 'thank yous' in every sentence. In those early days, before I became used to it, every 'I'm fine, *thank you*,' created distance, every 'Oh no, after *you*,' sounded like satire. In Chinese, the phrase 'you're welcome' (*ung sai haak hay*) translates literally as 'no need to be polite.' 'Polite', in turn, has the word 'guest' (*haak*) in it. That's because only a guest – someone you're not close to – would behave so formally, saying 'please' and 'thank you' after every tiny thing. In Chinese culture, it's bad form to act like a guest with people you're meant to be close to, like family. Instead of formality, there should be familiarity.

During that confusing first year in England, I returned to Hong Kong again and again in my dreams. I bought a plane ticket, a ferry ticket, a train ticket. I saw the islands and water of Hong Kong below my plane window, and told myself that never, ever, would I be taken from my home again. I woke up with such disappointment and yearning that it made me cry.

My mother tried her best to transplant our southern Chinese culture to cold England. She and I still spoke Cantonese at home.

'You are my daughter,' she always said, 'and you will speak to me in Chinese.'

One afternoon, Mom came into my bedroom clutching a stack of thin textbooks and set them down on my desk.

'I'm going to teach you to read and write in Chinese,' she said.

We spent hours going through those textbooks. Every evening, I wrote out the characters again and again, trying to connect the unfamiliar symbols to the sounds of my native Cantonese, which I had learned only by ear. Each character told a story. The more characters I learned, the more the past revealed itself as a land of endless stories, waiting for me to come back and live them.

~

The next morning, Matt, Fabio and I went on an acclimatisation hike up to 16,400 feet on Mulas Muertas, a hill not far from Laguna Verde. We stopped for sandwiches on a windy bluff overlooking the lake. As I bit into the sandwich with the altitude ringing in my temples, it occurred to me that there was a problem with Fabio's acclimatisation plan. We were going to spend three days at 16,400 feet, then shoot straight up to 22,615 feet on summit day. That was much too abrupt. We weren't going to have enough time to acclimatise.

As we descended Mulas Muertas, I rehearsed what I would say to Fabio. I had a feeling he wouldn't like my suggestion.

'Fabio,' I said over dinner that night, 'Would it be possible to stretch out our acclimatisation process? Maybe we could go for the summit one day later. That would give us more time.'
Fabio looked uneasy. 'Why?'

'I don't think three days at 17,000 feet is going to be enough to acclimatise us for nearly 23,000 feet on summit day. We have two extra days at the end of our programme anyway, for contingencies. We could use one of those days.'

Fabio gave me that fake smile again, then avoided my gaze. 'I think it's better if we go up fast, and come down fast. Then we can have more time at the beach after!' He stood up and walked out.

~

The tension that had been brewing within our team became overtly toxic after we reached Atacama Camp a few days later. Somewhere on the bumpy ride up to Atacama Camp at 17,200 feet, Fabio had changed. Or maybe his true colours had finally come out.

'Now the holiday is over,' he snapped as we came to a halt on the windy plateau. Fabio's earlier veneer of pleasantness was gone, like cheap paint rubbed off metal.

Matt and I leaped out, excited to be so much higher up the mountain. The summit of Ojos del Salado brooded high over our heads. In only a few days, we would be climbing across those snow rivers and battling our way to its crater.

Atacama Camp looked like a bereft fairground at the end of the holiday season. The dry wind had scoured the earth into sand. A red shipping container stood to the side. Clusters of multi-coloured tents looked wind-battered, as if they had been there for a long time. A few tents clustered around trucks and ruffled in the wind despite the low stone walls around them. A path covered in loose and deep dust led out of the plateau and zigzagged towards Tejos Camp at 19,000 feet, also known as high camp.

Most expeditions stayed at Atacama Camp for a day or two to acclimatise, before gradually moving up to Tejos Camp. Fabio had other ideas.

'We set up the tents quickly, then we go up,' Fabio said. I couldn't read his expression behind his sunglasses.

Matt and I grabbed our tents from the truck and flung them onto the ground. Under Fabio's orders, we set them up right next to the truck for maximum wind protection and tied some of the guy lines directly to the wheels.

When you've just arrived at this sort of altitude on a mountain, everything has to be slowed down. The more drastic your exertion, the likelier it is that your body will react badly to the rarefied oxygen, the burning sun and the higher risk of dehydration.

'Use the big stones to put in the corners of the tent,' Fabio said. We'd only just arrived at an altitude of 17,000 feet, and Matt and I were stumbling back and forth carrying boulders. The bigger the boulders, the safer our tents would be.

'Whew,' I said.

'Yeah,' Matt said, heaving what looked like a menhir onto his back.

Our tents looked pretty secure now. They weren't just weighed down with rocks shoved into the corners. I'd also build a mini-wall around mine, like the other campers, to prevent the wind from lifting my tent. I was ready to sit back and rest.

I had just sat down inside my tent when Fabio snapped: 'Get ready. Pack the camp equipment in your backpacks. We are going to Tejos high camp.'

Matt and I looked at each other and shrugged. After all, we had agreed to this itinerary.

By the time we started plodding out of camp, already sweating under our climbing clothes and 15-kilogramme packs, it was just after midday. We were roasting. I was forced to breathe hard right from the start. Our rucksacks were bursting with food, water, gas stoves, cooking equipment. I felt myself drying out with each breath, and awarded myself one Coca-Cola sweet from the front pocket of my fleece top with every turn of the track. Matt walked in front of me. This time, the rocket-fuel orange drink had no effect. As we rounded the last corner of the zigzag path on the steep slope overlooking camp, I glanced down at the now-tiny tents and vehicles below, next to which were a handful of ant-sized climbers standing in the sun. They craned up at us, looking astonished. We were the only group to head up further the same day as we arrived at Atacama Camp. All the other groups that had arrived that morning were taking a rest day.

It took 3 hours to lug everything to high camp. The path up to Tejos Camp winds through great sweeps of scree and giant shards of volcanic rock. As we climbed the wind picked up. Finally, we saw high camp, which consisted of two orange shipping containers welded together into an L-shape and plonked in a small rock- and snow-free clearing. We were now right under the nose of Ojos del Salado and the temperature was 18 degrees Celsius.

Fabio – this new, intense version – said only two words during the whole trip: 'Very good.' He kept checking his watch during the break, like a drill sergeant. When Matt later said warmly to Fabio, 'I think we have a strong team,' Fabio just shot him a baleful stare and said nothing.

'Oh yeah, that's totally doable. Definitely,' Matt now said as he surveyed the path leading to a rocky ridge and then snaking up in a zigzag up the mountain face towards the crater. The summit was still another 3,600 feet above us.

We unloaded the gear in the refuge and ate a quiet lunch sitting on the bunk beds. An hour later, we were striding back down to Atacama Camp.

Matt and I were jubilant. We schussed down through the deep sandy scree like alpine skiers and were back down at Atacama

Camp in 45 minutes. We flopped into a pair of wooden deck chairs and felt the mid-afternoon sun on our faces. We sipped warm flat Cokes. Matt passed around some crisps.

The ripe smell of warm urine stung our nostrils as it evaporated off the ground. I fought the urge to gag. Apparently people had decided it was fine to pee right next to their tents.

Suddenly, my temples started to ache.

No biggie. I was probably just dehydrated. I sipped some more of my Coke. It tasted unusually sweet.

Keep still. Don't move.

'You alright?' Matt asked.

The butterflies started. The vice around my head tightened.

'Yep. Just need more food and drink.' I swallowed. My saliva tasted sour.

The butterflies became wasps. Something was very wrong. I lurched to my feet and staggered towards the outdoor toilet. I only made it as far as the back of the refuge before I fell to my knees and vomited. In between the puking, I started to wheeze as I tried desperately to loosen the invisible noose around my neck.

After I was able to stand again, I asked to borrow Matt's pulse-oximeter, a device the size of a matchbox which clips over your finger tip. My blood oxygen saturation had been 84 per cent earlier, which is normal at an altitude of 17,000 feet. The red numbers which flashed up now were quite different. Now they read: 68 per cent. 69 per cent. 67 per cent.

'That's too low,' Matt said, reading over my shoulder.

It took a while, but Matt managed to convince Fabio to take me down to Murray Camp. *I can't breathe. I can't breathe. Get me out of here.*

~

The next morning, my headache was gone and my stomach had calmed down. Now Matt was the one with problems. We had spent the night back down at Murray Camp. Our modified itinerary was clearly not working – we needed more time to acclimatise. Over lunch of salami and toast, I asked Fabio again if we could attempt the summit a day later than planned.

'After all, we have an extra day built in, and neither Matt nor I really want to spend that extra time at the beach resort afterwards. Our aim is to get to the top of Ojos,' I said.

Fabio looked down at his plate, as if he were about to read aloud from it.

'Summit day is not fun,' he said. 'You are tired, you are cold, you are stressed. You should just enjoy every day, not only think of the summit.'

My stomach clenched in bright red anger. 'But you understand, I *need* to get to the top. I'm doing this to raise money. I need to get a photo of myself at the summit, holding the charity banner.'

Fabio smiled vaguely and then looked away, as if bored of the conversation.

When we returned to Atacama Camp the next day, it looked much the same. Our tents were still there, shivering in the wind. As we climbed down out of the truck, one of the French-Canadian climbers ambled over to see if we were okay.

'We were really surprised to see you go up after you'd only just arrived,' one of them said quietly. 'You guys had a tough day.'

That afternoon we took it easy. Fabio spent the day in one of the shelters ('for guides only,' he said).

I read. Towards evening, I walked over to the base of the zigzag path and stared up at the summit. 'What a difference a day makes,' I crooned to myself, picturing the orange shelter at high camp. It was a relief to feel fit again.

'Twenty-four little hours,' Matt warbled back. I turned to see Matt shambling over from the other end of the plateau. I'd forgotten how well sound carried in the mountains.

'How are you feeling?' I asked, smiling.

'Okay,' he said, wrinkling his nose. We stood there for a few seconds, looking up at the path. Ojos del Salado peered down at us. A soft breeze tickled my face. I took big deep breaths of the clean, arid air.

'I guess we'll know tomorrow whether we're well enough to move to high camp,' I said.

'I guess so.'

~

I'd been awake for hours by the time I heard Matt shifting around in the tent next to mine. The cold had woken me at 3 a.m. This time I didn't feel acute nausea but a bruising headache. I felt jumpy, anxious, wrung out and chilled to the bone all at the same time. It was a relief when the sun finally rose.

'Matt, how are you feeling?' I called through the canvas.

'Like crap,' came Matt's muffled voice. 'I didn't get to sleep until 5 a.m.'

I could hear the guides bustling around the refuge a few feet away, heating up water and chatting. It was time to drag ourselves over and face the situation.

Fabio had set up the breakfast table by the refuge. I walked over slowly and sank into a chair and closed my eyes, hoping to recharge my batteries using solar energy, like a cat. My brain was quite empty. Matt, sitting opposite, looked like someone whose mind wouldn't leave him alone, and he wished it would.

'I'm so tired of putting myself back together every morning,' he finally said. Since the beginning of the expedition, Matt had been doing yoga stretches twice a day to get the kinks out of his back.

I cracked open my eyes and looked at Matt. He looked very drawn.

'Yep,' I nodded. I closed my eyes again.

Fabio, who had been squatting on the ground making toast over the camping stove, looked up and studied Matt's face.

'What do you want to do?' I asked.

He paused. 'I'm not going up,' he said slowly.

And just like that, the Seven Volcanoes Project was over. This couldn't be happening. I couldn't let it happen. I made one last desperate attempt at salvaging the expedition.

Fabio now sat peacefully at the table, sipping his coffee and enjoying the view. I was probably fighting a lost cause, but I had to try.

'How about this,' I said to him. 'We still have an extra day for acclimatisation in the itinerary, yes?'

Fabio looked over the rim of his coffee cup at me.

'What if Matt goes down to Murray Camp, and Fabio, you and I move to high camp, and tomorrow morning we try for the summit?'

Matt shrugged an *Okay by me.*

But as Fabio put down his coffee cup, I realised my gut feeling had been right all along. This guy had never had any intention of reaching the summit.

Our guide leaned forward, clasped his hands together and turned to train his eyes first on me, then on Matt. 'We are a family,' he said. 'We are not three. We are one.' It sounded like something out of *The Godfather*. Then he sat back in his chair and looked away.

'Maybe there's a chance I can go up with one of the other expeditions?'

Fabio ignored me.

I wanted to tell Fabio what a prick he'd been. I wanted to smack him in the head with his six-pack of beer for taking us up the mountain too high, too fast when it clearly wasn't protocol. I wanted him to pay for screwing up the Seven Volcanoes Project and refund all the extra costs I knew I'd have to pay. I knew I'd have to come back out to Chile and attempt Ojos del Salado again if I wanted to get my world record.

But mountain sickness not only makes you sick, it makes you apathetic. I looked at Matt. He was still just sitting there, as if wishing he were somewhere else. I looked at Fabio, who stared out at the mountains looking about as regretful as a rock.

What did it matter? Matt was already sick. Fabio had made up his mind. There was nothing to be done. Was I going to let this cynical, petty man rob me of my summit attempt, and possibly my world record?

I stood up in disgust and walked back to my tent. The wind hummed over Atacama Camp, which was starting to bake in the morning sun. The smell of other people's evaporating urine floated on the wind, and it was growing more pungent with the heat. I sat down in front of my tent, no longer in a hurry to get organised or go anywhere. I turned on my IPod and played some Stone Temple Pilots and Guns N' Roses. The top of Ojos del Salado sparkled against the deep blue sky. Conditions looked perfect at the summit. I sat and watched the groups head up the zigzag slope one by one. They waved and then hunkered down, stepping slowly, conserving energy. In a few hours, they would be at high camp, and by tomorrow morning, possibly the summit. I sat by my tent, sweating in my climbing layers, and swiped at the corners of my eyes.

~

The next morning neither Matt nor I made any effort to interact with Fabio. Now that our summit hopes were over, there was a feeling of total disbandment. Our goodwill towards our guide had dissolved along with our summit dream.

After his morning stretches, Matt headed out to the balcony in his camp booties and non-climbing clothes. I went out to join him. We both sat on the sunny deck, staring at Ojos. The bloated plume of clouds which had laced the sky the previous evening was now gone. There was barely any spindrift coming off the summit, miles in the distance. It was a perfect summit day.

I felt for Matt, who looked downcast, his self-confidence dented from Fabio's bluntness.

Fabio came out, saw us staring at Ojos, and came over to sit opposite us. Matt and I ignored him. The mood was heavy and rank.

Damn you. Damn you with your weird negativity and Goat-Man drawings and your beer. You've cost us the summit. You've cost me the world record.

Speaking haltingly, he said, 'You know – I tell you the truth.' Fabio's usual half-sneer of bravado was gone. He looked serious now. Matt and I looked up.

'This year, the weather is very strange. It is much hotter than usual. You saw at high camp, it was 18 degrees Celsius. That is very weird.' He pointed at me. 'You are strong, but the heat make you sick. It was too much heat, not enough water.'

Yeah right. More like too much altitude, not enough time.

Then, looking at Matt: 'And you, Matt, I think you have something –,' he searched for the right words, 'some problems psychologically.'

The tension became acute. I sucked in my breath.

Fabio went on, 'You see, my wife has depression. I live with it. Every day. And every day I try to help her feel better, make life easier for her. I know what I am talking about.'

Matt still wasn't speaking.

'When you think things are bad, you think they are very, very bad. I think this is why you didn't want to go to high camp.'

Matt just stared at Fabio. I said nothing. I had not expected this. I didn't know if Fabio was telling us the truth, or just giving us more excuses for pushing us up to high camp too fast. Or maybe, he never wanted to come on this expedition in the first place.

What did it matter now? It was too late. I just wanted to get out of here.

'What do you want to do now?' Fabio asked.

Pause.

'Let's just head back,' I said. Matt and Fabio nodded.

~

We drove for 5 hours through the desert, back down to Copiapó and straight out to Bahia Inglesa, a touristy beach resort on the coast. Suddenly, we were surrounded by tanned children holding dripping ice creams, women in bikinis and humid, salty air. We drove down the main strip, past seafood restaurants and outdoor cafés.

'Hey look, altitude 800 metres,' said Matt, pointing to a sign.

'That's nothing. We can do 5,000 metres better than that,' I said.

He grimaced. I wound down the window to let out some of the stifling defeat. I was stunned. I normally loved being by the sea. But when I saw the Pacific Ocean bob up over the dusty horizon as we drove down the motorway to Bahia Ingles, I felt no joy. I hadn't come all this way to sit on the beach. I hadn't earned it. I certainly hadn't packed for it. I wanted to be back on Ojos del Salado, heading for the summit.

Bahia Ingles was so packed with summer tourists that Matt, Fabio and I were forced to share the same hotel room. We went out for dinner on the seafront and out of sheer politeness Matt and I treated Fabio to dinner. I sipped at a half-pint of beer, my first taste of alcohol in weeks. The three of us had nothing much to talk about. We sat there in our climbing clothes, watching the young couples and families with shrieking happy children run around in shorts and flip flops. We reeked of defeat.

That night I had the same dream on repeat: I packed my bags. I left the hostel. I rented my own truck and floored it right back to Ojos del Salado to attempt the summit again.

The next day, Fabio left. He had taken off two days early, leaving Matt and I alone with nothing to do but wait for our flights.

Like a bizarre, marathon blind date, Matt and I tried to kill time by browsing the street markets, visiting churches and searching for cafés that served proper milkshakes. It didn't help that Valentine's Day fell on that weekend and that we both wore wedding rings. People constantly mistook us for a couple, and when we changed hotels the receptionist couldn't understand why we didn't want a *sala matrimonial*.

On the second day, as we sat in the courtyard of a café, Matt rehearsed the talking-to he planned to give the climbing agency manager once we were back in Santiago.

But things didn't quite go that way. The climbing manager picked us up at Santiago airport, and we rode to the hotel in silence. When we checked in at the hotel, Matt just said, 'Thanks. Good night,' to the agency manager. 'Good luck, Sophie,' he said to me, then went to bed. That was the last time I saw Matt.

~

Twenty-four hours later, I walked through our front door in Denham and dropped my duffel bag on the floor with a thud. I was exhausted and covered in desert dust and the grime of many Latin American airports. Morag and Ethel, our two little cats, sidled up, astonished to see me. Morag, who has a little black moustache, pulled her Dismayed Hitler face. I sat down at the bottom of the staircase and watched as they scampered over to sniff the bag and sharpen their claws on the carpet. Built-in crampons. Then I went upstairs to run a bath. Steam billowed out of the tub and warmed the chilly bathroom. I sat on the edge of the tub and let out a deep sigh.

Now what? I had no money to return to Ojos del Salado. The climbing season there was ending soon. How was I going to save the volcanoes project? Could it be saved?

I savagely kicked my heel against the side of the bathtub. *Gracias por nada, Fabio.*

6

MOUNTAINEERING WITH MACHETES

There's a point in every adventure where things fall apart. The shipwrecked sailor clings to a raft of planks and canvas; the lost explorer embarks on the Sahara desert with nothing but a flask of water and a compass. I wasn't quite at that point, but I was starting to suspect my volcanoes project was doomed to failure. What was the point in carrying on if I didn't reach the summit of Ojos del Salado? I had to climb all the volcanoes, or I give up my goal of setting the world record. It was all or nothing. Something made me grit my teeth and carry on anyway. Maybe I have a problem with failure. The harder something is, the more I want to do it. I'd been told so many times as a child *not* to do something, usually because of my asthma, that I'd become unreasonably resistant to the idea of giving up. I still had time to climb Ojos del Salado again; the climbing season in Chile didn't end for another four weeks. So far, my lungs were behaving. I still had a chance.

I booked a new flight to Chile and requested a place on another expedition to Ojos del Salado. I was going to go thousands of pounds over budget. I had sponsors for the Seven Volcanoes Project, but I doubted they would cover another expedition. All the

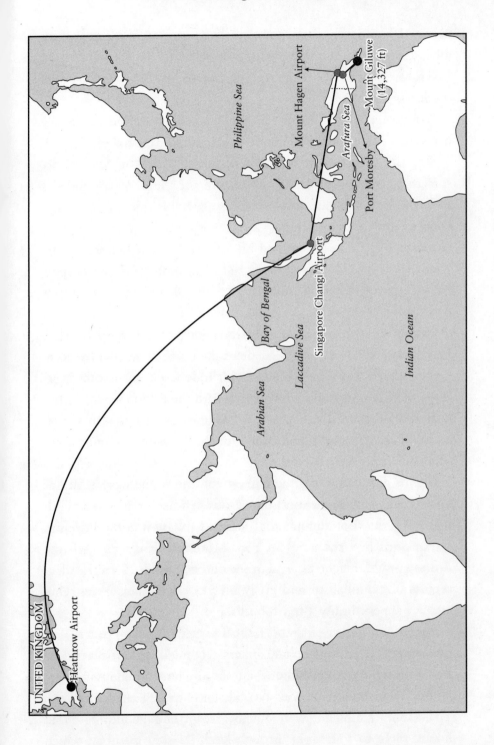

money I had saved from months of working in three part-time jobs, wasted. I cursed Fabio with every click of the mouse.

On top of that, Mom didn't approve of all this spending, and she let me know it.

'You're spending a fortune on these expeditions. Why don't you just *give* all that money to charity?' she asked over the phone.

'Because that's not how it's done,' I snapped. 'You have to do something memorable, that will inspire people to donate money. And it's not just about the money. It's about making a gesture. It's about commemorating Dad.'

'Okay, okay.' She recognised my tone and knew better than to poke more holes in my argument. In the meantime, I flew to Papua New Guinea to climb Mount Giluwe, the highest volcano on the Australasian continent.

Mount Giluwe lies on the eastern edge of the Ring of Fire, almost directly opposite Ojos del Salado in Chile. Papua New Guinea shares a western border with Indonesia, but is otherwise almost entirely surrounded by water, with the Pacific Ocean to the northeast. Technically, Papua New Guinea is part of Melanesia, a region that includes Fiji, Vanuatu, the Solomon Islands, New Caledonia and West Papua.

If Ojos del Salado was the highest volcano in the world, Mount Giluwe was among the most dangerous. It wasn't the actual climb to the 14,327-foot summit that worried me. It was the violence. Carjackings and robberies in Port Moresby. Urban gangs – the *Raskols* – with machetes. And in the outback, where I was headed, reports of cannibalism and grisly attacks on foreign hikers. One attack happened only a few months ago.

According to the news report, the 'frenzied bloody massacre' left two porters dead and several hikers wounded on the Black Cat trail between the township of Wau and the port of Salamaua. The injured hikers were not your typical sun-hatted weekend walkers. The Black Cat hikers were tough. Tough enough not to mind hiking three to four days through leech-infested territory, which one book has described as 'suitable only for masochists and Israeli Paratroopers.' Still, the hikers were lucky to escape alive.

What bothered me the most was that the attack had happened only 50 kilometres from Lae, Papua New Guinea's second-largest city. If this could happen so close to a city, what hope did I have in the highlands of Papua New Guinea?

On the map, Mount Giluwe looked as if it was in the middle of nowhere. As the crow flies, the volcano is about 40 kilometres from Mount Hagen, a city that was cut off from the outside world until 1933. Three Australian brothers – gold prospectors – stumbled into Mount Hagen's Wahgi Valley by chance and realised that over a million people lived there. Until then, the inhabitants led a way of life that hadn't changed since the Stone Age, including cannibalism and witch-burning. Even in 2013, a twenty-year-old mother of two was accused of being a witch and burned alive on a pile of tyres by an angry mob in Mount Hagen.

I did not want to go to Papua New Guinea. Volcanoes be damned. Douglas, meanwhile, had a new favourite joke: 'You'll be a well-seasoned traveller – geddit?! *Seasoned?* As in, at the bottom of a cauldron?'

I desperately looked for alternatives. Could I climb Australia's Mount Kosciuszko instead? Was 'Australasia' even a continent? But in the end I had to accept it: Mount Giluwe was the highest volcano in Australasia, and officially one of the Volcanic Seven. I needed to climb it if I wanted to set the world record.

It wasn't easy finding an agency to take me up this particular volcano. When it came to Mount Giluwe, the adventure tourism agencies became decidedly unadventurous. 'It's not something that any outfitter regularly does,' one agency wrote. Another agency said:

Hi Sophie.
Unfortunately I cannot recommend any operator to facilitate this trek for you. PNG is a very difficult area to operate in and it is hard to come by reliable operators in this area. Have an adventurous day.

After several inquiries, I received recommendations for Paiya Tours in Mount Hagen. We corresponded for several months, and the resulting and greatly shortened itinerary had me flitting around the country like a dragonfly: arrive in Port Moresby, zip straight out to the city of Mount Hagen, climb Mount Giluwe in two days and race straight back to Port Moresby to the fortress-like confines of the Airways Hotel, which was right by the airport and absolutely nowhere near town.

On 25 February, I boarded a plane to Singapore, where I then took an Air Niugini flight to Port Moresby. The journey took two days.

In the pre-dawn hours of 27 February, I stood in the immigration queue at Jacksons International Airport in Port Moresby. The dingy, fluorescent-lit little room was filled with grey-haired British tourists. They all looked in their fifties and sixties and seemed to have dressed for a cruise. The women wore sun dresses and silk scarves over their hair; the men ill-fitting tropical shirts and cheap shorts, their chalky legs planted in white socks and sandals. I was dazed, thirsty and sweating under too many layers of climbing clothes. I rummaged through my backpack and fished out a sheaf of documents: smile-free passport photos, multiple application forms, an invitation letter from Paiya Tours and 100 kina – the local currency – which had not been easy to acquire outside of the only country in the world that used it. Or had even heard of it.

The queue inched forward.

'How long are you here for?' I asked the couple behind me.

'Oh, two weeks,' the lady beamed. She smoothed her blonde hair, which was dyed too light for her skin. 'We're joining a package tour and staying at a luxury resort by the sea. There'll be swimming and boating most days. We've heard the food is delicious,' she said. She drew out the last word, as if savouring a long-awaited treat: *deliiiicious*.

My apprehension seemed ludicrous in the face of sun hats and golf shirts. I smiled. 'Whereabouts are you going? Have you also heard the same stories about the outback?'

Her face tensed slightly. 'Stories? No. We haven't heard anything.' She exchanged a glance with the man next to her who I guessed was her husband. He whipped out a yellow brochure.

'Hang on, there is something I read... somewhere...' he flipped back and forth through the pages. 'Something about cannibalism –'

'How long are you here for, love?' the woman interjected, her eyes flicking over my softshell climbing trousers and Salomon boots. The man continued muttering into his brochure. I could imagine these nice people sprawled over sun chairs next to a pool, gently turning pink behind high-security fences.

'Just four days.'

She raised her eyebrows. The conversation had to stop there as I was called up to the immigration counter.

The heavyset, po-faced man behind the counter frowned down at me. He held out his hand without saying a word.

'Here's my invitation letter – the photos are inside – and copies of my passport and an immigration form. I wasn't sure which address to use,' I babbled.

He shuffled through my documents and his face slackened into a smile. He waved a hand at me. 'No no, it's okay. We don't need all this. Just the passport.' He stamped a few pages with disconcerting force, then handed the documents back to me.

'Welcome to Papua New Guinea,' he said, pleased with his own efficiency.

I went through the gates and grabbed my bag off the carousel. My friends from the immigration queue came through as I was heading for the exit. The man waved his yellow brochure at me and shouted: 'You'll be fine, luv! Have a good time.'

~

'I recommend that you do not walk outside the airport,' Pym said as we sat down to coffee and hot rolls in the airport cafeteria. 'There is probably no danger, but foreigners always attract attention.'

Dawn had broken over Port Moresby. Pym Maimindi, head of Paiya Tours, and his wife Elisabeth were buying me breakfast. I had pushed my trolley into the dowdy arrivals hall expecting to be mobbed by aggressive minicab drivers, but instead there was only Pym and Elisabeth, beaming and holding up a cardboard sign with my name on it in big letters.

Pym had the physique of a retired rugby player. I asked him how long he had been working in tourism. 'Not very long. I wanted to build a tourist eco-resort in Papua New Guinea.' He bit into a beef roll. His cell phone rang again. It was only six in the morning, but his phone rang every few minutes. Paiya Tours clearly wasn't Pym's only business venture. He was an entrepreneur. Restless, keen to network, always hungry for information. I guessed that his employees learned early on not to test his patience.

'Are you a climber?' I asked him after he hung up. He shuffled through the newspapers littering the cafeteria table.

'Not really. I climbed Mount Giluwe once. It was very tiring.' His eyes shifting from me to the businessmen straggling off the hourly flight from Canberra. Australia is so close that its northernmost tip, the Cape York Peninsula in Queensland, almost tickles Papua New Guinea's underbelly.

I sipped my latte and watched as Pym waved to two of the Australian businessmen who had walked into the cafeteria. They waved back like old friends. Then Pym's phone rang again and he launched into another conversation. He hung up and stood up. They were preparing for a big tourism convention in a few days, he said. Then they wished me a good expedition and left, smiling encouragement at me but already preoccupied with other plans.

~

From the air, Papua New Guinea resembles the side profile of an elephant turned to the right. After Pym and Elisabeth left, I boarded a regional plane that would take me from Port Moresby (on the underside of the elephant's trunk) towards the elephant's eye.

There was hardly anyone on the plane. Across the aisle to my right sat a middle-aged businessman in an immaculate suit. A Chinese couple sat a few rows behind me, discussing construction projects. A young man sat a few rows in front of me. He looked like a personal security guard or a soldier. There seemed to be no tourists at all besides me. I fidgeted in my seat. I hadn't expected the plane to be so new, or the coffee so good, as if I'd expected to fly to Mount Hagen in a pig pen. I tapped my foot on the floor in a nervous staccato. I'd read so much about Papua New Guinea that I thought I'd prepared myself as well as I could, but I still couldn't shake the feeling that I was heading into the unknown. I was heading for a region of the West Highlands where tribal warfare still existed and internet access was virtually non-existent. I had no idea who I was meeting at the other end and no idea if I would be safe. I was completely on my own. For the next hour I pressed my face right up against the window, as if the view below would give me a clue of what to expect over the next two days. The ocean around Port Moresby morphed into dense kelp-green rainforest. The tropical vegetation was unmarked by roads, and as we glided along the land seemed to undulate and beguile, the valleys flowing like waves that merged and parted with languor. It was in rainforest just like this that the trekkers were attacked a few months earlier. I tried to see below the surface, but couldn't.

The safety belt light pinged on. We started to descend. It didn't feel like our pilot was guiding the plane lower; it felt as if the plane was being dragged down by an invisible chain into the depths of the mysterious country below.

'Ladies and gentlemen, we are now beginning our descent to Mount Hagen airport,' the flight attendant said over the speakers. A few buildings sprouted into view. We touched down.

Kagamuga Airport looked like a one-room tin shed. The security guard, the Chinese couple, the businessman and I disembarked from the cool dry air-conditioned cabin into humid warmth. I walked towards the building and I saw that I was right. The airport terminal was mainly one large waiting room with a few security guards dotted around it. I followed the other passengers, but before I could reach the building our bags overtook us on the back of a small trolley and were slapped like dead fish onto an outdoor bench.

A cluster of noisy people heaved around the bench like a sea of human piranhas, diving and snapping and emerging with pieces of luggage. I tried to peek over their backs but couldn't see my sailing bag. Where was the arrival hall? Was there one? Maybe they had kept it as oversized luggage. I wandered down a corridor around the outside of the building, only to realise that I'd walked clear out of the airport. I turned and fought my way back in again, past gigantic security guards who seemed not to see me. Then I walked into a man with blood-red teeth.

'SOPHIE?' the man shouted. He was frowning, which made me frown too.

'Yes?'

'I'm Luke,' he barked. 'I am your guide.' He wore a floppy sun hat, faded T-shirt and shorts.

Luke lunged at me. I instinctively took a step back, but he still managed to envelop me in a determined, unsmiling bear hug. I nodded helplessly in his death grip. He let me go, grabbed my sailing bag off the bench, and marched off. I followed. We walked to the small car park. Luke walked up to a white van with tinted windows. I could just make out the shadows of three men waiting inside. Luke walked to the back of the van, flung open the door and tossed my bag inside. He shouted something in a language I didn't understand and the other men nodded silently.

'Please, get in.' Luke gestured at the front seats.

I opened the passenger door of the van. The men in the back nodded silent hellos. They all had red teeth too. *Who are they? Why are there so many of them?* I raised my hand in greeting and climbed into the front seat, hoping my nervousness did not show. Luke climbed into the back with the others. The driver – a young, serious-looking man – stared at me for a second, then nodded and started the engine. We left the airport and beetled along the Highlands Highway towards Mount Hagen. We drove in silence for a few minutes.

'Those are farmers' wives coming back from the market,' Luke bellowed abruptly. He pointed at rows of women waiting by the roadside. 'They take the bus every day from the village to go to Mount Hagen market to buy food for their families.' Luke pronounced it 'Mount Hah-gen,' like the ice cream.

I nodded. I turned around with a smile, but Luke's impassive face and his blood-red teeth made me turn back to the front again. The other men started chatting, but I couldn't understand what they said.

Gaggles of women sat by the side of the road. They had laid out large pieces of fabric, upon which they had piled up a kind of fruit.

'The women are selling betel nut,' Luke shouted.

Betel nut juice. That's what it was. Luke's teeth were red from chewing betel nut. I almost smacked myself for not realising it sooner. What a relief. Had I actually expected his teeth to be covered in blood? Maybe.

'Those are children going to school!' Luke shouted. Again, the wild pointing. I nodded. For the next 15 minutes, Luke shouted titbits on the local landscape, people and crops. I noticed that when Luke spoke, the others shut up.

The humid air fanned my face through the window that was opened just a crack as we drove towards town. I was starting to relax. Maybe this trip wasn't so hazardous after all. Then I looked down at my feet.

'YAH!'

A stream of cockroaches was pouring out of the van's upholstery and all over my boots.

'Do not worry about them,' said the driver, breaking his silence. 'They do not bite.'

'But they fly, right? They're going to fly into my face,' I said. I was terrified of cockroaches. The ones I had grown up with in Hong Kong were always the diameter of casino chips, and seemed to fly towards the openings in my face – mouth, nose, ears – with fierce precision.

'No, these ones cannot fly,' the driver said.

'Are you sure?' I said. I didn't know what was worse, flying or crawling. For the rest of the drive, I crossed my legs so the cockroaches couldn't crawl up my trousers.

We rattled into the centre of Mount Hagen. The place was a bustling, happy little town consisting mostly of open space, broad tarmac roads and large two-storey buildings with corrugated metal roofs, some painted in the colours of the rainbow. It was hard to imagine that Mount Hagen was built on a single airstrip in the 1930s. The large enthusiastic lettering on the shop signs made me smile. They spelled out names that were almost, but not quite familiar: *Haris Stoa*, and *Klina Laundry Soap*, with soap suds drawn enticingly onto the tops of the billboard. There was even a 'Best Buy' that was definitely part of the US company. All around, rainforest smothered the low hills under an enormous deep green blanket. We passed the church, a long low building bearing a cross high above its freshly painted white roof. People were leaving the service. The men wore neat button-down shirts and the women skirts, their hair bundled up in colourful kerchiefs.

Then we turned a corner and saw the garbage. Huge festering piles of trash – mostly rotting plants and old tyres – steamed and burned in the sun. It smelled putrid. Bored-looking women squatted along the road outside under makeshift shelters selling vegetables. A large khaki-coloured enclosure like a cattle pen loured behind them, with a large conical funnel that looked like a chimney. 'Mt Hagen City Market,' said the weatherworn red capitals on the side of the building. I reached out to wind up my window, then stopped myself. Maybe I was being paranoid, but I didn't want to insult the men in the back of the van. I didn't want them to think that the stench bothered me. I couldn't read them. Other than Luke, none of them really met my eyes or seemed interested in talking. I had the feeling they didn't know what to make of me.

We pulled up at a tall metal gate. The driver honked the horn and the gates were pulled open by an older man who waved us through. We drove into a courtyard, in which there was a squat building: the headquarters of Paiya Tours. A few children milled about. The older man exchanged greetings with the driver, resumed his seat by the gate, and considered me.

I jumped down out of the front seat. 'Wait here,' Luke said. He went inside the house. I didn't know why I was waiting. I didn't know what Luke was doing. I felt disconcertingly adrift in this land of stark contrasts. Every time I started to relax, either cockroaches tried to crawl up my leg or strange men bared blood-red teeth at me or we passed giant burning piles of rotting garbage.

Just as I was considering looking for Luke, a man bounded across the courtyard towards me. Unlike the men in the van, he was smiling. Actually, he was more than smiling: he looked exhilarated, as if he had just found Jesus. He was over 6 foot tall and his meaty chest heaved as he jogged. Bulging arms protruded from his short-sleeved vest.

'Hello! My name is Joshua.' He grabbed my hand and shook it. 'I will be your chef.'

Chef and bodyguard. 'Nice to meet you,' I smiled. A few more men came out of the house, followed by Luke.

'Come! We go to Magic Mountain!' Luke barked.

Joshua raised his fists over his head. 'Yeah!' he shouted. He waved goodbye to the older man at the gate and bounced into the back of the van. I pulled myself back up into the front seat. Joshua said something in the local language that made the driver laugh as he gunned the engine. The gates parted and we left for Magic Mountain, our lodgings for the night.

The smooth tarmac road wound past villages of squat hut-like dwellings, some with thatched roofs, some with more modern materials. Most had neat farming plots dotted with green sprouting crops – potatoes, cassava – in small clearings hacked into the rainforest.

With Joshua in the van, the mood seemed to lighten. I had no idea what he was saying, but the intermittent laughter was relaxing and my shoulders started to loosen. Still, that edge of tension remained. As we drove towards Magic Mountain, I noticed that the people walking on the roadside were all turning to stare as we rattled past. Nobody smiled. The children, some walking in pairs, some walking alone, all seemed to glower from under heavy brows. I didn't think they could see me behind the darkened windshield. Still, I had the disturbing feeling that they were all staring directly at the spot where I was sitting, and frowning. I began to wonder if I was the reason they were frowning.

~

We arrived at Magic Mountain Lodge in the early evening. It was a pretty compound of large wooden villas ensconced deep in the humid foliage at the end of a bumpy earth track. Pym had taken care to make it look like a spa set in the rainforest. Colourful tropical plants lined the well-tended gravel paths, and each bungalow had an ornate little gate.

I pushed open the gate of my villa. A few wooden chairs sat on the porch, from which I had a view of thick, steamy vegetation. The moist air was laced with the scent of flowers and I breathed it in deeply, holding it in my lungs. I unlocked the door of my bungalow and walked through a bead curtain. Fresh soap and towels lay on the clean, comfortable beds. I could have been in a Thai spa resort, rather than the outback of Papua New Guinea.

Laughter and conversation drifted through my window from the hut next door. The moist air had begun to cool. I dragged the sailing bag onto my bed and pulled out my climbing clothes for tomorrow. For this trip, I'd downsized to a sailing bag rather than lug around my red

155-litre duffel. I didn't need an ice axe, crampons, harness or down jacket on Mount Giluwe. Papua New Guinea only really had two seasons – dry and rainy – and it was now the end of the wet season.

A thin whine of tension drilled into my head, unwelcome and unexpected. The resort was beautiful. The staff was welcoming. Everything had gone according to plan. What the hell was I worried about?

I was in a remote area of a remote country and completely alone. I stood out like a lighthouse. I was totally dependent on other people's goodwill, and even if I could defend myself, there was really nowhere to run to in the boonies of Papua New Guinea. But it wasn't just that. There was something strange about the people we had passed on the drive over. Something about the way they had stared nagged at me. In most rural mountain regions, the local children had waved and smiled at me. Here they scowled, as if they hated me on sight.

~

After unpacking, I scrunched over the gravel to the main building to meet Luke for dinner. The main dining room had latticed walls lined with photos of previous clients. No one was there yet, so I walked around the room, looking at the photos and then stopped as I suddenly recognised one of the climbers. I had seen the tall grey-haired man on the Russian 7 Summits Club website. I didn't know his name, but I knew he was a Russian climber who had climbed all of the seven summits as well as the two poles, and now it looked like he was after the seven volcanoes as well. I bristled slightly, wondering if he was out there somewhere right now on a different volcano, also trying to climb the seven volcanoes in record time.

Luke drifted into the room. He walked slowly, as if in discomfort. He stood at the head of the dining table and watched as I completed my tour of the photos. One of them featured a boy of about fourteen, standing on a windswept trail.

'He was a very strong climber,' Luke said abruptly, gesturing at the photo. 'I told him, "I am very pleased with you. You may come back anytime."' Luke had a way of speaking that was just slow enough that you were forced to pay complete attention. For some reason, the way he said this made me want to prove I could be a strong climber, as well.

Joshua breezed in, bearing plates of chicken and rice and a wide smile. He set the steaming plates down on the table.

'You are going out tonight?' Luke asked him.

'Oh no. We have a big climb tomorrow. I will go to bed early,' Joshua said. 'It is my first time climbing Mount Giluwe.' He flashed a smile. Luke nodded.

'Good,' Luke said. 'Come. Sit,' he said to me, holding out his arm.

I walked over and sat down at the head of the table. Luke had an oddly formal manner. I guessed he wouldn't appreciate small talk over dinner, so we ate in silence. Luke finished eating first. He stood up.

'Tomorrow, we meet at 6.30 a.m. for breakfast. Sharp. Then, we go to the mountain.' He stood up. 'Good night,' he said, and left.

I finished the chicken rice, returned to my hut, barricaded the door and went to bed.

~

The next morning I was in the dining room before sunrise. Luke's eyebrows went up as he came in and saw me there, already seated and spooning coffee powder into my plastic mug. He nodded hello, and reached for the pot of powdered coffee.

'You like strong coffee too, Luke?' I asked over the rim of my cup.

'Yes.' Finally, a hint of a smile crossed his face. 'Otherwise, it's no good.' He added another spoonful to his mug. Then he looked serious again.

'Are you packed?'

'Yes.'

'Okay. We go in ten minutes.' I nodded. We ate our eggs and toast in silence.

The air was crisp and cool after rain during the night. I carried my sailing bag out to the van as Joshua and Samuel strolled out of the main building.

'Woo!' Joshua yelled. That lottery-winner smile again. A robust fist-pump. 'Today we go to the MOUNTAIN!'

I laughed. 'How're you feeling? You ready to climb the mountain?'

'I'm good! I'm ready!' Joshua's exuberance was infectious.

We piled into the white van. Twilight soon surrendered to day as we drove through valleys a million shades of green. The sun gilded the muslin clouds as it rose, then it illuminated the fresh turquoise sky, burning away the heaviness of yesterday.

The tarmac road became a rocky track. Samuel, the driver, stopped bantering with the others as he concentrated on the road. We passed a string of bored-looking women by the side of the road, waiting for the morning bus. We also passed a string of children, but this time they had their backs to us, so I couldn't see their expressions. One of the children carried a machete almost 4 feet long.

A few minutes later, we pulled over to the side of the road.

'Come. We get out here,' Luke said.

I squinted. I couldn't make out any kind of trail head. All I could see were large bushes lining the side of the road.

Luke flung open the back door of the van and started hauling out the plastic bags of food and a big tin cooking pot. I scrambled out of the van to help him, then hoisted my sailing bag onto my back, lopping my arms through the straps like a backpack.

'I can carry your bag.' Luke held out his arm. He was already carrying three bags of food.

'Thanks, don't worry about it,' I said. Without a word, Luke turned on his heel – he was wearing galoshes – and disappeared into the undergrowth by the side of the road. Startled, I took a step after him. Hidden under the foliage were stone steps leading up the slope. I followed. As we climbed, the sound of children's laughter drifted down to us.

The village was full of children. They were everywhere. They giggled in the bushes, peeped out from the hunched little huts, ran around the bare earth clearing of the tiny village. Luke walked to the middle of the clearing and put down his plastic bags, and as he did the children clustered around him, shrieking and smiling. There were at least two dozen of them, some just toddlers, with big shy eyes. I walked up to Luke and lay my bag down next to his.

A little girl of about five ran up to me.

'Hello,' I said.

She shrunk away and hid behind her friends, her eyes fixed on me the entire time. I waved at her, expecting her to scowl at me. Instead, she broke into a wide grin, as if she couldn't help herself, and came back to reach for my outstretched hand.

'Good morning,' said a raspy voice. I turned to see a stout, older man with his hands on his hips. He looked at me as if I were an interesting new creature.

'William.' His self-assurance told me that he has the head of this village.

'Sophie.' We shook hands.

'How are you? Ready for the climb?'

'Yes. Can't wait.'

He gestured at two men behind him. 'Meet Gideon and Simpson,' he said. 'They will go with you.'

Two men walked ambled towards me and set down their bags. I had never seen two men with such opposite demeanours.

The man on the left stood very straight and wore a baseball cap and a lumberjack shirt. He looked business-like, as if he was keen not only to start the expedition, but also to ensure that it proceeded in an orderly and efficient manner.

The man on the right terrified me.

'Simpson is a bushman.' William gave me a proud, wide smile as he said this.

Simpson grinned at me. *Oh my god, he's going to kill me.* It wasn't so much his matted hair or blood-red teeth, or even the metre-long machete he was clutching. It was his expression.

Simpson possessed a manic grin. His eyes reflected a raw, unabashed exuberance that clearly eclipsed my own. I glanced down. Simpson was barefoot. His right foot was missing a big toe, the stump sheared off very cleanly. Whatever – or whoever – had cut his toe off had been very precise.

'Nice to meet you.' I stepped forward and shook his hand.

Simpson shook my hand. His bloodshot eyes bored straight into mine. Then he stepped back, shouted something to the others, and started laughing. The other men laughed as well.

What the hell am I getting into? Bad weather I could handle. Same thing for the risk of avalanches, rock fall and mountain sickness. But nothing had prepared me for spending two days camping with a barefoot, toe-deficient, machete-waving man in the wilds of Papua New Guinea.

Our Mount Giluwe expedition team was now complete. There were six of us: Luke, the head guide; Joshua, the cook; Simpson, the terrifying missing toe man; plus Gideon, Stan and I. We slung our bags on our backs. Just as we were about to head off, a young porter ran up and took his place at the end of the line, clutching a large weather-beaten kettle that clanked as he tried to stuff it into his white satchel.

'That is Stan. He is a porter,' said Luke, watching Stan wrestling with the kettle. Stan's satchel wasn't big enough to hold the kettle, so he simply decided to hold it in his right hand.

Why were there so many of us? It was only going to be a two-day expedition, and we weren't carrying that much gear. My stomach curdled with unease.

This wasn't going to be an adventure 'experience' like my other volcano expeditions. This was the real thing. There were no guarantees of safety. We would be invading the territory of local tribes who were probably not used to seeing outsiders on this rarely climbed volcano. Luke and Joshua weren't from the area, which meant the highlands of Papua New Guinea were probably as foreign to them as they were to me. The safety of our team depended on Simpson, who knew the local customs.

'Good luck.' William reached out to shake my hand.

'Thank you, I said. 'And thank you for letting us pass through your village.'

He smiled, gratified that I'd finally realised how instrumental he was to our safety.

'See you tomorrow night,' he said. It felt like an age away.

We left the clearing, Simpson leading the way. As we embarked on a muddy path leading out of the village, I passed a boy of about twelve. He scowled at me. I smiled and waved at him. The boy stopped frowning and grinned back.

~

We set out for Mount Giluwe. I'd never known a crazier climbing expedition. We were a ragtag walking cacophony of intermittent whoops and clanking saucepans. We wove through a high-walled gully of damp, dun clay that appeared to be a conduit for the village's waste water. A few minutes later, it spat us out into open land, the air lighter and drier as the view opened sideways to reveal small plots of farmland. Shortly thereafter, the path became narrower and steeper and led us into the led us into the steamy, buzzing forest. For 3 hours, the six of us blundered through the rainforest. We stumbled up gullies 2 feet wide, fell over moss-covered tree trunks and batted damp vines out of our faces. The whole time, Simpson yodelled incoherently from the front, prompting the rest of the men to shout and laugh wildly in reply. I had no idea what they were saying.

Simpson led the way. He skipped up the slippery mud track like he was off to a picnic. The vegetation and fallen trees covered in emerald moss were no obstacle. He simply vaulted over them. The path grew so narrow and the vegetation so dense that I was constantly whipped in the face by ferns and white beard lichens. I fought so hard to keep up with Simpson that there wasn't even time to wipe the sweat off my face. I squinted through the undergrowth. Simpson had disappeared. His barefooted steps were so light and swift that he barely disturbed the vegetation, yet I knew he was waiting for me because every so often he would let out a loud whoop. When the men weren't yodelling or shouting, they whistled with exertion. It sounded a little like wheezing.

'What's going on? Why are we stopping?' I asked Luke, who trudged a few paces behind me. Luke pointed upwards without speaking. I craned my neck. There, at least 20 feet off the ground, Stan balanced at the top of a thin tree. I had no idea how he had climbed up there so fast in his clumsy galoshes. He kept very still, eyes fixed on something hidden behind the leaves.

'Hunting. Tree kangaroo,' Luke whispered.

For a few minutes we watched Stan, who stood motionless at the top of the tree like a weathervane. Eventually, Stan shook his head and slithered down the tree. 'No tree kangaroo today,' Luke said. We walked on.

Joshua was hungover. He crashed through the forest like a boar. Every so often, he stopped to lean panting against a tree, his hand over his eyes. He had stripped down to his bright yellow sleeveless vest and carried only a light backpack, but his expression was that of a man in booze-induced pain.

'You okay, Joshua?' I asked. He flashed me a weary smile and exhaled.

'Tired,' he said. 'Last night I went out to the disco. Went dancing' – he made a few lethargic dance moves – 'Too many beers. Came home late.' He covered his eyes again and groaned.

I laughed. I thought he'd gone to bed after dinner, like the rest of us.

Gideon was solemn. He walked quietly, his eyes opened to their maximum, as if he were on the lookout for hidden enemies.

Luke, the head guide, was ill. As we walked, he slowly drifted to the back of the line and stumbled along in his big green galoshes. He didn't speak to anyone.

Everyone held big dangerous machetes, which they held as casually as if they were walking poles. I realised this when I turned a corner to see Simpson raise the blade over his head and bring it down, hard, onto something with a crack.

I froze. Simpson raised the dull blade over his head again, and once more hacked into something that splintered and rasped. He whistled as he worked.

'Err... What's up, Simpson?' I tried to sound casual.

He turned and grinned at me. He stepped aside to reveal the hacked-up copse of trees that had been blocking our path. Whistling again, he turned and pushed his way through the destroyed trees. I picked my way through and scurried after him. Behind me the sounds of machete splitting wood crackled through the forest.

The path became nearly vertical. My climbing poles were now a nuisance, so I tucked them into the straps of my bag and pulled myself up the slope with the help of dangling tree branches. The wet muddy track was now only inches from my face. Several times, my bag slipped from my shoulders and nearly dragged me down the slope with it. It was hard to get a firm foothold in the mud, which was as soft and slippery as clay. Sweat tickled the back of my neck and I could feel unseen tendrils – cobwebs? Bits of fern? – in my hair. I tried to brush away whatever it was out of my hair when a metallic glint caught my eye.

I turned to see an unsheathed machete 2 feet behind me. I'd been so focused on keeping my footing that I hadn't noticed young, quiet Stan walking right behind me. He was looking up, searching the treetops as he walked and paying no attention to me. Every time my gaze wandered, Stan's machete edged into my field of vision. As soon as the path opened up slightly, I stood aside.

'You go ahead, Stan,' I said. I hoped my nervousness didn't show.

Stan looked confused. Everyone stopped walking.

'You okay, Sophie?' Luke barked from the back.

'Yes. Can Stan please go ahead of me?'

'Why?'

I paused.

'Because he's got a really big knife. I'm scared that if I fall, I'll land on it.'

Luke stared at me as if I were complaining about earthworms. Stan didn't seem to understand. Luke muttered something to Stan, who glanced at me, nodded, and walked on.

'Come,' Luke said. 'We are almost at the up-road.'

~

The forest started to thin. The steamy air cooled. I looked up from the steep path and saw the pale blue sky through the tops of the trees a few hundred feet away. A light breeze tickled my skin and my sweat-soaked back where it met the sailing bag. Before long, the trees surrendered to open, slushy grassland dotted with tall tussocks of green and brown grass, large rocks, bogs and small rivers. We had reached the grassland.

'Now we have lunch.' Luke flung his bag onto a rock. I walked over to an outcrop next to him and did the same. It felt good to sit down. The treeline was now just below us, marking where the ice cap had once been. I sat back, enjoying the feeling of cool air drying the sweat on my forehead.

'Mount Hagen is that way.' Luke jabbed his hand towards the right.

The rainforest spread out below us like a vast shroud of green. From our hill to the horizon, there was barely a trace of human civilisation, except the faint outline of a small road here, a few squat houses there.

Joshua took out the plastic bags of white bread buns and passed them around with a flourish. The megawatt smile was back; he seemed to have recovered from his hangover. He smeared jam onto his bun and wolfed it down. I reached for one of the buns.

'Can I borrow a knife?' I asked.

Joshua grinned and handed me his 15-inch Bowie knife, which looked almost exactly like the one in *Crocodile Dundee*. I took it started carving up the marshmallow-soft bun.

I glanced at Simpson, who sat a little way off by himself and basked in the sun. He was not only barefoot, he had also carried more weight, far faster than us. He moved without sound, and I suspected he could be fearsome against intruders. The highlands of Papua New Guinea is home to hundreds of different tribal groups. Tribal conflicts occurred sporadically in the Highlands. Sometimes they involved spears, bows and arrows, or even rifles. Our route wound through several tribal territories. I knew, because I had seen the scratchings on the rocks we passed on the way.

We sat for a while, Simpson sprawled out on the grassy knoll above me, grinning to himself and shouting something every so often which made the others laugh. Joshua handed his camera to Luke, who took more photos of him in about ten different poses: serious Joshua, clownish Joshua, manly Joshua. He took pictures of me as well, so I did the same poses. Gideon preferred to keep his own counsel, walking around to look at the scenery, while Stan munched on the bread, shooting me curious looks every so often.

'Okay,' Luke said. 'We continue up the grassland, then go to Base Camp.'

We picked ourselves off the ground and set off again. Now that we were free from the closeness of the rainforest, the grassland seemed vast. There were few trees, and instead we walked through miles of straw-like grass which hid a network of tiny burns, the mud squelching in particularly sodden areas.

For the next 7 hours, we marched. The jet lag started to hit. I walked in a daze. Every few minutes I fell into a micro sleep – one second the ground was there, and the next thing I knew we were a bit further ahead, with no memory of what had happened in between. I slowed to a crawl, and when I tried to catch up to Gideon and Simpson I staggered like a drunk.

'I'm sorry guys, but it's 3 a.m. right now where I come from,' I said to Gideon and Simpson, who had stopped to wait for me. They watched as I lurched over a wet muddy patch like a drunkard. Gideon nodded at Simpson, and without a word he pulled the bag off my back, grinning and wolfish, and raced on ahead with Stan, the other porter. They pulled away, fleet and barefoot and silent. They soon disappeared behind a dip in the ground. It was like they had never been there.

'How much further?' I gasped to Luke, who was waiting for me sitting on a rock. He turned away from me and flung his arm out.

'Over there. Come,' he said, and marched off again. We were meant to be heading towards a ridge which would guide us all the way to Base Camp.

I was awed by the volcanic scenery. The smoothed-down surfaces of the rolling slopes gave way to huge eerie outcrops of deep brown rock, like the crests of enormous waves of rock. It was an odd landscape. The peaks did not seem to arise naturally so much as jut out at random places, like the giant rocky paws of a subterranean monster prodding its way through from underneath. There was no obvious peak in sight. Mount Giluwe was waiting unseen among the miles and miles of hills, ridges, valleys and ravines.

Giluwe is a shield volcano which, unlike the more cone-like Mount Fuji, is squat and broad due to the sludgy lava that oozed rather than exploded out of the Earth's magma, and is more common in Oceanic than continental settings. Giluwe last erupted 220,000–300,000 years ago.

We covered 20 exhausting miles that day. At one point I just stopped walking, irritated with the distance.

'I am tired,' Joshua said as he dragged himself up next to me. 'My head is very painful.'

'It is not far,' Luke said. 'You see that smoke? That is Base Camp.'

We squinted down into the valley from our position up on the ridge. A very thin line of smoke was coming out from behind a patch of forest, still a good few miles below the ridge we had been following for the last 10 miles. I shrugged and stepped off the rocky ridge and into the tall damp grass below. By the time we reached the source of the smoke about an hour later, we had sunk into so many rivulets that everything below the knee was soaked.

It was the weirdest Base Camp I had ever seen.

~

Base Camp was a straw tepee. It looked nothing like a mountain camp.

'You may stay here with us if you like,' Luke said. 'We can make room for you.'

The smoke didn't come out the top. It oozed thickly through the top. It looked like a smokehouse, only far more flammable.

He disappeared inside. I stood at the side of the door and looked inside. The earth floor was dry and sprinkled with straw, and a fireplace took up the centre. There was just enough room for a tall man to sit with his back up against the sloping roof and his feet at the edge of the fireplace. The others sat with their feet so close to the fire that sparks landed on them. I ate with the team in the tepee – boiled rice and other good stuff in a big pot directly on a wood fire.

I looked around at the warm, dry hut. 'I would love to, but I think I will stay in my tent,' I said. 'I have problems breathing sometimes.'

Luke gave me a solemn look. Without a word, he helped me set up the tent in a damp little clearing under the trees by the hut. 'Thank you,' I said and crawled in. I was a take-away meal, packed up and ready to go. How easy would it be for some cannibals to pull up my tent, wrap me up like a dumpling, and carry me off?

Darkness fell. I switched on my headlamp and zipped myself into the sleeping bag. I read for a while, but soon switched off the headlamp and lay there awake. *I'm camping in the highlands of Papua New Guinea.* Out in the darkness the insects buzzed, and a light rain started tapping on the canvas.

The humid air soothed my lungs like oil on a rusty wheel. Just as I was falling asleep, I remembered something Dad had told me about a sort-of relative – my cousin's ex-husband – who used to work in Papua New Guinea. Due to the nature of his job he didn't live in Port Moresby, but out in the bush.

'He used to live in a kind of fortress, because he needed all kinds of security to protect him from the locals,' he said. 'It's an extremely hairy place, Papua New Guinea.'

Wisps of smoke from the campfire in the straw hut seeped into my tent. It smelled like the kind of smoke you get from hay, or rough, dried grass. It smelled a lot like Chinese cigarettes – crude and acrid, deadlier and less filtered than cigarettes sold in other countries. That smell was a constant backdrop during my two years working as a foreign correspondent in Shanghai. I was being paid to witness the rise of the next world superpower, and I could not have been more excited. All my dreams had come true. I was fascinated by China. As a child, my Chinese grandparents had spoken little of the bad old days before they fled to Hong Kong. But here and there, I'd heard snippets of the chaos of the Great Leap Forward, the famine, the war. I was fascinated by China's drive to modernise, all while Marxism-Leninism continued to be taught in schools and people still suspected that Communist informants lurked at every social gathering – even family dinners.

One day, everything fell into place. I was fourteen. I was sprawled on a sofa on an idle afternoon reading *Alive in the Bitter Sea* by Fox Butterfield, former *New York Times* bureau chief in Hong Kong and Beijing. I had randomly picked the book from Dad's shelf, but as I read, I knew what I wanted to do with the rest of my life. It became clear in an instant. I would return to Hong Kong and become a journalist. I would be posted to China, and report from all corners of that vast country. I would be a respected, established foreign correspondent, documenting people's lives as they went through massive social and economic change. I would write books. I would start a family. I would fly my parents out every three months so we could have large, lively Chinese dinners once again. Tremendous changes were about to happen in China, and I was going to witness the rise of the next global superpower, and capture it in writing for future generations to remember. After that realisation, I went through high school and university homesick for the past, eager for the future, and counting down the years and months until I could return home. I wished the time away.

When my plane touched down in Hong Kong ten years later, I felt my universe snap back into place. Once I made it to Shanghai, I spent my days chasing stories, cultivating sources, covering the odd protest and seeing as much of China as I could. When I was sitting at my paper-strewn desk at 6 a.m., staring at the news stories on three screens and scouring that morning's Chinese papers for new developments, or chasing government officials for a comment at stuffy Communist Party conferences, or in a taxi zooming down a futuristic highway through smoggy Shanghai, I knew in my bones that I was exactly where I was meant to be. I had chosen my destiny years ago, and now it had become reality.

And after hours?

The loud, dark room boomed with classic American rock hits followed by Hong Kong pop tunes. The low table was littered with empty beer bottles and the lounge reeked of cheap cigarettes. A bunch of Chinese journalists – my colleagues – sprawled over the sofas. Yao Shifu was shouting the lyrics to *Meijiu Jia Kafe* ('Fine Wine with Coffee') at the giant karaoke screen, and as we sang along more beer was passed around. Another weekday, another work party. The reporter finished the song to applause, then handed me the microphone.

'Bitch! Bitch!' my colleagues cheered.

They didn't mean me. The hit song *Bitch* by Meredith Brooks was my go-to karaoke number, because it was the only song I could pull off drunk. The video featured a pouty female flouncing around a small German town, and as I took the stage I flounced around too. My colleagues clapped and whistled.

Hours later, we stumbled out into the clammy Shanghai night. The neon characters of the karaoke club glowed against the smog, the kind that tasted vaguely of sulphur and left a fine brown film on your face. Couples and adolescents chatted and laughed, while nearby the Uighur street vendors roasted thin skewers of meat on makeshift grills on the backs of their bicycles.

I adored living in Shanghai. I had a huge apartment, I partied a lot, and I was over the moon.

Yet something nagged at me. There was a reason why I tirelessly, almost frantically crammed as much as I could into those two years. Somewhere in my gut was the fear that everything I had worked for and loved would be snatched away. I wasn't wrong.

Those beery 4 a.m. karaoke sessions in Shanghai were a universe away from this 4 a.m. start on a mountain climbing expedition in Papua New Guinea.

Head torch, layers, anorak, hat. Rain. I scrambled into the smoky hut.

Snoring. Only Joshua was awake. He looked sheepish as he boiled water in the large metal pot.

'Luke does not feel well,' he said, waving at the nearest bundle of legs and arms. I detected the gleam of firelight on an eyeball observing me from the shadows behind him.

So much for setting off at 4.30 a.m. It looked like Luke's stomach problems had become worse. That explained his slow pace the previous day.

'It is raining, so it will be slippy at the summit,' Joshua added.

'Okay,' I said. 'I'll go back to sleep for a bit. Maybe the rain will stop soon.'

Two hours later, I was awoken by the yodelling of a madman. 'Hellooooo. Hellooooo!'

I crawled out of my tent to meet the boss. Luke was standing outside my tent in the heavy drizzle. He gazed balefully at me.

'It is raining. It will be slippy at the top,' he said. He did not seem keen to go marching through mud and reeds in the rain for 4 hours. I couldn't blame him.

'I'm sorry, but I have to go. I've come so far. I can't turn back now.'

Luke peered at me. 'Okay.' He did not look well. A tinge of something foul-smelling floated on the air.

We set off after half-an-hour. I took a puff on my inhaler, feeling Luke watching me.

There was a thick fog all around, and every step submerged my Salomons into ankle-deep muddy water, to the point where my feet were constantly immersed within the boots. It wasn't exactly cold, but the wind and drizzle didn't help. For some insane reason I hadn't packed my hardshell pants and before long I was soaked to the bone from the waist down. As long as my top half stays warm and dry, it should be okay. I'd been in much worse cold than this and although the guides kept complaining about the cold, it was nowhere near freezing – more like 8 degrees Celsius. Luke was wearing a raincoat which only came down to his bare calves, shorts and galoshes. As he climbed he struggled to pull down the flapping coat against the persistent rain.

'It is cold,' he said. We trudged on.

Before long we were joined by Simpson and Gideon, who had given us a half-hour's head start. We could hear their banter and shouting as they left base camp, and crashed through the mud and reeds. Every so often they would let out a piercing whoop. Luke always hollered back.

For the next 2 hours we made our way uphill.

'Is that Giluwe?'

'No. It's behind.'

Trudge.

'How about that one?'

'No. Behind.'

Some summit nights feel like the loneliest experience imaginable. Struggling through the dark, fighting for oxygen, each person locked in his or her own private hell and dodging demons long past the point of exhaustion.

This was not one of those summit climbs. If anything, our physical condition, the warm weather and banter made it feel like a community outing. I had reached the point where my body could just keep going without too much effort, the conditioning of the past few months paying off.

Weird shadowy forms appeared out of the mist, covered with reeds and rock. It wasn't until we were actually on the summit stretch that we could glimpse Mount Giluwe through the fog. Things got steeper, to the point where we eventually had to climb without poles using our hands and feet to grip the wet rock. Simpson shadowed me, watching, helping me over the slippery rock. He was still barefoot. The Gore-Tex in my boots, on the other hand, had stopped working. Each boot seemed to contain two inches of water. I developed tunnel vision. The only thing I could focus on was the next good grip in the slimy rock and keeping my balance.

Just then, a mad yodel. 'We are at the top!' someone shouted. Then there were a lot of whoops.

I looked up, to see Simpson leaning down from the summit just above my head, offering me his hand. I grabbed it and he hauled me up.

It was 1 March 2014. We had summited the highest volcano in Australasia. There was absolutely no view, we were so smothered in cloud. I shivered in the cold and wind.

'Congratulations,' Luke barked at me, shaking my hand and clapping my shoulder. I couldn't stop grinning. This had been the most enjoyable summit climb so far. We took turns posing for summit photographs, raising our fists in the air, whooping, smiling against the cold drizzle driving right into our faces. Then we began the slithery, slippery trip back down the rock face.

We moved extremely slowly – the descent being much more risky than the ascent – and within a few hours clambered back into the smoky tepee. Luke was now a lot more animated. He helped me hang up my socks to dry over the fire. Joshua helped me hang up my jacket. I noticed that Luke, Simpson and Gideon were glancing across at me every so often as they chatted.

'I was telling them that you are a very strong climber,' Luke said. I detected a hint of pride in his voice.

Luke was complimenting me. And smiling! 'Why, thank you,' I said and smiled at him. The young assistant shot me a shy grin as he washed the dishes.

We toasted our socks in the fire, dried out our sodden shoes (except Simpson, who just dried his feet) and ate lots of rice. The guides seemed happy with the speed of the climb, and I realised how acclimatised I still was. It was such a pleasure not to be gasping for breath. And after Antarctica, nothing felt that cold anymore.

'I am so amazed that you can walk and climb all this way with no shoes,' I told Simpson. Luke translated. Simpson threw his head back laughing and shouted something back to Luke. His eyes glittered.

'He says, if he wore shoes he would not be able to climb the mountain,' Luke said with a smile. I laughed. Simpson started bellowing. He grabbed Joshua's camera and thrust it at Luke, who almost giggled as he started taking photos of Simpson. He started copying Joshua's fashion-model poses, only on him the poses looked menacing.

We continued to sit in companionable silence. The straw felt good against my damp bare feet. Every so often Simpson and Luke would check my battered clothes as if they were smoking hams over the fire, turning them over delicately so they would dry all the way through.

'At 11 o'clock, we go,' Luke said, standing up.

We set out on our march back to the village. The mood was jubilant. Luke, Joshua and I surged ahead of Gideon and Stan, who stayed behind to put out the fire and tidy up Base Camp. By the time we had scrambled up to the top of the ridge overlooking Base Camp, the other two were specks in the distance, following us.

'HO!' came Gideon's cry from far below.

Simpson turned. 'WOO!' he screamed back, then cackled and resumed walking.

The 10 hours of hiking seemed longer this time. The mid-afternoon jet lag was starting to improve, but by the time we reached the rainforest my legs were so sore I had difficulty moving faster than an amble. We took a break on the rocks just above the rainforest, where we had had lunch the day before.

'How are you?' Luke asked.

'My legs are killing me. But I'm okay,' I said.

'Gideon, Stan and Joshua will take a break here. They are tired also. You, me and Simpson will go first. It is getting dark. We need to get back to the village before it gets dark.'

I nodded.

And so it began – the three most terrifying hours of the Seven Volcanoes Project. The sun may have still been up when we plunged back into the rainforest at 4 p.m., but I had forgotten that the dense foliage also blocked out a lot of daylight. The going was steep, and it was slippery after the rain. Several times I took a step only to fly straight off whatever stick, leaves, or loose mud I had set my foot on and land on my back. Most of the times I went off-balance, Simpson was there like a phantom, hands on my shoulders to save me from a fall. Though I fought to keep up with Luke, pretty soon he disappeared into the undergrowth and I would find him waiting for me further down, lurking in the twilight like an omen.

We stumbled down unending muddy paths and over fallen tree trunks. Night was falling fast.

'Hurry, it is almost 7 p.m.,' said Luke.

I tried to move faster, but couldn't.

Suddenly I heard someone following me. There was the snap of a twig that I did not make, the shushing of leaves that I had not disturbed. The metallic zing of a blade. I stopped. In my logical mind I knew I had nothing to fear. It was only the rest of the team catching up. But in that instant, fear had me by the neck. The primordial fear of being pursued by hunters far faster and more capable than myself. I cursed. I tried to speed up, but the more I tried the more I fell.

We had missed our sunset deadline. At the very moment that dusk turned to night, the insects started up and the jungle took on a chilling life of its own. A blood-curdling screeching started up. It sounded like someone screaming, over and over again.

'What is that?' I shouted to Luke. It was horrifying. It had to be something man-eating.

'Houseflies,' he said.

Man-eating house flies then. My ability to tolerate nature was being severely tested. Papua New Guinea is home to hundreds of species of snakes and lizards. Which of these lurked in the rainforest? Despite our head torches we couldn't see much. We blundered through a maze of trees which loomed out of the darkness. The noises invaded my head, blocked out everything but the fear.

Don't lose it, I told myself, *stay calm*. I crashed after Luke.

Half-an-hour later we erupted out of the rainforest and back into the village.

~

The next morning, I hobbled out of my hut to hear something I never expected to hear in the outback of Papua New Guinea.

'Do you know where I can plug in my laptop?' an Australian voice floated over the bushes. It pulled me up short. *What is a laptop doing in a place like this?*

I had showered and was finally back in clean clothes, but couldn't bear to put my boots back on just yet. They stank of swamp. I crept over the gravel to the dining hut to see Pym, hands on waist, talking to a woman with brown hair and a sunburned face holding a laptop. After just two days camping out in such wild countryside, the sight of a laptop – and the expectation of wi-fi – seemed ludicrous.

The Australian woman invited me to join her and a colleague for breakfast. I had been sitting alone on the balcony, lost in the view of the hills. We'd been through so much together. I didn't really want to leave. I'd come to love the wildness of the landscapes, the feeling of ancient hills and lack of people. I'd come out here with such feelings of trepidation, but over the last two days I'd come to feel almost safe here.

'So what are your plans out here?' she asked as I sat down opposite her.

'I've just come back from climbing Mount Giluwe,' I said, digging my fork into the scrambled eggs.

'What, by yourself? You're not with a team?'

'Oh, I was with five other people,' I smiled. 'A guide and the porters.'

She stared at me for a moment.

'How long have you been living here?' I asked.

'Five years now.'

'Do you think it's a dangerous place to live?'

She thought for a second. 'Well, you have your carjackings, and your robberies – she began.

'Didn't your daughter also get attacked?' interjected the colleague.

Now it was my turn to stare.

'Oh yes, some local guy ran out when she was running cross-country for her school. But she fought him off,' the woman said.

'She's feisty, that one,' added the colleague.

I swallowed. 'So I guess you heard about the trekkers who were attacked on the Black Cat Trail?'

'Oh yes. Yeah, that was probably a tribal territory dispute, over who gets the tourist dollars,' she said. 'Of course, if they caught anyone, they wouldn't go to prison.'

'Nah, it'll be the firing squad for them,' nodded the colleague.

I'd almost forgotten about the attack on the Black Cat trail. I'd been so busy just trying to climb Mount Giluwe that I hadn't had time to think of much else.

I finished eating and went out into the sunshine. Luke was chatting with some other guides in the yard.

Luke smiled when he saw me. 'Hello, strong lady,' he said. I smiled back and showed him the flower he had picked for me towards the end of our descent yesterday, which I had tucked into the side pocket of my backpack. Luke leaned forward and grabbed my boots from me. He started to scrape the mud off them with a stone.

'Oh, hey, it's okay. Let me do that, Luke,' I said. He shook his head and waved me off.

A few hours later Luke dropped me off at Kagamuga Airport in Mount Hagen.

'Thank you, Luke. Thank you so much,' I said. He nodded and shook my hand, solemn again. Joshua grabbed me in a bear hug, flashed his trademark bright smile and bundled into the white van. They roared off.

When I turned up at the Airways Hotel in Port Moresby that evening, I felt like a chimney sweeper who had snuck into the Ritz. I'd done my best to clean up a little, but my hair was still matted and greasy, my boots scattered little clumps of swamp mud everywhere and my clothes were rank. My face, though scrubbed with soap and water, looked haggard, the patches of tan and pale skin an uneven jumble from weeks of facemasks, sunglasses and goggles. Sunburnt nose, lily-white cheeks, chapped lips.

The immaculately dressed concierge didn't seem to notice the stench when I checked in at the glossy, wood-panelled front desk. For the next few hours I soaked myself, then my clothes in the paddling-pool-sized bathtub, and devoured huge chunks of pizza, onion rings and Coke. I washed my boots twice in the sink and stunned them with antiperspirant, but they still stank.

~

Forty-eight smelly, exhausted hours later, I was back in the UK. At Heathrow airport, I checked my email as I waited for the baggage reclaim to regurgitate my bag.

'We can do private climb of Ojos del Salado. We will confirm the guide later.'

Good. There was still hope. I was leaving for Chile in four days. Relief washed over me. There was still hope of salvaging the Seven Volcanoes Project and getting that world record. This was my second chance. I read the email again.

Actually, this was my last chance.

7

ROUTE LESS TRAVELLED

Only days after leaving tropical Papua New Guinea, I returned to the hazy heat of northern Chile. I was starting to get whiplash from changing country and climate every few days, and was happy for the relative familiarity of Copiapó. Desierto de Atacama airport looked the same as it had five weeks ago. Same sunshine, same warm air, same chattering crowds of passengers.

Still, there was one big difference. This time, I was here with an ally. I glanced at Douglas as we crossed the tarmac to the arrivals terminal.

'Mmmmm. Wonderful heat.' He lifted his face to the sun, eyes closed, and pulled off his sweater. He shoved it into his orange backpack, as if putting away the last of the British spring chill. I smiled. Life was so much better when I was with Douglas.

I had a feeling that things would go better this time on Ojos del Salado. Sure, I'd had to borrow thousands of pounds to come back to Chile. I'd shifted dates, booked new tickets, booked the cheapest flights possible, hired my own cross-country truck over the internet, and ordered dozens of ready-made meals and stuffed them into my duffel bag. I'd gone to extremes to get my second shot at the world record, and I wasn't going to waste it.

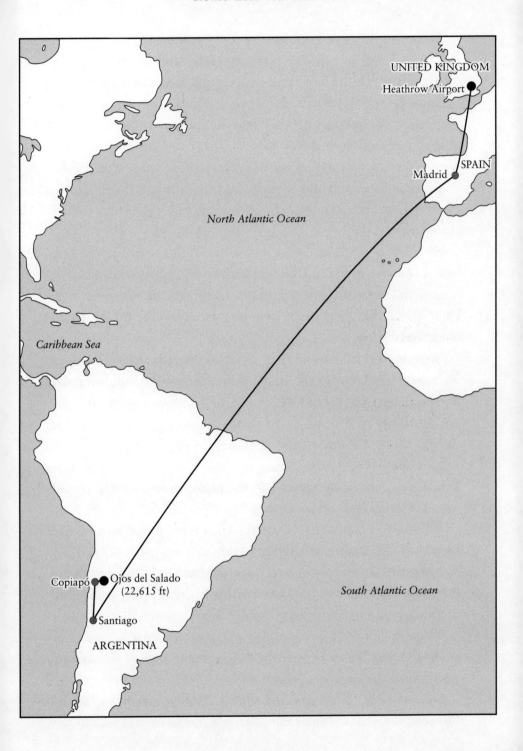

There was only one problem. I had no guide.

'Don't worry, I will find you someone,' the climbing agency manager had texted. I didn't care who I got, as long as it wasn't Fabio.

Douglas and I entered the cool, dark airport terminal. We dragged our duffel bags off the baggage reclaim carousel and as we pushed our trolleys towards the exit, I scanned the crowd. There were plenty of men with pony tails, but none of them were Fabio.

We pushed our trolleys back out into the sunshine. There, gleaming in the sun was the gleaming red 4x4 truck I had rented online.

We had no guide, and that was a beautiful thing. For the first time, I was free to roam. There would also be no awkward silences, no bullshit conversations or heavy metal music. We were free. I felt elated, like that burst of joy when school is closed on an unexpected snow day.

'We got wheels!' I shouted to Douglas. He grinned back at me. We tossed our bags in the back, wound down the windows and floored it for Ojos del Salado.

~

Valle Chico looked the same, only the grass smelt drier and the air cooler. Autumn was approaching.

'This is it! This is where we camped last time!' I said as we drove onto the field. 'I can't believe we found it!'

'Now this is *very* nice. And look at that sky.' Douglas threw the truck into reverse, backed up a little, then swung us around to the right.

'What're you doing?'

He grinned. 'So we can get the best possible view of the sunset.' He shut off the engine.

I leaned back in my seat and sighed. 'Now this is more like it.' I opened the little compartment between the seats and picked out one of the dark green avocados we had crammed inside. I turned around and rooted around for a plastic knife.

The back seat was piled high with plastic bags from the supermarket: fresh tomatoes, eggs, bread, a six-pack of beer, bottles of diet cola, miniature camping stoves, gas for the camping stove and a metric tonne of toilet paper. In the trunk, we had four extra canisters of fuel for the truck, wedged behind my duffel full of ready-made meals.

'Actually, first things first.' I grabbed the six-pack of beer and put it into a plastic bag. I jumped out of the truck and walked over to the river, and crouched down to tie the bunny ears of the shopping bag around some low branches, just as Fabio had done the last time.

'Next thing is to find out if this tent works.' We unpacked the cheap little tent I had bought online and set it up in the field among the horse droppings.

'You think you'll be okay camping?' I asked. 'You sure it's not too rough for you?'

Douglas laughed. 'I haven't camped since my Air Force days, and I didn't enjoy it then. But I should be able to cope.'

That evening, I cooked preserved beef stew on the little camping stove. I knew the stew was mostly made up of chemicals, but it smelled so good I didn't care. We ate in the front seats of the truck with our feet up on the dashboard, watching the sunset. A warm breeze brushed my face through the open window. My gaze wandered over the monumental gravel slopes cupping our little green valley and came to rest on the beer cans bobbing in the cool, narrow river.

Yes, it was all the same as before, only a million times better.

'This is fantastic. I just love this kind of scenery,' Douglas said. He took a sip of beer.

Douglas looked so contented. I felt overcome with gratitude that he was there. It hadn't been easy spending weeks apart from the person who keeps you sane.

'Douglas?'

'Yes?'

'Thank you for coming out here with me.' The words felt so adequate.

He smiled at me. 'You're very welcome.'

~

The next day, we set out to climb Goat-Devil Mountain. It was a rerun of the climb with Fabio a month ago. Same cloudless turquoise sky, same silent valley, the air so hot and dense that each breath warmed the throat like brandy. Our boots scrunched against the scree as we approached the base of the slope. Just before the path to climb, I stopped and looked up at the zigzag route. For the first time, I was the guide. I would set the pace this time, rather than following a guide whose plodding steps and lowered head told me they had done the route dozens of times before and were sick of it. No – this time I would take the lead, and that made this climb a real novelty.

'Here's where the climb starts,' I told Douglas, who had probably worked that out for himself. 'Seeing as how I'm the one with the walking poles, I'll take the lead. Sound good?' If Douglas heard the boarding-school-sports-teacher tone creep into my voice, he didn't show it.

'Sounds good.' He was dressed in casual slacks and a T-shirt, as if he were heading out for a day of golf.

'Now, if you start to feel the altitude, or need to stop for any reason, just let me know.'

'Sure.'

'You ready?'

'Yep.'

I turned back to the trail and started walking. We trudged up the loose rocky slope and followed the switchback back and

forth across the mountain face. The sun beat down and I began
to sweat. Why was I wearing so many layers? A T-shirt would
have been fine.

Douglas followed about 20 feet behind me, stopping every now
and then to take in the view. I waited for him to catch up, leaning
forward on my poles to hide my impatience.

'Have you ever thought of becoming a guide?' Douglas asked
as he walked up. He seemed oblivious to the 100-foot drop
beneath us.

I laughed. 'Nah. You need superhuman powers to become
a guide.' I shook my head, but part of me was flattered by his
question. 'How're you feeling? You okay to carry on?'

'Fine, thanks.'

'Okay. We'll reach the top soon and then we can take a break.'
I started off again. Like a true amateur, I made the mistake of
picturing myself as a mountain guide. Maybe climbing all these
volcanoes made me qualified to guide others.

That was when the trail disappeared. Perhaps the Goat-Devil
had a hand in it, but for the life of me I couldn't see the trail
anymore.

I froze. My downhill boot skidded a little, sending rivulets of
scree hurtling down the slope. My mind went blank. Where the
hell was the trail? I craned my neck and looked in front, behind,
up – anywhere but down – but all I could see was the steep faceless
slope covered in extremely loose and sliding gravel. My hands
started sweating around my climbing poles.

Douglas didn't say anything. He just stood there admiring the
valley, his hands on his hips. He didn't look frightened at all.

'Um. Just give me a second,' I called.

I peered at the rocks at the top of the slope. That was our
destination. How could I get us there without plummeting into
the valley? The scree felt as slippery as marbles. One false step and
I would tumble down a few hundred feet like a cartwheeling idiot.

Somehow, we'd overshot the trail and were now on the Dangerous Side of the mountain. Last time I was here, Fabio had pointed at this side of the mountain and said, 'That is where the Goat-Devil lives. We need to stay on the left side. The right side is very dangerous.'

I took a few more steps and felt my downhill foot slip. I looked down. The slope had gone from scree to sand on solid rock. With scree, you can at least take stable steps by packing down the loose stones. With sand on rock, you slide right out of control. The longer I stared down the slope, the more it seemed to tilt away from me. If I went on staring, the void might pull me down to my death.

I shut my eyes and clung to my climbing poles. The Goat-Devil had me in his goateed maw. I had better put my pride away before it killed us.

'Douglas…?'

Douglas ambled over. 'You alright there?'

'I've, um. I've lost the trail.'

'Oh.' He looked up. 'I think it's this way.' He sauntered past my stiff body and white knuckles along an invisible path only he could see. Before long, he reached the big rock about 50 feet above. He didn't even have any walking poles. I shouldn't have been surprised. After all, I had married someone from the Scottish Highlands. Douglas had spent his childhood running up and down slopes just like this. I inched forward, as if severely constipated. Meanwhile, Douglas reached the top of the slope and lay down on a rock to sunbathe.

'You alright down there?' Douglas shouted, his eyes closed as he enjoyed the sun. He looked infuriatingly relaxed.

'Yep. Absolutely fine.'

Inch by excruciating inch, I crawled out of the Dangerous Side and up to the safety of the rock where Douglas sunbathed. The moment I set foot on the smooth, sturdy rock, I crouched into a ball.

I brushed at the leaking corners of my eyes and said: 'And that is why I'll never be a mountain guide.'

~

A few minutes later, we reached the high plateau and ate lunch on a large warm rock. The heat waves shimmered over the blond sand. I felt a lot safer now we were off the cursed Goat-Devil Mountain.

Apropos of nothing, Douglas said, 'You know, a mountain cat could run out of nowhere and just have you for lunch.' He munched on a cereal bar.

Fabio had mentioned mountain cats before. He'd called them *pumas*.

'The 'puma's house' is just over in that valley.' I pointed to a dip that led into a rocky gully. 'Pumas stay away from humans though. If one attacks, we can just throw our food at him and run the other way,' I joked.

'You wouldn't have time to run.' Douglas looked grave. 'It would have you right away.'

I laughed. Then, I started to think about it.

A mountain cat. On a hot, hungry day. I glanced up the gigantic slope. Somehow this had never crossed my mind when I was hiking with Fabio and Matt. The puma could be hiding anywhere. It would be the same colour as the sand. We wouldn't see it until it was too late. I imagined the puma streaking towards us, teeth bared and ready. I gulped. It could probably smell us from a mile away.

In fact, it must already know we were here.

I stopped chewing. The back of my neck felt cold.

Beady eyes.

'Shall we head back?' I asked abruptly. Douglas was leaning against a warm rock, enjoying the sun.

'Mm?'

'I'd like to head back, if you're ready.'

'Oh, okay. Sure.' Douglas zipped up his backpack.

I slung on my pack and started walk-jogging to the top of the gully, like a deranged power walker. The puma's den was in the gully, but it was either that or Goat-Devil Mountain again. I scampered down like a frightened rabbit, dodging the bleached animal bones and the odd gnawed skull. Douglas crashed along behind me.

An hour later we returned to the safety of Valle Chico. I opened another packet of ready-made beef stew and cooked it on the camp stove, thankful to be back in the valley. Douglas ate standing up. He looked up at the steep sides of the valley.

'You know, if there were a flash flood or earthquake here we'd be goners,' he said.

I stopped chewing.

~

Travelling with Douglas was a lot like being on the run. We roamed the Atacama Desert like demented outlaws, crossing the high-altitude salt plains and zooming right up to the border of Argentina before crashing for the night by Laguna Santa Rosa and Laguna Verde. We clambered up windy slopes, cooked ready-made meals over the cheap dinky camp stoves and took photos of flamingos, vicunas and a sinister power plant in the middle of nowhere.

We sang a lot of questionable opera. Specifically, Gilbert & Sullivan operettas.

'LAAAAAAAAAAH,' Douglas bellowed as he pulled a U-turn like the Feds were closing in. The tyres kicked up a cloud of dust. We raced away from the road to the border and back down towards Laguna Verde and Ojos del Salado. '*Per chiiiiii – questi FIORIIIIII...*'

'La-la-la-LAAAAAA,' I hollered along. Dust from the road wafted through the open window and straight into my mouth. I giggled as Douglas floored it down the long, straight road, the Tres Cruces Mountains looming to our right and no one else around. He drove that truck the way he flew his plane – fast and precise – and as always in his company I felt as free as a daydream.

'Two bars! Oh wait, no bars. Crap! Back up!' It was our first phone signal in days.

Douglas jammed on the brakes, reversed the truck.

'THREE bars!'

'Okay!' He pulled over to the side of the road and jumped out to make his phone call.

Those six days with Douglas felt like more of an adventure than any other part of the Seven Volcanoes Project. Valle Chico, Laguna Santa Rosa, Laguna Verde. Somehow, it felt like I was discovering these places for the first time. We were free. The mountains belonged to us in a way I had never known before – as if until then, I'd assumed that only mountain guides held the keys to this magic realm. The more distance we covered, the more privileged I felt, as if I'd expected to return and discover that these beautiful places had existed only in my imagination, and that I'd see an empty theatre with stagehands rolling away the props and backdrop.

After a few days of marauding around the high desert, Douglas and I drove up to Atacama Camp, where I'd thrown up six weeks earlier.

We shambled up slowly. I had given up all pretence of being a mountain guide. We climbed until we felt the buzz of the altitude around our temples. Then we turned back, our matching Salomon boots sinking into the plush sand. We hung around in the car for a bit, wondering what to do next.

'How are you feeling?' I asked.

'Not bad. You can feel the altitude though.'

'Let me know when you want to head down. Best not to overdo it.' I could still smell the hot sand inches from my face as I heaved my guts out, at the spot just in front of our truck.

The season was almost over. The tent city at Atacama Camp was long gone. The dusty plateau was now empty, save for a couple of Spanish climbers and an empty tent. My brain echoed with phantom sounds: climbers talking, mugs clinking, the raspy flutter of dozens of tent flaps in the wind.

That night, we sat in the truck and watched the moon rise over Laguna Verde. The remains of our ready-made stew congealed slowly in a saucepan on the dashboard. The air turned chilly. Douglas and I drifted into silence, watching the moonlight-trimmed ripples glide across the lake. Behind it, the silhouettes of volcanoes waited under the darkening sky.

I looked for shooting stars, and thought of my father.

~

The next morning, Douglas and I stood next to our truck, staring up at Ojos del Salado. The massive volcano was smothered in cloud. Icy, fast-moving wind had covered the ground in snow overnight.

'What should we do?' Douglas asked.

I took a breath of chilly air. 'Doesn't look like a great day for a hike.'

'No, not really.'

We stood a little longer, mesmerised by the snow-spattered mountain behind cobwebs of fog.

'You think we've done enough acclimatisation?' Douglas asked.

'I don't know.' I tucked my hair behind my ear. 'I guess we could stay another night, and try to squeeze in one last hike tomorrow morning before heading back.'

Douglas nodded, still looking at the mountain. 'Yes. We could do that.'

Dad arrived in Hong Kong in 1970, and immediately fell in love with the city.

My father and mother, in the early days.

Dad was a lawyer. He always retained his curiosity and incisive intelligence.

My father and I. My mother told me that the day I smiled in recognition at Dad, he knew he loved me.

This is the approach to Pen Y Fan in Wales. The SAS train there – and so did I.

Clamshell tents were home to the various teams at Union Glacier Camp.

Above left: *The view of the lanscape from the plane. We were fortunate we did not have to make the journey to the volcano overland, which could have made the trip almost impossible for us.*

Above middle: *Camping in the crater of Mount Sidley.*

Above right: *Footsteps left in the snow after I had put out black plastic bags near the refuelling stop in Marie Byrd Land to mark it as a makeshift runway.*

Above right: *Wheeling over the crater of Mount Sidley, Antarctica. The plane we were in would be the first to touch down inside the crater, a hair-raising experience.*

Right: *It was a sobering thought that without the plane we would never have been able to return from Mount Sidley, the highest volcano in Antarctica.*

Below left: *On my way back from Mount Sidley in the Twin Otter.*

Below right: *The Load Master sitting at right angles to us in the Ilyushin-76 on the way to Antartica.*

*Above: Pico
de Orizaba, by
Eneas De Troy,
courtesy of Flickr
and Creative
Commons. The
volcano looms over
the nearby town.*

*Left: Packs front
and back, ready for
the next challenge,
this time in
Mexico.*

Mexican sunrise shining on the rock known as the Sarcophagus.

The crater of Pico de Orizaba.

Exhausted but happy at the summit of Pico de Orizaba (18,491 feet), Mexico.

Another temporary home, at Valle Chico, on the way to Ojos del Salado, and one with a lovely view.

The slopes around Valle Chico, Chile.

Laguna Santa Rosa in Chile.

Laguna Verde with its multi-hued waters.

We did an acclimatisation hike at Laguna Verde (14,200 feet), Chile.

On the way to Ojos del Salado, Chile.

Above: *Mount Kilimanjaro rises above the plains in Tanzania.*

Left: *Heading to Kibo hut (15,520 feet) on Mount Kilimanjaro, Tanzania.*

Aerial view of Mount Kilimanjaro in the evening, by Takashi Muramatsu, courtesy of Flickr through Creative Commons. The image was captured from a right-hand seat on a commercial flight at around 6.15pm on 8 February 2018.

Horombo hut on Kilimanjaro.

Above: Papua New Guinea's lush vegetation almost hides the village in the valley.

Left: Base Camp. The smoke meant there would be no risk of mosquito bites but I opted to sleep in my tent.

Below: 'Nah, THAT'S a knife mate!' Lunch on the way to Mount Giluwe, Papua New Guinea, using a borrowed knife that even Crocodile Dundee would proud of.

Back in Chile for my second attempt at conquering its highest volcano.

Sunrise at approximately 6am. We had already been climbing for hours.

Flying the cancer research banner.

Mount Damavand, Iran, by Greger Ravick, courtesy of Flickr and Creative Commons. At 18,403 feet, or 5,610 metres, Mount Damavand is regarded as the highest volcano in Asia.

Mount Damavand, Iran, by Reza Haghighi, courtesy of Flickr and Creative Commons. This shot displays the lush summer vegetation.

My guide Ali told me he had climbed Ghareh Dagh ridge on an unforgettable day.

Ghareh Dagh ridge can be seen in the distance as the sun burnishes the dome of the Goosfand Sara mosque.

Mount Elbrus in Russia, as seen from Mount Shatgatmaz, photograph by Konstantin Malanchevf, courtesy of Flickr and Creative Commons. Mount Elbrus is the highest volcano in Europe, reaching a height of 18,510 feet (5,642 metres).

Cheget village.

As my first attempt of Elbrus in April took place before the climbing season began, most of the other people there were soldiers undergoing endurance training, diehard competitive athletes and employees of local companies.

My temporary home in Russia.

Soldiers in training on the slopes of Elbrus.

My Russian guide Ivan skiing upward in front of me just before I bailed on my first attempt of Elbrus. I was feeling very despondent.

Climbing with an ally makes the most difficult journey more likely to succeed.

Victorious at last! On the summit of Mount Elbrus (18,510 feet), Russia, with climbing buddy Tina Bowman.

I caught a vague whiff of body odour and realised it was mine.

'Or... maybe we could head back and see if the hotel has a room for tonight,' I trailed off. Visions of the four-star hotel in Copiapó flickered before me. Real food. A hot bath. Soap.

Douglas glanced over at me. 'We could do that too.'

We looked at the mountain a little longer.

'Would you rather do that?' he asked.

'Would you?' We were doing that British thing of asking each other if they wanted the thing that we actually wanted ourselves.

'I'm happy with whatever you want to do.' Douglas paused. 'But if I have to eat any more of that ready-made crap I'm going to be sick.'

A few minutes later, the wheels of our truck kicked up a spray of gravel as we roared back to Copiapó.

~

The next morning, I met my new guide. The man looked in his mid-fifties, with a chest as deep as it was wide. His head was so bald it looked like it had been waxed and above his piercing, hooded eyes I discerned no real eyebrows. He strode across the hotel lobby and loomed over Douglas and me. After a second he smiled, bowed slightly and shook our hands.

'I am Matias,' he said.

'Nice to meet you,' said the long-haired girl next to him.

I'd been so focused on the man's bulk that I hadn't noticed the diminutive woman standing next to him.

'I am Amanda,' she said. She had large eyes the colour of swimming pools. 'Matias's English is not too good, so I am here to translate. I am the assistant guide.'

'Nice to meet you,' I said.

The four of us sat down around the coffee table in the lobby. Tourists walked by in summer clothes. We were dressed in long-sleeved climbing tops and trousers.

'I have a programme for the mountain,' Matias said haltingly. He took out a pen and a large notepad, and began writing down the dates of the next five days. He started speaking to Amanda in Spanish.

'Our goal is to get you to the top, no matter what,' Amanda translated. 'So, on the first day, we go directly to Atacama Camp at 17,000 feet. You say you are acclimatised, yes?'

Douglas and I exchanged a glance. I nodded. We'd done our best.

'Yes. We got as high as Atacama camp, actually higher, so maybe up to 18,000 feet,' I said.

'Okay. The first day, we go to Atacama Camp. The second day, we climb to Tejos Camp at 19,000 feet. The next day, we go back up, to 20,000 feet. Then back to Atacama Camp to sleep. And the third day, up to 21,000 feet. After that, rest day, then we move to high camp, then summit day. That way you will be acclimatised for certain before we go to the top.'

I felt like I had been locked into my shackles and handed an oar. *Now the holiday is over.* Fabio's voice butted into my thoughts like a fart.

I nodded. 'Sounds good.'

This was exciting. Everything would be fine this time. We were going to get to the top of the world's highest volcano. I was going to complete the Seven Volcanoes Project. I was going to achieve that world record in Dad's memory. The excitement buoyed me up until the next morning, even when I said goodbye to Douglas, who was heading back to the UK, and during the umpteenth trip to the supermarket before another long drive through the Atacama Desert.

Matias, Amanda and I sat down at a Formica-topped table in the café by the supermarket, plastic bags of food pooling at our feet. We nursed little cups of espresso.

Matias said something in Spanish.

'Matias wants to know why you want to climb Ojos del Salado,' Amanda said, eyes glued to her mobile phone.

'I'm climbing the highest volcano on each continent to raise money for cancer research,' I said. Matias nodded as he listened to Amanda's translation.

I watched Matias face as he listened. I don't know why, but then I said, 'And I'm doing it in memory of my father.' That was the part I usually left out. Somehow, I thought Matias would understand.

Matias listened, then looked at me as if he'd been stung. Were those tears in his eyes? He murmured to Amanda. She put her phone down and trained her turquoise eyes directly on me.

'He says, "What you are doing is beautiful."'

~

Matias took control of the expedition. He drove our rented truck the way a gladiator goads his horses, the four wheels straining to pull us through the mountainous valleys at high speed, across the salt plains, past the lakes of the high plains and straight back to Atacama Camp at 17,000 feet.

The further we drove, he more Matias's mood seemed to lighten. His brow lifted and he began talking a lot. In Spanish, which I didn't understand.

When we reached Atacama Camp a few hours later, Matias jumped down from the driver's seat with the relieved, satisfied smile of a man who had come home after a long day. He strode over to the shipping container and flung open the door. He beamed.

'This was his home for many years, when he was a ranger,' Amanda said from the back seat. I was still sitting up front, scrabbling around in my backpack for an extra pair of gloves.

'Wait, you mean he actually lived in the container?'

'Yes. For months each time.'

The refuge was nothing more than a shipping container reinforced with thick insulation and propped up on concrete blocks. The interior resembled a square cave. Small windows at the front let in some murky light above the makeshift sideboard where we balanced the camping stove at mealtimes. At the other end, there was a rickety wooden platform covered with thin mattresses, grimy from the ripe-smelling gunge of dirty climbers. Handmade shelves lined one wall from floor to ceiling. They contained a bazaar of obscure sachets of seasoning, packages of pasta, condiments, cooking oil, biscuits, milk powder.

'I built this myself.' Matias clapped his meaty hand on the cooking platform. Underneath it was a gaggle of empty plastic 5-litre water bottles, the kind I used to shove in my backpack on training hikes.

Matias cooed and hummed as he wandered around his former home. 'I made friends with climbers from all over the world here,' he said. 'But a lot of the time, I would be living here alone. I woke up early every morning, opened the door, and saw the snow covering everything, and looked up and saw the mountain.'

I looked around the container. It wasn't exactly homely. The container was just big enough for a single bed on a warped wooden frame at the back. The walls were covered in graffiti from climbers before us. 'Expedition, 1996,' said one. 'In Memoriam', said another.

~

The next morning, we shared a breakfast of eggs and bread on the little wooden table inside the container.

'Today, we hike to Tejos Camp,' Amanda said. 'It is important to acclimatise gradually.'

'You know, last time I was here, the guide took us straight to 19,000 feet from Murray Camp at 14,400 feet in one day.'

Amanda and Matias stared at me. 'Why the hell did you do that?' Amanda asked.

I shrugged. 'I really don't know. We just followed the guide's instructions. But that's how we – me and the guy I was climbing with – got sick.'

Matias shook his head.

An hour later, the three of us shuffled slowly out of Atacama Camp. Matias walked slowly. After the first hour, he stopped more and more often. He stood with his back to us, took a few deep breaths and resumed walking. As the afternoon wore on his breaks became longer, until finally he pulled himself off the side of the path altogether to retch.

'*Estas bien?*' Amanda called.

He waved her away. She turned back towards me, raised her eyebrows, and waited for Matias to recover.

Tejos Camp looked much as it had six weeks ago, crouched under the nose of Ojos del Salado. Amanda and I flung ourselves on to the camp beds inside the refuge and dug into our lunch packs. Matias hardly ate and just stood outside, breathing deeply and not saying much.

I looked at Amanda. 'We'd better not take too long up here.'

She nodded.

As soon as we got back down to Atacama Camp, Matias threw up. He said, 'I just need to rest,' climbed into the driver's seat of our truck, reclined the backrest as far back as it would go, and slept for the next 5 hours.

At sunset I went to check on him. He was still asleep in the truck, his exhausted pale, bald head resting against the dusty window pane like a grapefruit in a shop window.

~

On our third day on Ojos del Salado, I started to have my doubts about Matias. I woke up early with an altitude headache. It felt like a hangover, but without the party, which made me vaguely resentful. I walked out of my tent to see Matias washing water bottles and preparing breakfast. Yesterday, he had retreated to Laguna Verde to recover while Amanda and I made our second acclimatisation hike to Tejos Camp.

'*Como te sientes?*' I asked.

'*Bien*. Never better. Though I've never had worse mountain sickness than I did yesterday,' he said. '*Y tu?*'

I felt about as perky as a bathmat. 'I have a headache,' I admitted. We'd gone as high as 20,000 feet the previous day.

'Want to spend some time lower down today? We could go to Laguna Verde.' I suspected he was offering as much for himself as for me.

'Really? Do we have time?' I asked.

'Sure. Pack your stuff. Let's descend for a few hours.'

Laguna Verde was full of climbers, for once. A few of them knew Matias. He got out of the truck to chat with them, while I reclined the back of my chair and stared out at the glittering turquoise water. The air felt so much thicker here, like a duvet. The sun warmed my face and a cool breeze blew in through the gap in the window. I started to doze off.

Someone tapped on the window. I opened my eyes.

'Oh, crap.'

It was Fabio. He grinned at me through the dusty glass.

I wanted to pretend I hadn't seen him. Instead, I sat up and opened the door.

'Hello, Fabio,' I said. 'How are you?' There was so much I wanted to shout at him. If it weren't for him, I wouldn't be here now, attempting Ojos del Salado a second time. I wouldn't have spent thousands of pounds I couldn't afford. I wouldn't be spending more time away from home.

'*Hola*, Sophie,' he leered. 'I am good.' Infuriatingly, he seemed to have no clue that he was on my blacklist. 'My last client came to climb Ojos. Then she said, "It is too hard" and she cancel. So I was on holiday for one month.' He grinned, looking pleased with himself for having avoided more work.

'Oh. Good for you,' I muttered. He seemed to take this as a compliment, because he nodded in a self-satisfied way.

'I go to make lunch for my clients. I see you inside.' He walked towards the refuge.

I fumed. Maybe I could skip lunch. My stomach growled. No, I was too hungry. Might as well get it over with. I slithered out of the car and slammed the door of the truck, imagining I was slamming it in Fabio's face.

In the cool of the refuge, Amanda and Matias were talking in animated Spanish to the young climbers. Fabio stood at the counter cooking for his clients – a father and son from Italy.

Matias beamed as I walked in. 'I'm taking her to the summit,' he told the young climbers, who looked over at me curiously. '*Porque ella se lo merece.*' Because she deserves it. I smiled at Matias. I started to feel better.

'*Gracias*, Matias,' I sat down next to Amanda. Maybe lunch with Fabio wouldn't be so bad after all.

Fabio finished cooking, turned off the gas stove and brought the saucepan over to the table. Both father and son looked stunned into silence. Or maybe they were just shy. The son peered into Fabio's saucepan as if he expected a snake to jump out of it.

'Hi,' I waved. 'I'm Sophie. Nice to meet you.'

The men nodded silently. I tried again.

'You're heading up to Atacama Camp tomorrow?' I asked.

'Yeah,' the son said. 'That's the pla–'

'Sophie has tried *three* times to climb Ojos del Salado,' Fabio interrupted. He spooned the contents of the saucepan onto a plate. Father and son stared at me, as if they didn't know what to do with this information. Fabio looked up, shook his head at me and gave me a smile I wanted to hit with a brick.

I ate the rest of the meal in silence.

~

That evening, back at Atacama Camp, Matias, Amanda and I sat in the truck and watched dark clouds swallow the mountain. Our usual vista of endless blue was smothered by thick clouds that had oozed up from the valley. Ojos del Salado had disappeared.

'What's the last weather forecast you heard?' Matias asked Amanda.

'Nothing up to date. I don't know if it'll be calm enough to move to high camp tomorrow.' She shifted in her seat to get a better view of the sky.

We would have to see. Everything depended on the mountain's mood.

~

The alarm buzzed at 3 a.m. I no longer had a headache. In fact, I felt refreshed. This was it. My last chance to salvage the Seven Volcanoes Project and the world record. I jumped out of bed, eager and aggressive like a boxer just entering the ring. Matias and Amanda woke up and checked the sky.

'How does it look?' I asked.

Matias gave me the thumbs up. The expedition was a go. We began preparing for our attempt on the summit towering 3,600 feet above us.

Matias, Amanda and I stumbled around the L-shaped refuge by the light of our head torches and pulled on our warm outer layers. We normally slept in our day layers – soft shell pants, thermal top and sometimes long johns – and only really changed our socks. Amanda had a way of looking tousled and glamorous, and she looked slim even in puffy jackets. As she toasted slices of bread on the camp stove on the kitchen table, she looked like she had just had a shampoo and blow-dry.

It always takes longer than you think to get ready to set out for the summit. There is breakfast to eat, caffeine to ingest, several clumsy extra layers with and hand warmers, inner boots and long laces to contend with. Someone always needs to answer nature's call after they've strapped on their climbing harness. Somehow that morning, despite feeling well, we took longer than we should have. The digital clock in the truck read 5 a.m. by the time Matias drove us up to the end of the path at 16,000 feet.

We clambered out of the truck and heaved on our backpacks. I pulled the waistband and chest strap snug, so that the rucksack held my spine in a reassuring vice. I liked the feel of hiking with a backpack – far from being a burden, the weight anchored me to the ground and held me together.

Headlamps on, we started walking over small rocky ridge which blocked the road from the trail head. It was still dark, but the moonlight lent a dim light which at least revealed rock, dark and volcanic, and gravel. Matias walked slowly, taking a short breather every few minutes. I had no trouble keeping up with him and for once did not have to overcome any nausea, which usually struck during the first hour of a summit climb until I got a second wind.

Ojos del Salado is essentially a walk-up. In good weather, it takes around 7 hours to get to climb the south face and reach the crater. For the first 6 hours or so, we zigzagged back and forth across the mountain face. I started power-breathing soon after we passed the 20,300-foot mark.

There are some climbs where it all just comes together. The body rallies, the legs feel strong and the spirit light. Summit day on Ojos del Salado started out as one of those climbs.

'You have to find your rhythm. It is the same with everything. Once you have that, everything works,' Amanda said.

I kept my eyes glued to the path just in front of my feet, glancing up only briefly after each hairpin turn to gauge the distance until the next corner. I didn't look up at the summit, I didn't look below. Hours passed.

It all started to go wrong, as it so often does, because of the altitude. Once we neared 20,000 feet, I wasn't able to think clearly. We were now four-fifths of the way up the face of Ojos del Salado, somewhere around 22,000 feet, at the base of two parallel ice streams. The narrow glacier on the left petered out into nothing, but the right-hand ice stream fed into the broad glacier below, which then plunged abruptly over cliffs.

'Nobody goes onto the glacier,' Fabio had told us in February. 'It is crazy – very dangerous.' Between the two ice streams, a waterfall of giant boulders. Matias started to cross the snow field.

'Is there any way we can avoid going on the glacier?' I asked.

'This is the usual way,' Matias replied, hands on hips.

I looked at the snowy expanse again. It looked icy and unstable. The drop to the rocky ledges beneath looked even steeper up close.

'Can we at least wear crampons and rope up?' I called.

'No, no need for crampons or rope.'

I'll never really be sure of what happened that day. Either I had made a sound safety call, or it was the altitude muddling my perceptions, or Fabio and several others had been wrong about embarking on the glacier so close to the cliff. For some insane reason, I chose to believe what Fabio had said.

'Look, let me put it this way: I am not walking across that.'

Amanda stared at me. This was her first time climbing Ojos del Salado, which meant she deferred to Matias.

'Is there another way up?' I shouted.

Matias looked at his boots, then looked at me. 'We can go up via the rocks.'

I looked up. A colossal waterfall of boulders, spilled down from the crater miles above our heads and swept down the mountain face.

'Okay,' I said. And we embarked on the hardest, most punishing struggle of my life.

I had never fought so hard against an invisible enemy before. We had passed 20,000 feet long ago. Every time I raised my boot to haul myself up onto the next boulder, the altitude sucked a little more energy from the marrow of my bones. A heaviness grew within me like a wetsuit filling with water.

After every stride the three of us stood there, gasping, feeling as if we had been punched in the stomach. That the large boulders were not fixed to the face of the mountain made it that much more dangerous. Every so often, without warning, massive chunks of dark rock suddenly unmoored themselves and hurtled down the steep slope. We were barely making any headway.

'Wait, stop,' I called up to Matias. He glared down at me. 'This can't be right. This is much too hard. It's dangerous too. Can we cross to the glacier now that we're a bit higher up?' He shook his head.

'But this is ridiculous,' I shouted.

He shook his head sullenly.

'*Vamos*,' he said with an impatient jerk of his head. He turned his back on us and resumed fighting his way up.

It was already past midday. Above us the crater rim was still far away. It would take us hours to wind our way through this maze of moving rock. 'This could cost us the summit,' I suddenly realised.

'Matias,' I tried again. I stopped to catch my breath. My legs were burning. I was wearing an invisible lead cloak. 'This is taking too long.'

What Matias said next was an ice-cold slap in the face.

'*Sabes, Sophie, no creo que puedes ir a la cumbre. No tienes la fuerza.*' He glared at me.

I don't think you can make it to the summit. You don't have the strength.

I'd never been good at anticipating a crisis.

~

'Do you plan on staying out there forever?' Dad asked in the winter of 2006. I was back in the UK, visiting my parents for ten days. This time, I'd brought over my Chinese boyfriend. My parents knew what this meant.

Dad sat on the sofa, eyes closed, listening to a classical symphony. Next to him lay his dog-eared copy of *I Shall Bear Witness* by Victor Klemperer.

'How do you mean?' I asked.

Dad got up, walked over to the stereo and turned down the music. I glanced out the windows at the moth-eaten weather, the damp little houses.

'In China. Are you planning on being there for a long time?' He sat down again on the sofa, getting ready for a long, lawyerly interrogation. Dad had retired at forty-five, but had never got used to it. He spent his days weaving brief conversations with my mother, snippets of Radio Four and unnecessary trips to the shops into a tenuous fisherman's net to trawl his vast oceans of free time. But his net was never fine enough, and time slipped through all the same.

Dad wasn't happy. After a year of living in England, he wanted to leave again. He hated the bad weather. He hated the cold. Most of all, he was dismayed to find himself a foreigner in a country that was no longer his.

In his first year back, my parents had dinner with some friends in London. One of the friends had a new girlfriend. Dad never forgot what she said.

'She thought I was Dutch,' he said at breakfast the next day. He looked as if someone had thought he was Batman.

I started laughing over my bowl of cornflakes. 'Really? Why would she think that?'

Dad stared into space. 'I have no idea. She said, "You speak very good English for a Dutchman." So I said, "Thanks." I thought she was joking. Then she said, "When did you first arrive from Holland?"'

'So she was serious?' I asked.

'Apparently.' I started giggling at my father's confused expression, but in hindsight, I realised it really wasn't very funny.

England no longer recognised my father, and it sure as hell didn't recognise me. By the time I was transferred to Shanghai, my parents were preparing to move to the north of France, near Rennes.

Dad was greyer now. He took off his reading glasses – when had he started wearing reading glasses? – and set them down on the sofa next to him. He leaned forward, elbows on knees, cigarette in his left hand, and waited for my answer.

'Well – I don't know, really.' I used a phony-jovial tone, trying to convince Dad that an awful thing is really a good thing. 'I mean, I'm getting much further in my career than I ever would have if I'd stayed here. I want to be bureau chief one day.'

Dad took a drag on his cigarette.

'You left too, at my age.' I stared at my nails. We were not good at sharing our feelings. 'I mean, I never wanted to come to Europe in the first place–' I started to say, but then I looked up. I saw the lines on Dad's face, the stoop of his shoulders. The shoulders that used to carry me around our garden in Hong Kong as a child. Suddenly, my mother's words crashed into my brain.

'Your father and I never expected you to go back,' Mom had said the day before. 'And it's so polluted. Why would you take a step back?' To my parents, China was still the chaotic, primitive place people tried to get away from, a land of famine and chaos and revolution. Why had I left them for a place like that?

So I stopped talking. Just then my Chinese boyfriend and Mom came into the room and we all switched to phony-jovial mode, making phony-jovial conversation.

A few days later, we said goodbye at Heathrow Terminal 3. I hugged my parents tightly. 'I'll call as soon as I'm home – I mean, back in Shanghai,' I said. I could not wait to dash through the departure gates and return to my future. Much later, Mom told me that after I'd walked through those gates, Dad had silently wiped tears from his eyes.

Like I said, I've never been good at anticipating disaster.

~

'You know, many people consider this to be the summit,' Amanda shouted against the wind.

The actual summit of Ojos del Salado is at the top of a rocky outcrop jutting out from the rim of the volcano. To reach it, you need to climb approximately 100 feet up a steep rock face on a fixed line. By the time Matias, Amanda and I finally reached the rim of the volcano, we were too exhausted to make the final push. We never reached the summit of Ojos del Salado.

The sense of failure was crushing. The wind was so ferocious that it was almost impossible to stand upright, and in any case we were so strung out that we would have been blown off our feet.

As soon as we ourselves over the rim of the volcano, gasping and retching with exertion, Matias flung himself into the shadow of a large rock and grimaced against the wind. His hands shook as he wrapped his arms around himself against the cold.

Tears ran down my cheek. I was dizzy from hunger, but at the same time the idea of food made me nauseous. I was exhausted, to my bones, to the ends of my nerves. I fumbled with the Cancer Research UK banner as the wind tried to tear it out of my gloved hands. Amanda took photos of me holding the banner, and as I tried to smile my face felt doughy and swollen from the elevation.

Amanda looked exhausted as well. She glanced first at Matias, then at me.

'Look, guys,' she shouted. 'We are tired, yes. But look how far we've come! We still have food. And we all have head torches to get back after dark.'

Matias glared at her from under his rock.

'I mean, we're here now! We can still make it!' she said.

I loved Amanda for her optimism, but only Matias could make the decision for us. He shook his head wordlessly.

'Then at least let us get into the caldera and have a break there. It'll be less windy,' Amanda pleaded.

I waited. After a few seconds, and with great effort, Matias pulled himself to his feet. Leaning against the wind, we struggled down into the crater. Matias could barely walk in a straight line. Directly above us, no more than 100 vertical feet away, was the summit of Ojos del Salado.

What was wrong with me? I had felt so strong that morning. Now I could hardly take five steps without veering off the path. I had no control over my legs.

'We can try, eh Matias?' Amanda said.

Matias shook his head.

'Well, maybe we could at least try.' I tried to walk over to her, but stumbled off the path and collapsed onto some rocks.

Matias shook his head. 'It's too dangerous. We're too tired. There's ice on the rock face.' He wrung his gloved hands, looking ashen.

It was over. The three of us stood, defeated, in the crater of the highest volcano on Earth. I had tried my best and still failed, even with a guide like Matias. As the three of us stared up at the summit, I could feel despair settling on our shoulders like drizzle.

All it takes is one wrong decision, one wrong step, to destroy everything. Like taking the wrong way to the summit of a mountain. Or leaving for Shanghai when your father is dying. Either way, it was a disaster.

8

COCA-COLA TRAILS

The day dawned with a sky so innocent and blue that I almost felt guilty about wanting to kill someone. I woke early, despite my exhaustion. I lay in the lower bunk, thinking murderous thoughts as I listened to Matias snoring in his cot at the end of the dormitory. My volcanoes project was truly screwed. There was no time to climb Ojos del Salado a third time. The climbing season in Chile ended in a few days, and even if I had the inclination to put myself through another climb, I didn't have the money.

Amanda rustled in her sleeping bag opposite me and mumbled something in her sleep. Matias looked sickly and exhausted. The three of us had barely exchanged a word last night before passing out. By the time we stumbled back into Tejos Camp, we were barely able to walk in a straight line. I had thrown up so hard that my contact lens had flung itself off my eyeball and into the darkness, lost forever. My feet throbbed in pain, the toes dented after hours and hours of descent.

Amanda was the one who'd kept me going.

'I want you to really focus, okay Sophie? This is not very safe. Step where I step,' she shouted as we crossed the glacier – the one I had refused to cross on the way up. Matias walked several hundred feet ahead of us. Every so often, he sat down and stared into space.

The glacier was steep and covered with a layer of snow, which the late-afternoon sun had melted into an uneven, slippery swamp. Even with crampons on, I slipped in the slush and fell onto my back several times. My legs felt like they belonged to someone else. When a hole appeared beneath my right foot, revealing a drop of several hundred feet, I was so delirious that all I could do was giggle.

Amanda turned to see why I was laughing.

'Use your ice axe! Dig a seat and sit down, dig in your heels, don't fall.' Amanda strode back to me and grabbed my arm. 'This is not safe,' she muttered. Step by painful step, we crossed the glacier together.

We reached the trailhead an hour later, just as night fell. Matias was already sitting in the truck, his mouth clenched into a thin line. We had driven 300 feet to the trail head that morning to save time. Amanda and I climbed into the back.

Matias turned the keys. The truck lurched forward, then stopped. The wheels turned but nothing happened. We had driven straight into a ditch.

'*Bastardo*,' Matias shouted. He wrenched the wheel around, swore, stamped on the accelerator again. The truck tried to climb out of the rut, its engine revving like a wounded animal. It strained, shuddered, and rolled back into the hole.

'The car is stuck,' Matias said. 'We'll have to walk.'

Amanda and I didn't move. I closed my eyes, pretending I wasn't there.

'Come on! *Vamos!*'

We stumbled out onto the rutted road to camp. Not even the beautiful night sky cheered me up.

~

Breakfast was a silent meal of toast and coffee. Matias wrapped his hands around his thermos and stared out the window. Amanda busied herself with making toast over the camp stove. I sat on the bench and stirred my coffee. We could take our time, now there was no more mountain to climb.

Matias stood up.

'I'm going to get the truck.'

I nodded.

Amanda glanced at me, then at Matias.

'Hey, Matias, did you know Sophie is planning to climb Kilimanjaro next?' she asked.

Matias paused on his way out and looked at me properly for the first time that morning. I glanced up. He leaned forward and slapped me lightly on the shoulder. 'You can do it,' he said with a gentle smile. He pulled on his hat and walked out.

I smiled, but my stomach was full of lead. What was the point in carrying on with the volcanoes project? I may as well give up, fly home and apply for jobs.

Amanda began clearing the table.

'You are a very strong climber,' she said. 'There I was complaining so much about my cold hands and feet, but you just kept going, never complaining.'

She looked at me, as if sizing me up.

'We need more strong women climbers like you.' Amanda nodded. 'I think you should definitely go and climb Kilimanjaro.' She went to the dormitory to pack up.

~

Five days later, I landed in Arusha, Tanzania.

Kilimanjaro is a beautiful anomaly. It is not only the highest peak on the African continent; at 19,341 feet above sea level it is also the highest free-standing mountain in the world. Unlike Ojos

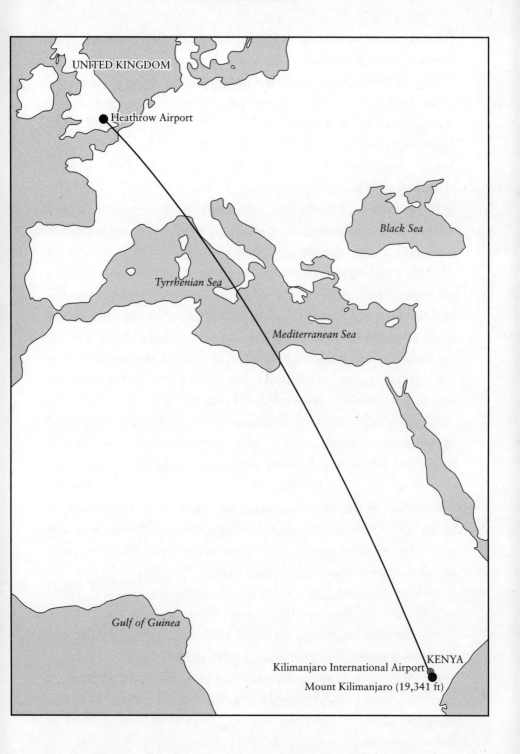

del Salado in the Andes, or Mount Elbrus in the Caucasus range, Kilimanjaro stands alone.

'My name is Dismas, like "Chris'mas" with a D,' said the stout-chested man dressed in khaki shorts and a T-shirt. He stepped forward and shook my hand. Dismas was my new guide. Kilimanjaro is one of the Seven Summits as well as the Volcanic Seven, which meant I was greeted by a well-oiled tourism industry accustomed to solo climbers.

I'd arrived in Arusha late last night. After a restless night's sleep, I'd eaten a lonely breakfast in the hotel's vast, shiny-floored restaurant. Now, I felt jetlagged and adrift as Dismas and I stood in the lobby and went through the usual pre-expedition pleasantries.

'Very pleased to meet you,' I said. Dismas was nearly 6 feet tall and didn't smile much. His skin was so smooth that his shaved head resembled new leather. The morning was fresh after heavy rains during the night, and the hotel courtyard smelled of clay as Dismas led me to a small white van. Four porters were crammed inside. They nodded and smiled as I climbed in.

We drove through the neat, busy streets of Arusha and headed towards the outskirts towards Kilimanjaro National Park. Dismas turned to ask with rehearsed politeness: 'Is this your first time in Africa? Is this your first mountain climb?' I answered his questions, but for the most part I was happy just to sit and take in the scenery. An hour later, the mighty bulk of Kilimanjaro came into view. Its flat-topped summit was necklaced with snow, while its mauve lower reaches disappeared into the haze.

Hello, old friend. Unexpected tears came to my eyes at the sight of Kilimanjaro. This was the mountain that had changed my life. It was the first big mountain I had ever climbed. When I decided to climb it nearly five years ago, I had no idea that it would be a gateway to years of mountain climbing that helped me process my grief over losing Dad. Funny, how a decision made on a whim can have such far-reaching consequences. Would this second climb of Kilimanjaro measure up to the first?

We drove through the tall, triangular entrance gate of Kilimanjaro National Park. I leaned back in my seat and clenched my calf muscles. The months of travel were starting to take their toll.

Funny how such a formidable-looking mountain was now treated as just another item to tick off the bucket list. It had been five years since I climbed Kilimanjaro, but I still felt the same awe and respect as the first time I saw it. Now that I had blown my chances of setting a world record, I wasn't really sure why I was persevering with the remaining climbs. All I knew was, something was pushing me to carry on this strange journey through the volcanoes.

~

The start of Kilimanjaro's most frequently climbed route is a work of art. The beginning of the Machame route (also known as the Coca-Cola route) is a paved path the colour of burnt brick, about 8 feet wide, and even as a pavement. It doesn't look like the start of a mountain climb.

'In high season, you almost cannot walk on the path,' Dismas walked like a man on his post-dinner stroll. 'There are hundreds of climbers. Sometimes there is too much traffic and you cannot move.'

The path wound through the humid, warm forest, the morning sun filtered down through the thick green and lit up the moss on the trees, which swished and whispered with unseen creatures. Our porters were long gone. They had taken the shortcut to Mandara Camp, leaving Dismas and I to follow the meandering scenic trail.

Every year, around 20,000 tourists walk along this path, or around 40 per cent of all people climbing Kilimanjaro. Who are all these people? Thousands of amateur adventure-seekers whose bucket lists tend to include 'Go bungee jumping' and 'Swim with dolphins' – and of course, 'Climb the Seven Summits'. Kilimanjaro has become a symbol of modern-day commercial climbing.

In August 2009, nearly a year after Dad died, I was among those hordes. I had no idea about mountain climbing, but I'd heard of

Kilimanjaro. I knew I wanted to do something that felt daring, without actually being dangerous. My decision to climb Kilimanjaro set in motion a chain reaction that changed everything else in my life.

Losing a parent for the first time is the Continental Divide of happiness. Everything changes. Before and After are different universes. I stopped caring about climbing the career ladder. I gave up on my dream of being a foreign correspondent in China. Mom became the main factor in my life. I had to take care of her now, because she needed me. It was the two of us against the world.

It had given me an odd sense of freedom to give up all my dreams. What do you do when everything you've worked so hard for disappears? I booked a nine-day climb of Kilimanjaro. Mom bought me new running shoes.

After I booked a place on the Kilimanjaro expedition, I joined a gym near my office in Paris. It was a cross between a sauna and a sardine can, crammed with Parisians in Spandex. Every second evening I walked the three blocks from the news bureau, and as I panted on the treadmill I tried not to choke on the musty air.

I created a training plan and ran away from my sadness. Every week, I made the runs longer. When the runs began to get easier, I upped the incline on the treadmill. I braved the airborne machismo of the weights room and learned how to use the machines. The more punishing the workout, the better I felt. My skin improved and my resting pulse dropped. My asthma subsided. I slowly shook the Shanghai smog out of my lungs, like dust out of a carpet.

Over the years, my training regimen grew to epic proportions. Every year, I climbed a new mountain in Dad's memory. In between climbs, I trained like a madwoman. In late 2013, I drove to Wales to climb Pen y Fan (2,907 feet) with 26 litres of water in my backpack.

It was a sparkling winter morning as I heaved myself over the top of Jacob's Ladder, the near-vertical rocky steps before you reach the summit of Pen y Fan. I wore a big rucksack on my back and a smaller one hanging in front, like a koala. There were other people around, mountain runners, couples, a few families. The breeze tousled my hair as I strode up to the stone monument that marked the summit.

'Excuse me,' I called to a grey-haired couple. 'Please could you take a photo of me and my friends?'

The woman smiled and walked over to take my camera. Trying to smooth down my hair, I knelt down by the monument. She looked through the lens and then drew back.

'Hang on – where are your friends?' She looked left and right.

I grinned as if I'd just tossed away my straitjacket. 'Here they are.' I opened my backpack with a flourish. I pulled out bottle after bottle of water and lined them up in front of me: 26 kilogrammes of water weight that I'd carried up the mountain. A personal record. The couple started laughing in surprise, and the woman took my picture.

Climbing Kilimanjaro started as a lark, but it became a lifeline.

~

Kilimanjaro is increasingly advertised as an adventure open to anyone, regardless of fitness or climbing ability. People didn't come to Kilimanjaro expecting a strenuous mountain climb with its inherent risks. Kilimanjaro was just something else to do between safari week in Kenya and a spa getaway in Zanzibar.

Kilimanjaro has become the darling of commercial climbing agencies, which have blossomed thanks to the Seven Summits fad and tourists like Anka and Nina, and of course myself. In the late 1950s, there were fewer than 1,000 climbers on Kilimanjaro per year. In 2012? Over 50,000. At the end of an expedition, the guides and assistants often sing and dance for the clients, in the hope of receiving more tips. It was as authentic as the paved start of the Coca-Cola trail.

A major problem with commercial climbing is the waste it creates. Everyone knows that climbers eat a lot, and all that food has to go somewhere. In 2006, around 125 tonnes of solid human waste was deposited on Kilimanjaro. That's a lot of faeces. A lot of it gets into the local water, especially when climbers relieve themselves in the wild rather than using park facilities.

In addition to the faeces and the trash was the impact of the explosion of tourism all over the wilderness. A few decades earlier, there was no tourist infrastructure. The only way to get to Kilimanjaro was by days of hair-raising travel on broken-down buses. Even the last time I climbed Kilimanjaro in 2009, I had to take a gruelling 5-hour bus ride from Nairobi to the mountain. The highway had run out after 2 hours, after which we trawled through dusty townships at night filled with bored men standing in groups, using outdoor toilets, warming their hands over fires in tin barrels.

These issues are not restricted to Kilimanjaro. Take the lurid yellow pee hole we left behind in Antarctica, for example. 'It's just a question of aesthetics,' Pete, our guide, had said in the cafeteria. 'All the waste at Union Glacier Camp gets exported to Chile, so tourists can think of Antarctica as this pristine wilderness. But really, all you're doing is moving trash from one place to another.'

~

I met Mountain Gazelle on the second day. It was evening, and I was sitting by myself in the dining hut at Mandara Camp, my first stop. I was reading a bad police novel and drinking hot chocolate while the rain clattered down. The rangy man walked in, clothes steaming. Dismas, sitting opposite me, jerked his head at the man. 'Today, Mountain Gazelle jogged all the way up here from the park entrance. Even the porters could not catch up with him.'

The man nodded to no one in particular and sat down at the table next to ours.

I leaned forward. 'Hi, I'm Sophie.'

Mountain Gazelle stared at a spot just above my head.

'Did you really just run all the way up here? That's impressive.'

'Oh. Yeah. I had a long weekend, so I thought I would do it now.' He had a vaguely European accent that I couldn't place. He was a middle-ranking cultural attaché on secondment to Nairobi. He wore fluorescent athletic gear and had the hungry, lean face of a long-distance runner.

'You're planning on climbing Kilimanjaro over three days?' I asked. That was pretty fast.

'Well, Nairobi is already at almost 6,000 feet above sea level so I think it will be possible,' he said. 'Tomorrow I'm heading straight up to Kibo hut,' – high camp at 15,420 feet – 'and then going to the summit tomorrow night.'

Too many people think Kilimanjaro is easy. It's true that most trails are walk-ups with no technical skills required. Every year, hundreds of people attempt to climb Kilimanjaro in faster and faster times. People set other records too, including Climbing Kilimanjaro Backwards in the Fastest Time, and First Bearded Hippy Riding a Unicycle Up Kilimanjaro.

Too many people underestimate that monster called Altitude. There's also no real vetting for fitness or climbing experience, or knowledge of mountain safety techniques. Which means a large number of amateur climbers are in no shape to tackle Kilimanjaro. Every year, around 1,000 evacuations and 10 deaths occur on Kilimanjaro, mostly due to acute mountain sickness, or AMS. If ignored, AMS can lead to pulmonary oedema – where fluid builds up in your lungs and you quite literally drown on the inside, my worst nightmare – or cerebral oedema, where the brain swells with fluid. In both cases, death is a swift possibility.

I looked at the sporty young diplomat in neon clothes and running shoes. He was aloof, as if he needed to prepare mentally for the climb ahead.

~

I met Nina and Anka at breakfast. The porcelain-faced Danish girls had just finished university. They were on a three-month volunteer posting to a small Tanzanian village. They lived with a local family, had bright blonde ponytails and blue eyes, showered once a week and taught English at the local school.

'So, why are you climbing Kilimanjaro?' I asked.

Nina ladled some porridge into her bowl. 'Oh, people kept telling me, "You're living in Tanzania, you've got to climb Kilimanjaro!" So here we are.'

'Have you climbed a mountain before?'

'This is our very first mountain,' Nina said. 'How about you?'

'I've climbed a few.'

I look out the window and saw Dismas striding around in the morning sun, waving at some people, giving orders to others. Wrapped up in his big neon yellow parka and navy baseball cap, he looked purposeful, impatient. I smiled.

'There's the boss,' I stood up and grabbed my backpack. 'See you on the trail.'

Dismas and I set out for Horombo Camp (altitude: 12,140 feet). We wound our way through the dense, damp forest, still following the brick-coloured path, which had started to form mini-crevasses from the rains and had become trickier to navigate. There was little sound aside from the wind rustling the trees dripping with strands of Spanish beard, and before long the trees opened up and petered out, revealing rolling green expanses of the moorland. Odd, tall palm-like trees that sprang out of the vegetation like signposts. The air became cooler and dried the sweat on my face.

Halfway to Horombo Camp, Dismas stopped at a few metal picnic tables next to a wooden toilet hut. We unpacked our lunches, tearing into the fried chicken drumstick, packet of crisps, sandwich and mango juice in a little box.

Twenty minutes later, two or three large black crow-like birds suddenly appeared overhead, followed by Anka and Nina, and their guides. Nina and Anka looked flustered and tired. Both wore earphones, as if to block out the exertion of the hike. They had stripped down to their bikini tops. Their faces were red and they took small steps, as if their skin-tight trousers were too tight.

'Uff.' Anka slumped onto a big rock. She removed the little white earphones. 'I didn't think it would be so hard.'

Frowning, she checked her appearance in a little mirror and tried to neaten her ponytail.

'Me too,' said Nina as she set down her bag. 'I thought I was fit from the gym.'

I nodded. As I did, I dropped a piece of chicken on the ground by accident. One of the birds hopped over and gulped it down without hesitation.

'Did you train a lot for this climb?' I asked.

Anka shrugged. 'I walked around a lot. I didn't think it would be this tough.' She looked at one of the menacing black birds. It sidled closer to her, eyeing her drumstick. 'Shoo! Shoo!' Nina giggled.

Dismas walked over. 'Ready to go?' I nodded and stood up. Dismas turned towards the trail, and we resumed our walk to Horombo Camp.

'Aaaaah, get those birds away from me!' Anka shrieked as we headed up the path. The smell of the toilets lingered in the air long after we left the picnic area.

~

The men at Horombo Camp were giving me the Death Stare. I was obviously intruding. This hut was only for mountain guides, and irritating, high-maintenance tourists were not allowed.

'I'm – I'm just here to get the key to my hut?' I asked.

The gigantic man with his back to me turned around, glared, and slapped a large key into my hand. 'Here,' he barked. He consulted his checklist and shouted something in Swahili. One of

the younger men scrambled to his feet. 'I will show you the way.'
He jogged out of the hut.

Horombo Camp resembled a ski resort. The perfect path led
to large clearing, and as we walked across it to the registration
hut we passed two massive chalets which served as dining halls.
The snowy summit of Kilimanjaro peeked over the horizon, while
to the right Mawenzi Peak loomed over the camp, the savage,
fang-like edges of its crater lacerate the African sky.

At maximum capacity, more than 100 people can stay in
Horombo Camp. During high season, porters carry up tons of
food and water on their backs, at twice the speed of the tourists.
That wasn't the only thing porters carry. Last time I climbed
Kilimanjaro, two porters passed us carrying solar panels, beach
chairs and barbecue sets on their backs.

'What are those for?' I'd asked my guide.

'They've been hired by two ladies. Company directors. They
paid a lot of money so they could bring up a barbecue and sit
in beach chairs.'

That night in the dining hall, I asked Dismas what was going on.

'Is something wrong?' I asked. 'The guides in that hut seemed
really, um, pissed off.'

Dismas poured me some more tea. 'Sometimes, the staff have too
much work. And the clients ask for very strange things.'

'How do you mean?'

Dismas thought for a second, as if wondering whether to tell me.

'One time, my clients wanted us to get them marijuana and
vodka,' he said. 'They were in the tent at high camp, and the man
said, "Get me some weed as fast as possible".'

'Really? What did you say?'

'We told them, "No". So he began shouting at me, he threw
money at us,' – Dismas made a flick of the wrist – 'And said he
had more money and would pay us more to get the weed and the
vodka to him.'

'Wow. Did you do it?'

He laughed and shook his head.

~

We saw Mountain Gazelle a few days later, as Dismas and I passed the Mawenzi Ridge on the way to Kibo Hut. He looked like a different man, and by that I mean he looked destroyed. His face was sheet-white, his hair tufted and sweaty. He looked about twenty years older.

'Hey! How'd it go?' I called.

He stopped. 'It was… tougher than I expected.' He swallowed, as if keeping down the vomit. He looked past me again at the miles yet to cover, and the ravages of summit night encrusted his nose and mouth in snotty clumps. 'It is good to have it behind me,' he said. 'Good luck.'

~

Twenty-four hours later, I wiped the white vomit from my mouth and wished Dismas would stop shining his torch in my face.

'I'm okay.' My breath sounded slightly raspy. 'Just give me a minute.'

We were halfway to the summit. We had left Kibo hut hours ago and now I was sick as a dog. And I thought I was already acclimatised after Ojos del Salado.

Dismas was in an unusually chatty mood.

'You know, all the people who want to become guides on Kilimanjaro have to enter a contest,' he said as we left Kibo hut. We started to pick our way up the path, our head torches the only pinpricks of light in the vast inky night.

'Yeah? What do you have to do?'

'We have to climb Kilimanjaro carrying heavy packs. Actually, we need to be strong enough to carry our own packs, and the client's packs too, just in case.'

'Wow.' I was using short sentences to conserve my energy. 'How many people try out each year?'

He thought for a second. 'When I did it, it seemed like there were maybe over a hundred of us. We have to climb up as fast as we can, then down as fast as we can.'

'And you were picked. It sounds almost like army training.' Even in the dark, I could tell he was smiling.

'Yes.'

The more we climbed, the more painful my stomach cramps became. It got to the point where I had to stop, doubled over, every 10 minutes and breathe. Other people passed us, and at some point I saw a climber being led down. He'd given up.

Hours of hell later, we reached the rim of the crater. I'd almost given up a few times, but Dismas had talked me out of it. He'd also taken my pack.

'How do you feel?'

'Terrible. But I'm okay,' I dragged my sleeve across my mouth. 'How about you, Dismas? You okay?'

I saw the silhouette of his head turn, but couldn't see his expression in the dark.

'Of course I'm fine.' I could sense him shrugging. 'I only go *pole pole* for you.'

~

A few hours later, I fought back tears as Dismas took my picture at the summit of Kilimanjaro. For the second time, I was standing at the highest point in Africa. The warmth of the rising sun seeped into my bones after hours of intense cold.

I dug in the pocket of my down jacket and pulled out the folded Cancer Research UK banner. It opened out like a kite, almost taking me for a flight. Another climber stumbled over and we held it up for the camera. After a few camera clicks, I could feel the other climbers waiting to take their turn and stepped off the summit mound. Dismas put away the camera and offered me his hand.

'Iron lady.' Dismas held out his hand to help me down.

Other people stepped up to pose for photos. We had made it in under 7 hours, and despite all the pain and vomit it wasn't a bad time. Dismas smiled and swept his arm across the view. 'This is my office,' he said. 'I am here all the time.'

'And that makes seven, buddy!' came an American voice sailing on the high mountain winds. 'How do you feel?'

Suddenly they were everywhere: a dozen American climbers collapsing on rocks, giving high-fives, gasping for breath.

'I'm never doing this again. Why the hell did I do this?!' one woman shouted. She met my eyes and laughed.

'It took me five years to climb this again,' I shouted to her over the wind. She gaped at me. 'You've done this *twice?!*'

The first guy was not be outdone. He pointed at his friend and shouted, 'This guy's done it *three* times!'

I waited for Dismas to announce that he had climbed Kilimanjaro 200 times. But Dismas just listened to their boasts and smiled to himself.

~

Dismas and I met Anka on the way back down. She had only just reached Gilman's Point on the crater.

'Hey! Well done guys.' Anka grimaced as she hunched over her knees. 'My feet are killing me.'

'What happened to Nina?'

'Oh, she turned back halfway up the first slope.'

We spent a few minutes together, letting the sun sink in, drinking water, eating chocolates. My nausea was gone. I breathed in deeply and smiled in relief.

Dismas smiled. 'Strong lady,' he said to me. 'You say you are tired, but you are very strong. Besides the stomach, we are making very good time.'

After we skied back down the loose scree, there were still a few kilometres of slippery sand between us and Kibo hut. The sun was fierce. Dismas led me to cave hidden under a huge rock – the Hans Meyer Cave – where I had thrown up 8 hours earlier. While I had been puking, Dismas had found a coin in the cave and pocketed it with delight.

We sat down on rocks and drew out our water bottles. I heard something go *ping*, then turned to see Dismas scrabbling around muttering to himself.

'Where did it go?' he said.

'You lost your coin?' I glanced at the ground. No sign of it.

'Yes. In the same place where I found it.'

I took a swig of water. 'Well, maybe it just didn't want to go down with you.'

Dismas scrabbled a bit more, then stopped. He started chuckling to himself. The assistant guide looked at us. Dismas translated what I'd said into Swahili, and started giggling. The assistant guide started giggling as well. The more we giggled, the funnier it became. A few seconds later, the three of us were holding our stomachs, laughing in the cave like unchained lunatics.

~

Dismas and I set off for Marangu gate the next day.

Dismas seemed to know everybody. As I followed him down off the moorland and back into the rainforest, almost every guide and porter nodded to him, almost deferentially.

'*Shikamoo*,' one of the porters said to him, hand on chest. It was the third time that morning.

'*Marahaba*,' Dismas replied with a slight bow.

It was our last day. We were heading back down to Marangu gate and Dismas was in a good mood. I was too, except that my throat was on fire. Every so often I croaked for more mango juice, which he dug out from his backpack.

We marched down a few more steps and Marangu gate came into view.

'So what's *shikamoo*? Was that Swahili?'

Dismas stopped walking. 'It is Arabic,' he said over his shoulder. He looked up at the sky, thinking.

'It means, "Can I kiss your boots." Or in Swahili, it means, "I am below your feet".'

'I see. Wait, what?'

'It is something you say to older people, who have experience,' he explained. 'And when I say "Marahaba", it means, "I accept".'

'You accept their kissing your boots?' I said. 'So it's a gesture of respect?'

He nodded. 'Yes.'

I burst into a firework display of coughs. Dismas fished around in his backpack and brought out a box of mango juice and handed it to me.

'Thanks. So, do you mind if I ask how old you are, Dismas?'
His face collapsed into a smile. 'I'm forty-nine,' he said. 'I know, I look young.'

'And you, you are not too big or too small,' he continued. 'You are strong. When I first saw you I said to myself, that person, she will climb well.'

It was such an unexpected compliment that I couldn't stop smiling for the rest of the hike.

~

I arrived home a few days later. The stone steps were slick with English drizzle, and before I could take out my keys Douglas flung open the front door. His grinned and held out his arms for a congratulatory hug.

'Very well done! Urgh!' He recoiled as I erupted into a spluttering cough in his arms.

'Thanks. Sorry,' I pulled away to avoid spluttering on him. Everything went fuzzy – was it the rain? Or the tears in my eyes from coughing? – And suddenly there wasn't enough air.

Douglas took a step back and looked at me.

'You're mountained out, aren't you,' he said.

The next day, I went to see the doctor.

'Let's measure your lung function,' he said. The doctor was one of those terribly polite types, which meant I mistrusted him immediately. He handed me a peak flow meter. It's a device shaped like a hairdryer, only instead of air coming out of the barrel, you stick it in your mouth and exhale as forcefully as possible. The effort threw me into a coughing fit.

He made me do it twice, then checked the readings in silence. I tried to sit still, but it felt like my hands had taken on a life of their own and wringing each other over and over again in my lap. The sounds of babies wailing and shrieking echoed down the corridor. The doctor prodded his glasses further up his nose and turned to me.

'Your lung capacity has dropped to 74 per cent,' he said.

I'd always known that sooner or later, my lungs would try to kill me again.

9

MOUNTAIN SORCERY

The white-tiled consultation room smelled like a pharmacy. It had no windows or exits, like all dead ends.

'How did this happen?' I asked.

Even before the doctor answered, I knew it didn't matter. Asthma does what it wants. I could medicate. I could live in a hospital, sealed off from dust and smoke and animal dander and pollution. I could inhale steroid-laced vapour. None of it mattered. Asthma would still reach down my throat and close its fist around my lungs if it wanted to.

The doctor shrugged. 'The short answer is, nobody knows for sure. It could be seasonal change, or something new in your environment triggering the symptoms.' He didn't look at me.

'But I *need* to get better. I'm leaving soon for a mountain climb.' A tickle crawled up my throat.

'Where are you going?' He peered at my patient file on the computer screen. 'Will you be at high altitude?'

'Iran. Yes.' The harder I tried to suppress the cough it the more it fought me, like a gremlin trying to tear its way out.

'And what is your trip for?'

'It's to raise money for cancer research. My father'– the cough exploded out of my mouth. I bent over double, shuddering as I hacked again and again. My eyes burned.

'Okay. Let me prescribe you a daily inhaler. That should help.' The doctor scrawled familiar drug names on an officious little notepad. His hand was crab-like and dusted with age spots.

Nightmare. Taking daily medication meant you were a sick person. All I wanted was to be normal.

The doctor finally looked at me. His face revealed nothing. Then he swivelled away and reached down for his briefcase.

'And let me find you a tenner. As a donation.'

~

I took the prescription and went to the pharmacy, where I was given two boxes of daily medication. The brands had changed since I was a child, but the ingredients were the same. I was back to sucking on vapour twice a day just to breathe properly.

'Please take care,' Douglas said when I returned from the pharmacy. 'If you feel you're in trouble, just get off the mountain and come home.'

I nodded. A few days later, I was sitting at a coffee stand in the very modern arrivals hall of Imam Khomeini International Airport in Tehran. The Iranian sky hung like dark velvet behind the windows. Men in suits and women in silk head scarves hauled their bags off the carousel. I, on the other hand, was a mess. I hadn't been able to find a silk headscarf to cover my hair. The best I could do was fish out a dowdy gingham scarf and bandage my head like E.T. in the flying bike scene. I even had deep, dark circles under my eyes like E.T. Families walked by, laughing, chatting, dragging suitcases. They shot me curious glances.

'So, are you climbing much these days?' I asked Ardeshir Soltani, the director of Damavand Info, who was assisting me with the

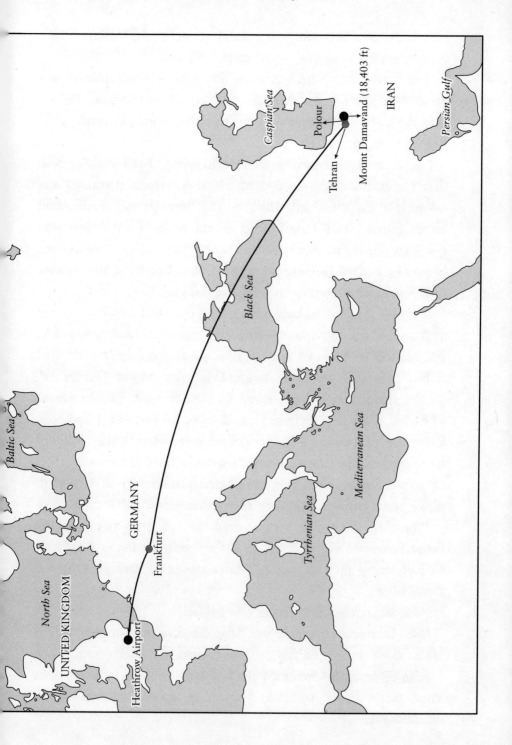

expedition. The beginnings of a cough scratched my throat and my ears itched from my badly-tied scarf.

'Every week. If I don't go climbing once a week, I don't feel good. It is like a need,' Ardeshir handed me an espresso. Behind him, the night sky beyond the floor-to-ceiling windows slowly gave way to twilight.

I nodded. I was having trouble focusing. Even the espresso didn't help. I felt light-headed. Maybe it was the antibiotics I was taking for my chest infection, or the new asthma medication, or the painkillers I'd swallowed on the plane. I didn't feel that I was recovering so much as temporarily patched up. A wheezing, beaten-up tractor running on nothing. Was I really at the summit of Kilimanjaro with Dismas only five days ago?

Ardeshir was still talking. I leaned in, tried to focus.

'You will go up Mount Damavand tomorrow with our guide, Ali. He will be here in a minute, he is parking the car.'

Just two more volcanoes to go. This week, Mount Damavand, Asia's highest volcano at 18,406 feet. Next week, Mount Elbrus in Russia. That was it. Then I could go home and rest. I had been living out of a suitcase for so long that mundane things like hot baths and indoor heating seemed exotic, almost decadent.

'So you must climb Damavand pretty often, then?' I tried to make polite conversation despite my wooziness.

'Yes.' Ardeshir set his little espresso cup back on its saucer. His brow furrowed slightly. 'But it is very strange. Every time I go to high camp on Damavand, I have the same dreams. Only on Damavand.'

'You mean, the same dream every time?'

'No. Different dreams every time. But for that single night, it is the same dream, on repeat. I go to bed, I have a dream. Then I wake up from the dream. When I go back to sleep, it is the exact same dream again. And then, I wake up again. This goes on the whole night.'

I nodded. Hypoxia. Mountain sorcery, caused by lack of oxygen.

'That is why I now go only once a month to high camp. The mountain does something to my head.'

I nodded again, but all I could think was: Two more weeks and I was done. The Seven Volcanoes Project, the rhythm of my life, was nearly over. I was growing more exhausted by the day.

~

The moon was still glowing as we roared through the empty streets of Tehran. My guide Ali gunned the engine as our little hatchback shot past slumbering low buildings tinged blue from the twilight.

'I have chosen the best guide for you,' Ardeshir had said at the airport. 'I know you are doing an important project with the volcanoes. Ali has climbed Damavand over a hundred times.' Clearly, Ali was also a man who processed reality a hundred times faster than anyone else.

'Yah!!' An oncoming car sliced past us. Ali laughed and shook his head.

'He cannot drive!' he shouted merrily, making a rude hand gesture for good measure before yanking us back to the right side of the road. Ali spoke little English, but what more do you need to know about someone who shrieks with laughter at imminent death?

Mount Damavand lies about an hour's drive north-east of Tehran. The volcano was born amid the thrust and fold of the Alborz range, where the Eurasian and the Arabian tectonic plates collide. Before researching the Seven Volcanoes, I'd never heard of mountain climbing in Iran. I had no idea what to expect, but I did know that Mount Damavand was an active volcano that emitted sulphur. And it goes without saying that sulphur is about as good for asthma as fire is for a house. But right now that all seemed moot anyway. There was a good chance we would wind up a fiery ball of twisted metal and never get to the mountain.

Dawn broke as we left Tehran and the road began to climb, turning into a dual carriageway that clung to the sides of the Haraz Valley. We passed through Pardis, Rudehen, Abali – small towns not far from Tehran but which already felt like mountain outposts, spread out and open to the sky.

Camp One on Mount Damavand is not actually on Mount Damavand. It is in the small village of Polour, which sits at an altitude of 9,974 feet and consists of a handful of two-storey white houses with yellow and orange roofs arranged prettily around a river. We pulled up at a gigantic echoing building run by the Iran Mountain Climbing Federation. All the windows had bars on them. It looked a little like a psychiatric institution. Or a convent. Or perhaps that perfect marriage of the two: a girls' boarding house. On the horizon, Mount Damavand pierced the deep blue sky like a frosted arrowhead.

Ali slammed the car to a stop outside the building and cut the engine. There was no one around. The air smelled of snow. Ali looked satisfied, unfolded his tall, wiry frame out of the car, grabbed my rucksack out of the back and threw open the glass-paned front door of the asylum.

'Come.' He put on a pair of sunglasses with his free hand. The metal door clanged shut behind us.

Ali led me down one a long white corridor. We passed a few climbers, all men, single and in pairs. They chatted quietly among themselves. They looked sinewy and more experienced than anyone I saw on Kilimanjaro last week.

'Ali, have you really climbed Damavand over a hundred times?'

He glanced at me and laughed. 'Maybe two hundred, soon.' He opened a door at the end of the corridor and ushered me into a dormitory.

I had the dormitory all to myself. It was austere: three bunk beds, each with a neatly folded duvet and two pillows on top. The narrow windows were so high up that you had to climb on to the upper bunks to see through the bars. Pale sunbeams filtered through the bars in the windows. I walked to the bottom bunk and threw my backpack on it. The room was so silent, it felt like it had been expecting us.

'Tea? *Chai?*' Ali asked. I nodded and followed him back down to the end of the corridor, where he ducked under a fabric partition and past the prayer room to the high-ceilinged living room dominated by a mural of Mount Damavand. The painting was covered in myriad routes, some for climbers, some for cross-country cyclists. I sat down on one of the leather chairs, while Ali brought in a tray of delicate tea glasses, a teapot and lumps of sugar and set it down on a low table.

An hour later, Ardeshir arrived as I gulped down my fourth glass of sugary tea.

'Ah, welcome Sophie, to Polour Camp.' He walked in with a confident smile, as if I was a guest in his mansion. 'You have had some tea, yes?'

'Yes, thanks.' I gestured at the mural. 'Damavand really is beautiful.'

Ardeshir poured himself some tea.

'You know, when I first tried to climb Damavand, everybody told me a lot of myths,' he said, adding a lump of sugar. He settled into the chair facing me.

'How do you mean?'

'They had so many strange beliefs. Like, "Damavand can only be climbed at night, never during the day," or "Damavand can only be climbed when there is a full moon",' he said, listing each one on his hand.

'Really? So how did you first start climbing?'

'The first time I tried to climb Damavand, I had almost no experience. I joined a group, and because it was so crowded in the shelter I slept right by the door. Now this was a mistake, because everyone was going to the toilet, and of course they woke me up on the way out.'

My throat was starting to itch again. I took another sip of tea.

'When we did start climbing it was very late at night, and very dark. The people in front, even my guide, walked faster and left me behind. After a while, I lost them completely and was all alone on the mountain,' he smiled.

'I was very tired, and I was lost. So I said to myself, "I will sit by this rock and I will take a rest." I woke up in a very strange place,' he said. 'This time, I knew which way to go. So I climbed, and soon I was at the summit.'

Ardeshir spoke of Damavand with the same awe as other people spoke of deities. His enthusiasm seemed to sparkle around him and for a second his reverence for the mountain was palpable. He sat back, staring up at the huge painting of Mount Damavand. It might have been the lack of sleep, or my deteriorating health, but at that moment I felt as if I had entered a world in which mountains were wreathed in spirits and legends. They weren't just targets to tick off a list. This journey had taken me so far from my beginnings. Antarctica felt like another life, with its logistics and schedules and the petty rivalries with Vladimir. Even my obsession with getting a world record had faded. My memories of Dad still hovered at the edge of my mind but they felt more distant, more ghostly. It was disconcerting.

'I need to have a nap. I didn't get much sleep on the flight.' I hurried towards the door.

Ardeshir nodded amiably. 'Of course.'

As soon as I left the tea room I broke into a jog. My steps thundered in the silence of the building and echoed around me as I ran down the long corridor towards my room. My diaphragm spasmed, and I held my breath hard to hold back the paroxysms I knew were coming.

I had only just managed to unlock the door to my dormitory when the coughing took over. I tore off my headscarf and sat down on the lower bunk, doubling over as I surrendered to the spasms. Tears flooded my eyes. I couldn't breathe.

I grabbed one of my sacks and tipped it upside down. Energy bars, anti-blister food plasters, a small tube of sunscreen and packets of instant coffee tumbled out. I picked out a small dark vial of antibiotics, unscrewed the cap and swallowed one of the little white tablets.

Slowly, painfully, the coughing subsided to erratic little bursts and then stopped altogether. I sat back on the bunk bed, exhaling slowly. The wan light fell through the barred windows on my upturned face, but I felt no warmth. I felt like a blunt pencil, being steadily worn down to a nub.

~

The next morning, Ali and I piled into the front of a small blue jeep with a strip of fake fur lining the dashboard. It was so cramped that my forehead was only a foot from the cracked windshield. Our driver heaved himself in, squishing Ali in the middle seat. The only way the three of us could fit was if Ali more or less spooned the driver. The driver said something in Farsi. Ali laughed and nearly put his head through the windshield as we juddered out of Polour Camp and onto the main road.

The sharp, fresh air stroked my face through my open window. I was feeling much better today after a long sleep and I felt almost relieved. I started to enjoy the sounds of Ali bantering in Farsi and wound my window all the way down to enjoy the breeze. Mount Damavand reared up before us like a perfect frosted cone, and the mares' tails of yesterday were now gone, leaving a flawless deep blue sky. We turned off and started to climb a winding tarmac road.

'You see the flowers?' Ali leaned over to point out my window, and for a second I thought his weight would topple the truck over.

I looked.

'Poppies!' I said. Remembrance flowers. 'Yes. Very famous in Iran. Every year, the tourists come to see when the flowers are all here.' Ali beamed. 'When flowers all here, it is very beautiful.'

I smiled and squinted at the snow-covered slopes. The slopes of Mount Damavand looked deserted. It was still only April; the high season was not until June. We might be the only climbers on the south route today.

The higher we drove, the chillier the air became. The tarmac road morphed into a rocky mountain track and I clung to the door handle, partly to keep from sliding into Ali and partly because it looked like the door might fly off. The track then became a bog, which seized our truck and stopped us from driving any further. We hopped out. The driver laughed and pulled my rucksack out of the back of the truck.

'We're starting from here?' I said. The driver handed me my bag with a smile, as if he were handing me a bouquet of roses.

Ali laughed. 'Yes. Truck cannot go up anymore.'

I loved it. This was nothing like Kilimanjaro. There was no one around and even the path had vanished. Everything felt more personal, less commercial. Just us and the volcano.

The driver climbed back behind the wheel and revved the engine. Ali walked over, leaned his gangly frame against the passenger side door, grabbed the top of the truck and shook. Every time he revved the engine, Ali gave the truck a shove, until it broke free of the mud and spring slush. Then the truck turned around and puttered out of sight, the driver waving gaily through the open window.

The air smelled of expectation and the blue sky beckoned. Ali and I began plodding up the mountain. I wondered whether, once we arrived at the summit, I would be able to look over the top and see the Caspian Sea. Besides the light crunch of our feet on the ground it was utterly quiet. It felt utterly different from the hustle and traffic of Kilimanjaro. Ahead, Mount Damavand sprawled like a glorious gigantic dessert, deep chocolate laced with white snow icing, and behind it the deep blue sky.

The air was so clear that it seemed to make my vision sharper. For the first time in a long while, I didn't make lists of things to do in my head. I didn't think of what was to come. I was finally clear and present. Nothing else mattered, except what was happening right now.

We reached Goosfand Sara mosque, which sits at an altitude of 9,700 feet. Its courtyard was partially embedded into the side of the mountain, with a dark green roof and gold minarets.

'In summer, many people here.' Ali walked to the door of the mosque. 'No one.'

'It's very peaceful,' I said.

We started up the path behind the mosque and embarked on the stony switchback. My rucksack seemed to weigh more than usual. The mule-track was littered with rocks and in tiny rivulets in places and gradually, we left the good weather behind and climbed towards the beckoning tendrils of the low-drifting cloud.

Ali plodded in front of me. Then he stopped, and turned to face the valley. I did the same, and what I saw took my breath away.

'Look. I climb that in one day.' Ali pointed across the valley.

'Wow. You climbed that?'

It was the most beautiful sight I had ever seen. The snow-covered ridge on the other side of the valley resembled a glittering, silver-white bridge in the sky. I pictured Ali, on the magical day where he walked the narrow ridge where the pristine path met the infinite sky, and tears came to my eyes.

'Ghareh Dagh ridge, fifty kilometres long. I walked all the way. It is very dangerous, easy to fall. But to me, it was... peaceful,' Ali said.

'Beautiful,' I breathed.

Ali smiled. 'Yes,' he nodded. 'Perfect day.' Then his smile faltered. He raised his arm again, and pointed to the right side of the range.

'My friend. He fall there.' Ali cleared his throat. 'Nobody find him.'

I felt the cold clutch of dread in my stomach as I turned to look at him. Ali's face was now expressionless. I stared at the place Ali pointed to where his friend had perished, somewhere in the beautiful folds of snow and rock.

'Oh, no. I'm so sorry.'

He shrugged. His eyes traced the jagged top of the ridge, remembering his departed friend.

~

A few hours later, Camp Three came into sight. The concrete building couldn't have been more than 300 feet away, but it may as well have been on the moon. Camp Three, otherwise known as Bargah Sevom Camp, is at nearly 13,800 feet. I'd been well above this altitude in the past few weeks, but the altitude was still killing me.

'Dammit,' I muttered. My head was pounding from the altitude, my legs were killing me and my backpack felt a lot heavier than usual. The sun was gone now. We were so close, but I was barely able to cross the final stretch of deep snow.

My hands shook as I reached down to tighten my belt. My clothes felt looser these days. I needed to catch my breath for the hundredth time that day. Ali was already at the massive stone fortress. He leaned patiently against the side of the building, chatting to another guide.

Half-an-hour later, I finally shuffled up to the building. Ali took my backpack.

'Very good,' Ali said. 'Come, now you rest.'

I heaved myself onto the bottom rung of the metal staircase, which led to the front door. Why was it taking me so long just to climb a ladder? Maybe the new medication wasn't working. Our breath formed icy clouds as we clattered through the entrance of the slate-grey building into the dark hallway. Behind the heavy metal doors leading off the entrance, people rummaged in food bags and prepared meals.

The main hall contained nothing besides a few plastic chairs and tables. The stone walls were covered in black and white photos of climbers. Several of them were female climbers, posing on snowy mountain sides, their headscarves draped over their climbing jackets.

I walked closer to the photos. 'Ali, who are these climbers? Did they win awards for climbing? Break records?' There were inscriptions in Farsi beneath each photo. Ali walked over.

'Ah. No...' he tried to find the words in English. 'They are... dead. On mountain. The photos are for them.' He walked down the corridor to one of the store rooms.

I turned back to the photos. The chilly air grew colder against my face. All these people, dead.

I took a step back. The faces seemed to watch me. It was a wall of photos to honour great climbers who had perished on Damavand. I understood very well, and at the same time I didn't understand at all.

Why do we honour the dead? Why do we light candles in their memory, bow our heads to their photos, carve their names into stone? Memory was what made us human, yet its meaning continued to elude me. I was climbing volcanoes in Dad's memory. But as I stood in that chilly stone building on a mountain in Iran, the impulse had never seemed stranger. Our desire to bear witness to the life of someone who no longer exists is so innate that I had never questioned it.

I thought of Dad's tombstone in Somerset. That stone was perhaps the most symbolic gesture of all, because it stands over an empty grave. My grandmother had asked for the stone, as a gesture of remembrance for the son who had left England so long ago. That tombstone bears my father's name, but he is not buried there. His ashes are in a shiny black urn in Mom's house.

But Dad is no more in that urn, than he is buried in a churchyard in Somerset.

He exists now only in memories. And the urge to restore those memories had driven me to climb mountain after mountain, perhaps because I wanted to prove that death has no dominion over love.

~

Ali appeared next to me. 'You want food?'

He led me into one of the storage rooms. Hazy white rays pierced the tall glass windows and bathed me in pale light.

'Hi!' someone chirped. I squinted to see a tall, lanky man and a diminutive woman huddled around a table spooning what looked like gruel out of plastic bowls. They were bundled up in thick winter clothing and looked like a pair of balled-up socks.

'Hello,' I said. 'How was your climb up?'

'Oh, not bad.' He sounded Canadian. They both looked perky, as if they'd just come in from a picnic.

'How long did it take you?' I blew on my hands, tried to sound casual. Truth was, I felt completely drained.

'Oh, two-and-a-half, maybe three hours,' he said.

I'd taken twice as long. I winced on the inside and just nodded, praying he wouldn't ask me the same question.

'How about you?' he asked.

'Oh. Um,' I fumbled with my jacket. 'Five hours.' Their eyes widened. 'But I've just got over a cough,' I added with a reassurance I didn't feel.

'I'm just going to head upstairs to rest,' I said. They nodded and went back to spooning their gruel.

My own austere little chamber had high stone walls. The floors were cold and my breath formed clouds in the air. It reminded me of a monastery, high on a mountain and miles from civilisation. I collapsed onto the bottom bunk and fell dead asleep.

~

Ali pounded on my door at 5 a.m.. I woke from another night of oblivion and as if on autopilot, clambered out of the cocoon of sleeping bag, insulating bag, and blanket and pulled on my outer climbing layers. I didn't dream anymore. I didn't have the energy. The room was well below freezing.

I joined Ali in the next-door room. He had prepared a breakfast of coffee, peanut butter and flatbread.

'We leave after six,' Ali said. Beyond the window, lightning flashed across the sky.

'Hey Ali, there was lightning just now. Is it still wise to go?' I asked.

'No, it's okay,' Ali said with confidence. 'The lightning will happen only once.'

'Only once?'

'No problem,' he said. 'No black clouds, only white.'

Ali was right. The lightning happened only once. At 7 a.m., we left camp and trudged upwards through the snow and rock. The sky grew light. I fought against the wind that whipped bitchy little splinters of ice through the crack between my goggles and face mask. The mist blocked out the upper slopes of Mount Damavand.

As we passed 15,000, 16,000, and 17,000 feet and the oxygen grew thinner, I fell slowly under the mountain's spell. The wind became stronger, and the cloud started to thin. Gossamer spindrift whirled around us and glinted in the sun. Just as we were negotiating some big rocks, the sun broke through and my high-altitude euphoria began.

Intermittent white-gold sunbeams lit up the snow and turquoise skies. The clouds formed images that had the haunting familiarity of half-remembered dreams. Mountain sorcery had set in.

Blue and gold. The colour of Dad's eyes before he died. Suddenly, I was back in his hospital room. His emaciated hand reaching out from under the bed sheet to hold mine as I told him I was flying back to Shanghai. I could hear his voice, I could smell the hospital linoleum.

Dad, Dad, Dad... You're gone but I'm still here. Mom and I are still here. Where are you?

The euphoria came and went for the next few hours. Sometimes I was lost in memories, other times I thought of nothing but the crunch of rock under my boots.

Ali and I reached the summit plateau 5 hours after leaving camp. I started to feel nervous. My lungs had felt fine so far, but now we were getting closer to the sulphur. We had climbed above the clouds and the crater appeared, like a mini-Stonehenge of dark brown rocks against the unblemished sky. A thick column of smoke, the colour of stale urine, billowed out of the crater. The plume changed direction abruptly with the wind. We could smell the rotten-egg sulphur smell from 300 feet below. The sulphur had stained the rocks that dotted the slopes the colour of horse manure.

Ali and I plodded towards the summit. The sulphur smell grew stronger. We eyed the teetering plume, in case the wind blew it straight down onto us. My throat began to clench. Somehow, through a combination of extreme watchfulness and cunning footwork, we reached the summit of Damavand without getting gassed.

'Yes!' I shouted as we stepped into the crater. 'Volcano number six!' Ali grinned and shook my hand. The crater of Mount Damavand is not particularly big, perhaps 1,000 feet across. It was surrounded by rocks cloaked in sulphur. The inside wall bore plaques in memory of past climbers. I dug in the pocket of my down jacket for the Cancer Research UK banner. I held it up while Ali took a photo, pirouetting and flapping to get away from the sulphurous tendrils invading our stone fortress.

'We go soon,' Ali said. 'The weather is not good down the mountain.' I folded away the banner and picked up my walking poles. We left the summit, and that's when the sulphur attacked us. It happened before I knew it. My immediate reaction was to hold my breath to protect my lungs.

'STOP! Do like this!' Ali shouted. He bent over and covered his face with his mittens. We stayed frozen in position. My throat felt itchy; it wanted me to cough. The cloud didn't dissipate. If anything, it was getting thicker. Where did all this sulphur come from? I was terrified of inhaling, but I soon wouldn't have the choice. I couldn't hold my breath any longer. I gasped involuntarily and at the same time the sulphur forced its way into my tortured lungs. I started to choke. My chest convulsed.

'Go! GO!!' Ali screamed. He made a break for it, and I forced myself to run after him. Both of us were swearing; me in English, Ali in Farsi.

Our mad dash lasted a good few minutes. Gradually, the air cleared and we could see down the mountain again. For the next hour, I smelled sulphur on my breath every time I exhaled into my face mask. It smelled like rotten eggs and vomit.

~

We climbed back down into the mist. The descent took about 3 hours, but most of the time we could see barely 3 feet ahead. We walked in a thick white soup. All I could think about were luxury toiletries. I listed them as reasons to go on as I battled the fog. 'Bath salts,' I muttered. 'Lavender soap. Chamomile face mask.' I told myself I would experience them again. This gave me hope.

Ali trotted ahead of me, crossing rock and snow, turning and urging me to watch where I put my feet. I tried my best, but I was starving, and I had no energy, and I was in pain. All my joints – knees, spine, neck – jangled with every step down. It was as if the sulphur had poisoned my system and pooled in my legs. My chest felt tight.

I stopped to rest after every thirty steps. It was the only way I knew to lessen the pain in my legs. Ali drew farther and farther away, until he became a dark speck far down the slope. He was stumbling too. I knitted my brows and concentrated on stepping in his tracks.

When we finally reached Camp Three, Ali slowed down, threw me a concerned glance and stepped aside, so I could be the first to return in a display of triumph.

'No, Ali, you go ahead. I'm the slow one.' My voice was barely audible.

'Good summit,' Ali said. 'Even with bad weather, we come down not too slow.'

A few feet short of camp, I lurched to the side of the snowy track and retched. Nothing came out except for a thin white sinew of phlegm. In the background, I could hear Ali gagging. I scooped up some snow and tried to clean the bitterness from my mouth.

Almost done. You're almost done. Just one more mountain to go.

~

The next afternoon, I returned to the UK. I had a few days of rest before flying to Russia for the last expedition. On my first evening back, I sat down at my laptop at the kitchen counter, showered and smelling of lavender soap.

I randomly decided to check out the 7 Summits Club website. Had anyone else started climbing the Seven Volcanic Summits? What I read make me taste the sulphur all over again. There was a new entry on the 7 Summits Club website that filled my stomach with cement.

'*...it appears quite clear that the highest volcano in Asia is in China, in the mountains of Kun-Lun. Ka-er-daxi is 5,808 metres high.*'

What? I'd never even heard of Ka-er-daxi. I'd always read that Mount Damavand was the highest volcano in Asia. My hands jittered as I googled the Chinese volcano. Didn't everyone already know the highest volcano on each continent? Wasn't this already settled?

I couldn't find much information on the mysterious Ka-er-daxi. The volcano was located in the 3,000-kilometre Kunlun mountain range, at the northern edge of the Tibetan plateau. It was a mere 430 feet taller than Mount Damavand. According to the 7 Summits Club, Ka-er-daxi was a recent discovery, which explained why I had never come across it.

The good news was, nobody had climbed Ka-er-daxi yet. Maybe I still had a shot.

The bad news? I'd just climbed the wrong frigging volcano.

10

GOING TO THE SHOP

Some places are perpetually in a bad mood, and Cheget village was in the worst funk of all. The place was quiet as a graveyard and twice as dead. It looked nearly deserted and everything – the buildings, the trees, even the few people – seemed to come only in shades of lead. Cheget village lies at the base of Mount Elbrus, the final volcano on my long journey. While Elbrus is technically Europe's highest volcano at 18,510 feet, it is barely on the European continent. Mount Elbrus is nestled in the Caucasus mountain range, which runs from the Black Sea to the Caspian Sea and snakes between Russia, Georgia and Azerbaijan.

A few days earlier, I traced my finger along the Caucasus range on the map as I sat at the kitchen counter at home. After I realised that I'd climbed Damavand by mistake, all I could do was giggle like a lunatic at the ridiculousness of it all. Here I was trying to set a new world record, and I couldn't even climb the right mountains!

The volcanoes project was a complete mess. I'd tried and failed (twice) to climb Ojos del Salado in Chile. I'd climbed the wrong volcano in Asia. I was physically drained and my lungs felt like wheezy tortured little bagpipes. Perhaps climbing Damavand, Kilimanjaro and Elbrus in the same month had been a little ambitious.

And yet, every time I thought about packing it in, something stopped me. I'd already come so far. Maybe I couldn't salvage the Seven Volcanoes Project, but I could at least finish it. That's what Dad would have told me to do. That thought had pushed me onto the flight to Moscow, where I took a connecting flight to Mineralnye Vody, a small town deep in the south of Russia. From there, it was a 3-hour drive to Cheget village.

The arrivals hall of Mineralnye Vody airport was grim, the people grimmer. Everyone was dressed in dark, scruffy clothes. We shuffled into the haphazardly whitewashed baggage reclaim hall, and as I waited for my red duffel the other passengers sneaked not-so-friendly glances at me. Little children wandered about, shrieking and making nuisances of themselves. Most of the men had either mullet-like hairstyles, or shaved heads. The women seemed to have all dyed their hair the same shade of custard.

I walked out of the airport and looked at the bleak sky. A wiry man just over 5 feet tall rushed up.

'Welcome,' he said in English. 'I am Ivan. Your guide.' He bowed slightly and shook my hand.

'*Dobre ultra*,' I said. That was all I knew in Russian.

Ivan had the kind of face that looked more natural when it was smiling. His shaggy brown hair spilled over his forehead, which made him look ridiculously young, especially as he was much shorter than me.

'Nice to meet you,' I said. Ivan seized my duffel bag, turned and marched off. I followed.

It hadn't been easy to find a guide to take me up Elbrus in April. The climbing season hadn't even started yet, and conditions on the mountain were icy.

'If you are a novice I do not recommend to come too early,' one agency wrote. 'Elbrus is icy before mid-May. Climb may really require mountaineering skills that time – crampons, rope belay and so on.'

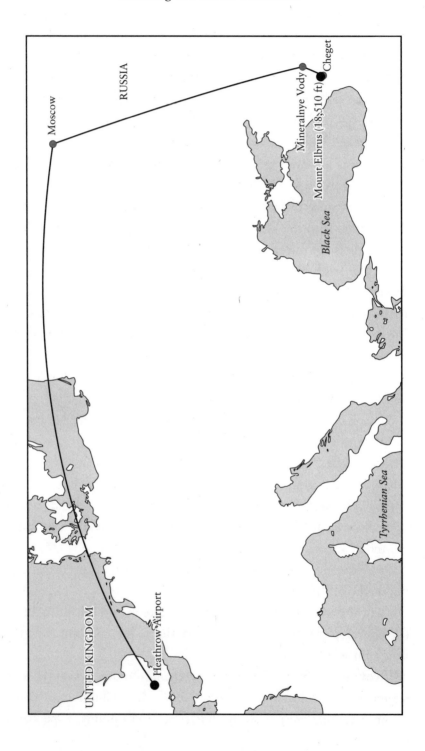

I'd ignored the advice. I found a different climbing agency that was willing to take me on a special pre-season climb, which is how I met Ivan.

Ivan led me to a battered black Volga, a Soviet-designed, squat box of a car with dark windows. Its trunk didn't look deep enough to fit a spare tire, never mind my duffel bag. A driver with a paunch and a cigarette in his mouth clambered out of the car, shook my hand and helped Ivan jam my duffel in the trunk. The three of us folded ourselves into the low-slung vehicle.

We left Mineralnye Vody and drove into the moody green Baksan valley under an overcast sky. Ivan and the driver sat in the front and chatted in staccato Russian. We drove through several army checkpoints to get to Cheget. A few years earlier, there were several bombings by Islamist separatists in the region. Nothing seemed to have changed since I was last here. The security risk felt as acute now as it had in 2010.

And yet, nothing, not even the ambient tension, could keep me awake. I tried to watch the scenery but couldn't keep my eyes open. For the next 3 hours, I slept. I didn't rest so much as float in unconsciousness. My exhaustion was so complete that no amount of sleep could assuage it. Since Kilimanjaro, I'd napped whenever I could, but I'd still woken up tired.

I only woke when our car reached the bumpy roads of Cheget village. The town square looked familiar in all its sullenness, but at the same time the alienness of my surroundings unmoored me. I couldn't understand a word of the conversation between the strange men in the front of the car. I couldn't read the hostile Cyrillic signs. There was a layer of smeared plastic between me and the world. I'd felt alone a lot these past weeks. I'd also been constantly surrounded by strangers, which amounts to much the same thing.

~

Just outside the centre of Cheget village was a monstrous concrete skeleton that looked as if it once intended to become a luxury apartment complex, but had somehow missed its destiny. Now, in its dilapidated state, it was hard to tell whether it was being built or about to be torn down.

A giant tarp hung uselessly over it, and as I walked past I felt its rows of hollow sockets bearing down on me. The exposed spines of the walls ran vertically through the structure and ended in blunt concrete pillars pointing baldly at the sky, like stakes awaiting their victims. 'Rostelecom,' the tarp read. 'More possibilities,' it added underneath. Between these two proclamations was an untidy gash in the fabric, through which unfinished concrete balconies jutted, like vertebrae through flesh.

I had to walk under this spectre to get to our hotel. Hotel Teberda was a newly built, echoing stone building buried in the forest outside the village. Like most hotels in Cheget village, it managed to look imposing but unfinished, as if it had been built in a hurry.

'Here is hotel. We eat dinner at 7 p.m.' Ivan heaved my duffel bag onto his back. He smiled – that big, empty smile again – and led the way into the hotel. The tiled lobby reverberated with the blare of cartoons. A young boy sat on the floor and played with a truck. He frowned when he saw me and shouted something. A woman, who had been sitting on the sofa staring at the television, heaved herself upright and slouched over to the front desk. She looked me up and down without smiling.

~

That evening, I joined Ivan in the dining room in the basement. I was post-nap: 4 hours of blissful unconsciousness when I had dreamed that I was asleep in my own bed. At the far end of the otherwise empty room, a wall-mounted television broadcast the

State-run news channel *Rossiya-1*. Russia had just annexed Crimea. Ivan, who was from the Ukraine, remained silent as he watched footage of Ukrainian rebel groups fighting Russian troops.

'How long have you been a mountain guide, Ivan?' I pulled out a chair opposite him at the small table.

'Actually, I was engineer.' He tore apart a bread roll. 'But, I love mountains. My wife also. Many years ago, we enter national mountain climbing competition. We choose toughest route, climb together, sleep in bivouac on side of mountain rock. Three days.'

'Wait – Ivan, you and your wife are national climbing champions?'

'No, no, we only win silver medal.' He said it as if he'd won second place at the county fair. 'After competition, somebody from climbing agency come to us and say, "You want job with us?" Now we both work with same agency.' He shovelled in a mouthful of borscht.

I swallowed. I was about to go climbing with a national mountaineering champion. 'So, I guess climbing Mount Elbrus must be very easy for you,' I said.

Ivan paused.

'For me, climbing Elbrus is like going to the shop.'

~

The next morning, I felt rested for the first time in weeks. Maybe the new asthma drugs were finally kicking in. Weak sunlight filtered through the conifers outside my window and landed on my threadbare bedsheets. I sat up and cracked open the window to let out some of the stale hotel room air. Yes, today would be a good day. I changed into my climbing gear, grabbed my keys and ran down to meet Ivan.

Ivan wanted to climb to 15,000 feet to help our bodies adjust to the altitude, then head back to the valley and spend a second night in Cheget village. Tomorrow, we would move to high camp. The following night was summit night. A short and sharp expedition.

An hour later, Ivan and I sat in a gondola that looked like a cheap tin box. The only other people riding with us were locals, with dark hair and intense expressions. They greeted each other – *Salam Alaykum* – but ignored Ivan and I. Two of the young women in headscarves were taking crates of beer and food up to the café at Mir station. The only other man wore jeans and a jacket much too flimsy for the cold. As we trundled up, he fiddled with latch of the cable car doors and nudged them open an inch or two. He peered through the crack, as if he were curious whether he would survive if he fell into the valley far below.

Our gondola trundled into the maw of Old Krugozor station, 9,700 feet up Mount Elbrus. Ivan walked over to his huge backpack, which sat upright in the corner of the gondola like a multi-coloured synthetic slug. He leaned against it, put his arms through the straps, bent forward and heaved it onto his back with a grunt. The backpack was nearly bigger than he was. We changed to a second cable car, which took us to Mir station at an altitude of 11,500 feet.

As the cable car lurched up the valley, everything was monochromatic and harsh. The only other people on Elbrus were cross-country skiers in catsuits and soldiers in training. I peered closer, just as a fierce gust of wind flung snow against the window pane. Angry clouds smothered the sun. The conditions looked terrible. My positive mood evaporated. Tiny ice pellets sandpapered our faces as we stepped off the rickety gondola. Visibility was minimal. We could barely see the slopes of Elbrus. As we left the cable car building we sank up to our knees into the fresh snow, which swirled like sand.

A few men ran full pelt up the side of the mountain in thin catsuits, stabbing the slope with climbing poles. They looked fit but insane. I was clearly the only tourist here.

'Training for Elbrus race,' Ivan said, nodding at the runners.

We needed to take one last chairlift to Garabashi station at 12,200 feet, but the creaking, single-seat chairlift was out of order. The single chairs swung from the wire like hangmen.

'You wait here. I will ask for snowcat.' Ivan thrust his skis at me and lumbered towards the line of hulking snow bulldozers. The drivers were smoking in a nearby cabin. Ivan soon disappeared into the icy mist.

Behind me, two French climbers snapped their boots into their skis.

'You're going up in this?' I asked.

'Yes!' declared one. The other shouted: 'It is wonderful conditions! I do not know why everyone else is back in the café down in the valley!' They laughed, waved at me and started trudging up the slope on skis. Within seconds they disappeared into the cloud.

Ivan returned.

'We have to wait. No driver.'

I nodded. The wind whistled like a dismayed coyote, chucking snow against our face masks, down our necks. The visibility was getting worse, but I could still make out the debris that litters the lower flanks of Mount Elbrus.

I knew what awaited us at Garabashi station, our destination. The camps on Mount Elbrus are surprisingly derelict and messy. Barrels Camp, which is next to Garabashi station, used to have running water, steam baths and Jacuzzis. But glacier shifts over the last few decades have rucked up the concrete around Barrels Camp, like a carpet. Broken slabs of concrete litter the grounds, while the kitchen hut is propped up under one corner by a hastily jammed in pile of rocks. The view of the mountains is beautiful, but it is marred by several rusty, weather-beaten pylons. It is hard to take photos without some ugliness getting into the shot. The thought of the awaiting dilapidation depressed me.

'You know what, I don't want to go up in this,' I said.

'What?' Ivan looked less surprised by my decision than my tone.

'I don't want to climb for five or six hours in these conditions. I'm already acclimatised anyway.' I headed back into the gondola station without waiting for Ivan to follow. Snow blew into my ears as I trudged up the frozen stone steps.

Ten minutes later, we re-boarded the gondola and bobbed down to the valley, our skis dry and unused. Tongues of snow roamed like dry ice over the rocky cliffs above us. The two French men I'd spoken to were heading down as well. As we descended out of the clouds, the deserted monochromatic valley rose to meet us. Here and there the dull mud infected the snow, tainting it brown and turning it to sludge. Ivan said nothing the whole trip.

We arrived at the base station. A few minutes later, the Volga pulled up and the driver lumbered out, a rank cigarette jammed in his mouth. He shot a questioning look at Ivan as he helped me stash my skis in the trunk. We piled into the car and drove silently back to the hotel.

On the way, Ivan said he needed to stop in Terskol village to retrieve our climbing permits. He ran up the steps into the permit office while the driver and I waited in the dusky Volga. The dark curtains on the inside of the back windshield were partially drawn and the black synthetic upholstery stank of smoke.

The driver pushed 'play' on the cassette tape player. The dull thumping of house music pulsed through the car like a migraine. We listened in silence. A nightclub ambiance at 9 a.m.

The last time I had listened to house music was the day after I'd climbed Elbrus for the first time. It was a sunny day. I was sitting with five other climbers, packed into a bright yellow van weaving through the Baksan valley on the way back to Mineralnye Vody. Our guide sat in the front with Susan, one of our teammates. From where I sat, I could see both of them reflected in the rear-view mirror. Now that we had climbed Elbrus, Susan had discarded her climbing clothes. She now wore a glittery, skin-tight top. She was barely recognisable under her purple eye shadow and cover-up the consistency of mashed potato as she slouched against our guide and stroked his face. Both of them looked stoned. I was too far away to see properly, but it looked like his hand was up her shirt. I'd turned away, nauseated.

The two of them had vanished for nearly two days as we were snowed in at Barrels Camp. It turned out that they had found their own separate cabin and emerged only for coffee and snacks. It wouldn't have been so bad if he hadn't spent the rest of the time talking about his wife and how great she was. My memories of Elbrus were both sordid and strenuous, which partly explained my lack of enthusiasm for climbing it again.

Ivan returned to the car, snapping me out of the memory. We drove back to the Hotel Teberda. I went straight to my room, wondering how there could still be two more days to go. Time seemed to have slowed right down. I collapsed onto the bed and sank into oblivion.

~

The weather the next morning was calm and cold. It was our last chance to train for the altitude. Our summit attempt was in less than 24 hours.

When Ivan and I arrived at Mir station we were once more engulfed in cloud, but this time Ivan commandeered a snowcat and shoved me, our duffel bags and our skis onto the back of the snorting machine. We rolled up past Barrels Camp, passing men in fatigues shuffling uphill on skis.

'They are soldiers,' Ivan said. 'This is training for army.'

We trundled higher. Suddenly, the clouds disappeared, revealing a deep blue sky streaked with mare's tails. We could see all the way down the mountain for the first time. I caught my breath as I saw Elbrus. The mountain was laden with far more snow than I'd anticipated.

Mount Elbrus sits like an icy two-headed giant astride the border of Georgia and volatile Kabardino-Balkaria. Its twin peaks were created by separate volcanic eruptions: the west summit (*Zapadnaya*) at 18,510 feet and the east summit (*Vostochnaya*) just 69 feet lower. The summits are swathed in an immense ice sheet, 1,300 feet thick in parts, making Elbrus look like a pair of beautiful snow cones separated by a low saddle. Or as some Russian climbers put it: 'Russia is a woman and Mount Elbrus is the breasts.'

The snowcat came to a stop outside a long metal barrel painted blue and yellow. Ivan jumped off. I followed. The beauty of the scenery had energised me. Maybe the climb wouldn't be that tiring. Maybe all that sleep had helped.

'Here is high camp.' Ivan waved a proud hand at our new camp. It was essentially a long cylinder half-buried in the snow. The interior was separated into two sleeping quarters, one at each end, and a seating area in the middle. At a guess, we were at an altitude of around 14,000 feet.

'Where's the toilet?' I asked.

Ivan grinned. 'Everywhere.' He gestured at the clean snow around us.

We ate some slices of cheese and salami, then strapped on our skis. Ivan was determined to reach the top of the Pastukhov Rocks, the curving parallel dorsal fins of a lava ridge that starts at around 15,000 feet and ends at 16,000 feet. We were doing the bare minimum of altitude training before attempting the summit tomorrow, but it was better than nothing.

'We go?' Ivan said.

'Okay.'

Ivan pointed his skis uphill and started slithering up the snowy crest. I followed about 30 feet behind. My legs were heavy and my head was fuzzy.

Come on. You're almost done. Just one more big climb tonight, and you can rest.

Ten minutes in, Ivan started pulling further and further ahead. I cursed and spurred myself on, but my legs were stubborn. It was like wading through mud. Ivan looked back and stopped when he saw the gulf between us.

'I will slow down,' he called with a smile. 'Sorry.'

I nodded and gave him the thumbs up.

It's a nice spring day. It's a nice spring hike. Now come on.

Even at a slower pace, Ivan continued to pull ahead. The harder I tried, the slower I became. I felt so light-headed that I ground to a halt several times, but I always started moving again before Ivan saw me. The gap grew ever wider.

I hate this.

I lifted my head. Ivan was a speck on the slope. Though the sky was blue, the looming summit of Elbrus was swallowed up in a huge, glowering cloud. *Hello*, the mountain seemed to say. *Your nightmare awaits you.*

'Ivan, could you please wait?' I shouted.

He stopped and turned. 'No problem. Anytime you want break, just tell me.' He waited while I shuffled up to him like a zombie.

'Are you tired because of sulphur?' He sniffed the air.

I shook my head, took a swig of water and shoved some candy into my mouth. We hadn't even reached the bottom of the Pastukhov Rocks yet. We set off again.

Come on, get your head right. Keep going, dammit.

I'd never felt this awful on a mountain before. I felt as if I had been hollowed out on the inside.

'Ivan!' He was already so far ahead.

This time he climbed down the slope to me.

'I don't know what's wrong with me, Ivan. I just don't feel right.' Ivan gave me his blank smile again.

'I don't feel safe.' The underlying drumbeat of panic quickened. *I'm scared.*

But most of all, I was tired. I was so fed up of being shunted about. Of living according to someone else's schedule, eating unfamiliar foods, trying to communicate with strangers. I was tired of being trapped in hostile environments. I missed Douglas. I missed familiarity. Most of all, I was exhausted. I just wanted to crawl into bed and shut out the world.

'I want to stop.'

'We have to go to top of Pastukhov Rocks. It is very important.'

'I know. What I mean is –,' I took a quick breath, 'I want to stop the climb. I do not want to climb Elbrus anymore.'

I knew I had good reasons to finish the volcanoes project. I knew that I was lucky to have got this far, despite my bad lungs. I needed to climb this final volcano while I had the chance.

But I didn't care anymore. I didn't care if I didn't finish the project. I didn't care if I let Dad down. I just wanted out.

Without another word, we headed back down to camp.

~

That night, the wind roared at 50 kilometres per hour and the temperature sank to minus 37 degrees Celsius. Ivan and I were sharing the barrel hut with a group of rowdy men from Andorra, and when they headed out for the summit at 3 a.m. I remained unmoving in my bunk. I woke to the slam of the metal door, then listened to the wind scream outside the cracked window just behind my head.

If ever there was a time to lose your nerve, this was probably a good one.

Normally I took summit nights as they came. Until they arrived, I tried to think of them as little as possible, as a form of self-preservation. This time was different. Somehow I just hadn't been able to get summit night out of my mind. I still remembered everything from my last climb of Elbrus four years ago. My mind had ferreted out every memory of every slope and struggle along the way. The prospect of doing it all again overwhelmed me.

Hours later, when the sky was calm and blue again, I dragged myself out of bed. Ivan was slicing cheese and salami. We ate in silence. I sat at the wooden table, cradling a cup of coffee and staring at our skis, which were propped against the wall.

Ivan hailed a snowcat and bundled me on to the back. I rode the machine down to Mir station while Ivan skied alongside us. I watched him carve graceful wide arcs in the virgin snow with ease and strength, and felt diminished in every way.

By the time we reached the valley, my stomach was full of despair. How could I have given up so easily? I had the summit within reach. At the same time, I felt overwhelming relief at being off the mountain. Ivan and I sat on some steps to wait for the driver. I realised that I had forgotten to empty the bottle of urine under the bed in our hut.

The Volga pulled up and honked. The driver got out, shook my hand, chortled and said something to Ivan in Russian.

'What did he say?'

'He asks, are you lazy,' Ivan said without expression.

I shrugged and got into the car.

That evening I walked down to the village in search of food. We had come down a day early, which meant the hotel hadn't prepared any dinner for us.

'I will meet you at 7 p.m. for dinner,' Ivan said. We retired to our rooms to unpack.

Seven p.m. came and went. Perhaps Ivan had lost track of time. I sat on the bed and waited, famished. Ivan never showed up.

At 9 p.m., I sat at a table in an empty café, watching Russian music videos on the overhead TV while the cook made what I hoped would be chicken kebab. A dried fish lay on a plate on top of the bar, its withered lips puckered mournfully at me. I stared into my black coffee, which was missing the milk – *moloko* – I had asked for.

Today would have been summit day. Not only that, it would have been the culmination of the Seven Volcanoes Project, four months after climbing Mount Sidley. Antarctica felt like a long time ago; I felt like I'd aged ten years. I stirred my coffee.

I should never have come here.

~

That night, all I could think of was a comment one of Dad's friends had made, many years ago.

'Some women lose their nerve when they get older.' The statement had stuck in my mind ever since.

There is more than one way to lose your nerve. Sometimes it snaps, wetly and invisibly, like an overstretched tendon. Sometimes, it withers from lack of use, from avoiding challenges.

Mountain climbers often talked about strength. Strong people were able to carry half their body weight in a backpack. Strong people could break trail through fresh snow for hours, and still have the energy to build ice walls around camp.

Strong people did not allow their nerve to break.

It was one thing to claw at the edge of my courage, fighting to nail down one flapping corner before it all blew away. It was quite another to watch my courage wither and recede, and do absolutely nothing about it.

What did that say about me? Why is it that, when I needed to make just one final push to climb the last mountain, I had simply given up?

~

Ivan and I checked out of Hotel Teberda early the next morning. As Ivan emerged from his room a few doors down, a stale plume of beer drifted down the corridor towards me.

'Morning,' I said.

'Good morning.' No smile.

The hotel manager peppered Ivan with questions as we checked out. She trained wary eyes on me as she spoke in Russian. Ivan replied something about the Pastukhov Rocks. She nodded and stared at me. Ivan didn't bother to translate.

We drove back to Mineralnye Vody in silence. It felt like weeks since I'd first arrived. I leaned my head against the window and stared out at the semi-industrial villages and Soviet-style half-builds dotting the Baksan valley. How could a place with such natural beauty look so ugly?

Three hours later, we drew up at the entrance of Mineralnye Vody airport. The departures hall was large and modern, the opposite of the grim arrivals hall only four days earlier. I stepped out of the car and into the sun. My climbing clothes were stifling now we were back at lower altitude.

Ivan helped me drag my duffel bag to the waiting area. Check-in for my flight had not yet started. All around, relatively well-dressed people bound for Moscow milled about, chatting, drinking coffee, browsing the shops. Doing normal things.

We sat down on a pair of plastic orange seats in front of the check-in desks. After a pause, I turned to Ivan.

'Listen. It's not you, it's me,' I began, as if it were a bizarre kind of break-up. 'I don't know why I am so tired.'

Again, the blank, polite smile. I suddenly realised that Ivan didn't give a damn.

'And if you want to leave now that's okay. I can check myself in–'

He was gone before I could finish my sentence.

~

Back in the lush greenery of Buckinghamshire, I tried not to think about what had happened on Elbrus. I still couldn't figure out why I had given up. Was it exhaustion? My lungs? Lack of courage? I didn't know, and I didn't have the energy to think about it.

All I knew was, I couldn't face another desperate, freezing night of fighting to the summit.

Everyone told me I had made the right decision.

'Elbrus was the one I was worried about because of the weather conditions, but I didn't want to discourage you,' Douglas said. 'I think you're just really exhausted. You need a rest.'

'I suppose you're right.' I turned away and walked into the kitchen. 'Want some lunch?' I didn't want to talk about climbing.

Douglas looked at me for a second, then nodded.

I immersed myself in everyday minutiae. I laundered my climbing clothes and left them in a big messy pile in the storage room. I watched my favourite TV sitcoms. I ate every 2 hours. I now weighed less than 53 kilogrammes, which meant I was underweight. The rolls of fat around my waist were long gone. I looked pale and skinny. Not in an athletic way, but like someone who has lost too much weight too quickly due to illness.

~

Over the next few days, the universe sent me signs that I was right to give up mountain climbing. The first came in the form of an email from Mom. She had forwarded me the link to a news article.

'There is a report about an experienced woman climber (a doctor) who fell off the highest peak in North America,' she wrote. '38 years old. VERY DANGEROUS BUSINESS this is!'

I clicked on the link.

'Oh my God,' I wrote back. 'I know her.'

Sylvia and I had climbed Mount Elbrus together in 2010. I could still picture her standing below the Pastukhov Rocks, hands on hips, waiting for the rest of us to catch up.

Sylvia had died trying to climb Denali in Alaska. Both she and her partner were amateur climbers, but rather than take the conventional

West Buttress route, they had attempted a much riskier climb. They were caught in a vicious storm and became separated. Sylvia fell to her death from Denali Pass. It took over two weeks to bring home her remains. The pair had embarked on the climb before climbing season had really started, which meant that none of the park rangers were acclimatised enough to retrieve her.

I closed my laptop, my mind churning. So much about mountain climbing depended on luck. If ever there was a sign that I should forget about mountains, this was it. It wasn't worth it. Too dangerous.

That wasn't the only sign. My whole reason for embarking on the volcanoes project was to keep the memory of Dad alive. I'd thought that regaining memories of him was the only way I could feel closer to him, and make up for my absence during the last years of his life. The problem was, not all the resurrected memories were happy ones.

As a child, I often sensed a coiled anger in Dad. He lashed out if he felt slighted. Even some of the happier memories have an angry lining to them. Even on those perfect summer days in the south of France, roaring around the villages in his open-top convertible. The sun burned the top of my head, glinted off Dad's sunglasses and watch. There was a smell of baked earth and warm Orangina. Dad would take the corners at an insanely high speed and I'd shriek in excitement, which made him laugh as well.

Truth was, Dad was an angry driver. The cars he bought were always aggressive, powerful machines. Or maybe I just think that because of the way he drove.

Dad took charge of the car, the same way he dominated everyone in his life. He drove the fastest after dark, when he would hurl the car at turns the way a slalom skier throws himself down a mountain. It was a dare. He wanted to scare me, so he could laugh at my lack of courage. My sharpest childhood memories are of those late-night drives, headlights illuminating insects in mid-flight in the murk, the velocity nearly flinging the car screaming off the tarmac. It was then that I felt him taunt: *Scared, little girl?*

For years I sat, a stony-faced child, as we careened through country roads. I never gave him the satisfaction of seeing my fear. I locked it in a box.

Stay calm. Stay calm. Don't lose it.

I didn't like these memories. Some things were better forgotten.

The worst memory, though, did not technically include Dad. It was something Mom had said during those dark days after Dad died. We were sitting in our shared bedroom on a dark evening.

'You remember that time you said you were considering returning to Europe?' Mom said, almost as if she were thinking aloud.

I looked up. 'Wait, when did I say that?' This was news to me.

'Over the phone. You said you'd had a bad week in Shanghai and were thinking about coming back. Dad couldn't stop smiling for days.'

I hadn't said that. Had I?

I tried to remember. There had been so many phone calls. Then suddenly, I remembered. I'd had a bad work week. I was venting to my father on the phone. Something about a bad interview. Or maybe it was office politics. What had I said?

I shut my eyes.

The memory returned. At the end of my rant, I'd said, 'I may as well pack it in and come back to the UK.' Something like that. I hadn't meant it. It was just one of those frustrated, throwaway comments.

'Dad was so happy,' Mom said. 'He was like a changed person. It was like a new lease of life for your father and I.'

Oh my God. The whole year before his death, Dad had thought I was coming back. He must have been crushed when he realised I had no intention of returning. My stomach twisted.

A horrible thought surfaced. If I hadn't left for China to pursue my career, would Dad still be alive? Had I stayed, would his health have been better? Had his sadness at my departure somehow contributed to his getting cancer? And the worst thought of all: If I hadn't left for Shanghai to pack up my apartment, just after he was diagnosed, would he have died so suddenly?

I wanted to scream.

Your father died of a broken heart, a voice whispered, *and it was all your fault.*

~

While I brooded at home over the past, I realised how much I had missed of the present.

The first sign: My cats no longer recognised me. Morag and Ethel, only sweet kittens a few months ago, were now fully-grown cats. I had been away so long that I was now a stranger to them. Every time I called them they gave me a catty scathing look.

Second: I discovered that one of my close friends was having a baby. She was already seven months pregnant when I heard the news. I'd been so out of touch that I hadn't even known she was trying to start a family.

Third: Even Mom had developed new hobbies. She no longer answered the phone as if she had been waiting next to it; sometimes I couldn't even reach her.

'Ma? Where were you? I called several times.'

'Oh, sorry. I was out walking with the neighbours again,' she said.

'You went on a walk? But you hate going on walks.'

'Well, turns out it's actually quite fun. We walked five kilometres today.'

'Five kilometres? Really' I stared into space, dumbfounded.

'Do you even have shoes for walking?' I pictured Mom striding across the French fields in high heels.

'I dug out my old gym shoes. They still fit!' She laughed.

While I had been stuck up on some mountain or other the past few months, the world had moved on without me. I was absent so often that I was missing out on the lives of my loved ones, just as I had during the years I spent chasing a journalism career in Hong Kong and Shanghai.

'By the way, I want to give you the money for another attempt on Mount Elbrus,' Mom added. 'The idea of you climbing mountains scares me, but I know it's important to you and I want you to complete your volcanoes.'

I blinked back tears. 'Thanks, Ma. I really appreciate it. But I don't know if I can go away again. I'm just so grateful to be home. I've missed so much.'

'I know. You've been away for a long time. But still, think it over.'

~

All of a sudden, it was mid-May. I had brooded long enough. I knew I had to do something big, something difficult, to wake myself up.

'I want to come flying with you,' I said to Douglas.

'Sure, alright.'

'And I'd love to do some aerobatics with you as well,' I added. He usually avoided doing manoeuvres when I was in the back of his plane. They made me nauseous, the same way climbing gave him vertigo.

Douglas tried to hide his surprise. 'Okay then.'

So one beautiful evening in May, I went flying with my husband.

We drove to Denham Aerodrome. Douglas rolled out a single-propeller plane the size of a canoe. I squinted against the sunlight as we clambered into the two-seater Vans RV8. He was in front, I was in the back. I buckled myself in and put on my headset, then reached up and pushed the glass canopy forward to Douglas. He reached back and pulled it shut. We took off.

Ten minutes later, somewhere over Amersham, Douglas started throwing the aircraft into a series of barrel rolls. Then, a nosedive.

We were a thousand feet up in the sky, staring straight at the fields below. We were essentially standing upright, encased in a tiny plane, watching the fields and villages of Buckinghamshire through the windshield below our feet. Like a dagger falling out of the sky, our plane rushed to stab the ground below.

Don't react.

The altimeter plunged. Douglas laughed as we pulled out of the nosedive, like it was nothing.

'You alright?' his voice buzzed in my headset.

'Fine.'

Ten minutes later, we landed at the aerodrome and taxied off the grass towards the hangar. 'Did you feel sick at all?' Douglas asked.

I bit back the vomit. 'No.'

'Really? Not even a bit?'

'Nope.'

'Good for you! You'll get used to it.'

'I hope so.'

We stopped outside the hangar. Douglas shut off the engine. We looked out at the bright green airfield, which was lit up by the late afternoon sun. I watched Douglas quietly jot down the flight time in his logbook. He was the bravest person I knew.

For him, throwing a tiny aircraft around the sky was like going to the shop.

~

That evening, Douglas and I cycled into Denham to pick up some groceries. It was a warm evening, but I hardly noticed as I stormed past him on the home stretch.

'Ha-ha!' I shouted as I overtook him, pounding the pedals like a piston train. My quads felt firm and thick. 'I win!' I coasted the last few feet, taking my feet off the pedals. The amber evening sunlight warmed my shoulders.

Suddenly Douglas flashed past me in a blaze of sweaty T-shirt and swinging plastic grocery bags. He blew a raspberry as he passed. He beat me to the house, jammed his brakes on and then turned around, grinning, and held up two fingers.

'Nice!' I shouted, laughing. I drew up alongside him and got off my bike. The bottle of rosé in my backpack pressed on my spine. We put our bikes away and I realised that I felt well again. Better than well. And then I remembered something Ardeshir Soltani had said to me in the car, the day after I climbed Mount Damavand.

'Sometimes, it is good. Sometimes it is very hard.' He'd stared straight ahead as we drove down the highway. 'I tell myself during the hard times, "Never, ever will I climb again."'

He turned and smiled at me. 'But then you wait a day, two days, and you start to feel better. And you forget the pain. And you remember how much you love the mountains, and you go back.'

NOW

Mountain climbing is a bit like childbirth. Both are physically painful, and more to the point, both cause a strange kind of amnesia. The exhausted climber watches the sunrise from the summit and forgets the brutal climb. The mother holds her new baby and forgets the pain of labour. That's the only way the climber can ever climb again, or the mother consider having another baby. To recover, you have to forget.

I was therefore happy to return to Cheget village after five weeks and find I barely recognised it. The bitter cold of April was gone. The muddy roads had dried up and the dull earth at the centre of Cheget village had given birth to green. Mount Elbrus's twin peaks bobbed like two seal heads and the sky, once so stark and white, was now a gentle blue, cradling a glowing sun.

Chairlifts chugged up and down the green and white slopes. A lively little market in Cheget village square sold hand-knitted woollen socks, sheepskins, T-shirts and local produce. Summer tourists stood around smiling, chatting, taking pictures. I felt alert. My breathing was better. Cheget village was alive again, and so was I.

'Today would have been a great summit day,' I said. Next to me, Tina nodded under her white sun hat. Tina, my ally from Pico de Orizaba in Mexico, had come to join me on Elbrus. I'd called her at the last minute and told her of my breakdown. She didn't hesitate. Tina few from California to Heathrow airport, scooped me up, and flew with me to Russia.

This is usually the part in the movie where all the loose ends are tied up, but I was not fooled. Something was definitely going to go wrong on my last expedition, because something had gone wrong on almost all of my mountain climbs. Postcard-pretty Mount Elbrus was plotting something. That evening, I was proven right.

'The weather on the mountain is not good,' said Igor, the assistant guide. 'Your guide Anna, is still on Elbrus.' Tina and I were in the dining room of our hostel, eating borscht. We exchanged a glance.

'How bad is it?' Tina asked.

'The weather on the summit is very bad. There is a lot of wind and snow. She cannot get down so she will wait on Mount Elbrus.' Tina frowned down at her borscht.

'When will you know more, do you think?' I asked. Our mountain guide was stranded on Elbrus. Not good.

'When we know more, we will tell you.'

~

The next evening, Tina and I met a woman wearing the tallest, spikiest pair of high heels I had ever seen. Her long, peroxide-blonde hair fell across her shoulder and down past her waist like a bright yellow streak. Her face was heavily made up with black kohl eyeliner rimming her huge blue eyes. She was dressed to go clubbing. My first thought was that she was coming to tell us that our guide was still stuck on Elbrus.

'Hello, my name is Anna. I am your guide,' she said. Tina and I looked up. We were sitting on the floor, surrounded by climbing gear.

'You made it down off Elbrus!' I stood up and went to shake her hand. Anna did not smile. I hoped it was only because she was tired.

'How was the acclimatisation hike today on Mount Cheget?'

'Fine,' I said. The climb had been easy.

'I check your gear now, yes?'

Tina and I nodded.

'Ice axe!' Anna said.

'Yes!' We brandished them from different ends of the room.

'Crampons!'

'Yes!'

'Boots!'

'Right here!'

Finally, a smile. 'Okay. Tell me your names again?'

'Tina!'

'Sophie!'

Anna's face softened behind the heavy makeup. She peered at me. 'Sophie is the name of my daughter,' She smiled at me, then cleared her throat.

'Okay, then I wish you ladies good night. We meet tomorrow for acclimatisation climb.'

Anna whipped her bright blonde hair around like a cape and clattered back downstairs.

~

The next morning, we waited for the chairlift to open. Tina and I watched as Anna smoked with another guide as they sat on a wooden bench. We had already reached an altitude of nearly 13,000 feet on Mount Elbrus. It was warm; the low cloud was stifling. I slung my backpack to the ground and took off my outer top. Behind us Mir gondola station hummed and clanked. It spat out a few more climbers.

'Girls, put your backpacks on please.' Anna stubbed out her cigarette. Tina and I strapped ourselves into our rucksacks and followed Anna up the bulldozed snow track to Barrels Camp.

'Okay girls, today we go to 14,000 feet,' Anna shouted. 'We go slow to acclimatise, no hurry.'

I hadn't done any training in five weeks. I wasn't acclimatised, unlike Tina, who had been hiking in the Sierra. I wasn't even sure if my new asthma medication was working.

We trudged up to Barrels Camp, then continued across a wide snow field. The three of us fell into a rhythm. Every so often, a cool breeze freshened our faces and sought out the crack between our collars and our necks.

In mid-June, the area around Mir looked more like a village square than a cable car terminus. The rickety little stands by the chairlifts sold handmade clothes, sunglasses and trinkets. A headscarf-clad woman in non-climbing clothes slumped in a folding chair, smoking and beckoned to us to inspect her wares.

Behind her, the dark doorway of a shipping container-turned-café leaked drum 'n' bass music. Snowcat drivers, climbers and guides sat on the wooden bench outside the container. I realised I could now read Cyrillic writing. 'Café,' said the spray painted sign over it. 'Chai.' Whooping men zipped around on skidoos, going nowhere in particular. They waved at Anna as they yodelled past. Far above us by the Pastukhov Rocks, miniscule climbers dotted the slopes like ants.

An hour later, the snow field grew into a steep slope. Anna stopped to talk to another guide and waved us on. I took the lead.

We climbed past the yellow and blue barrel I'd stayed in at the end of April. Was my 5-litre bottle of urine still tucked under the bed? We overtook the exact spot of my breakdown. Suddenly, I felt unstoppable. My arms pumped in precise rhythm with my legs. High as we were, the air felt thick with oxygen.

I turned to see how Tina was doing. To my surprise, she had fallen behind.

'Hey, sorry,' I called. 'I didn't know I was going too fast. I would have slowed down.'

Tina grimaced and shook her head, breathing hard. 'It's fine.'

Anna panted up to us. 'You are going very fast.'

'Sorry, I didn't realise,' I said. 'I was just really enjoying the climb.'

'No, no! It is good!' Anna looked relieved. She took the lead again, and for the next few hours the three of us climbed like clockwork.

When we reached 14,000 feet, Anna gestured to Tina and said, 'You are so strong, like Terminator. Tina the Terminator.'

The expedition was off to a good start.

~

For the next two days, the expedition went suspiciously well. Tina and I acclimatised without any problems. My lungs were fine. The weather was good.

Summit day, however, brought storm clouds to the top of Elbrus. Everything had been so easy so far that I was not surprised by the change of weather.

Tina and I went through the usual preparations. Anything to distract us from the big climb awaiting us. We tipped out our rucksacks and combed through our gear. I dug out my chemical foot warmers, extra supplies of carbohydrate, extra gloves and clean socks, and checked all my clothes for damage. When we were done, we laid out everything we were going to take with us neatly on an unoccupied bunk bed. We finished our novels. We napped. We drank lots of water.

For our last meal, Tina and I sat with a group of German climbers at high camp, which was a shipping container. Tina chatted with the Germans about the night ahead. I was so tense I could hardly talk. My earlier confidence had vanished. Tina looked at me and understood. I took a breath and hoped there wouldn't be a repeat of my last breakdown on Elbrus.

Anna huddled with the other Russian guides and examined the weather forecasts, which changed by the hour. They pointed to maps of the summit, apparently arguing over the condition of the slopes. Anna stood up and stared down into her cup of tea.

'Summit day,' Anna muttered, as if to herself. Then she exhaled, shook her head and gave Tina and me a forced smile. 'We do briefing, yes?'

Tina and I sat up straighter.

'Alright. Weather looks okay for tonight. Maybe some snow, but wind is not strong. We will see. Please remember to pack your mittens, your balaclava, your harness, and all your warmest layers. We leave wearing crampons and harness.'

Anna had the kind of gaze that gave you courage. She looked at Tina, then at me.

'Your condition is good. You are ready.' She nodded. 'I will see you for breakfast at 2 a.m. Good night.'

~

That night, I couldn't sleep. Maybe it was the altitude, or the dread of the summit climb. Tina and I lay in our bunks in the pitch dark, trying to fall asleep. My mind wouldn't leave me alone. I kept revisiting the first time I climbed Elbrus, in 2010. Specifically, I kept replaying something our guide had said as we sat in the dilapidated kitchen hut at Barrels Camp.

'Some mountains, when I'm up there alone at night, it's like being on the moon,' he said. It was the only time I'd seen him with a serious expression. 'Mountain climbing cleans your mind.'

I knew the feeling. Over the years, I'd stared at the moon from the slopes of so many mountains. I'd lain in my tent on Aconcagua with my head outside, staring up at the glittering night sky. Or watched the moonlit waves of Laguna Verde. I loved the beautiful isolation of the mountains. But the problem with being on the moon is, everyone I loved was far away. They were all back on Earth, moving on with their lives. Every step I took on some moon-kissed trail was a moment I sacrificed to the mountain.

Mom was right. Had I been around more, I would have had more memories of Dad. The less I witnessed, the less I had to remember. Even now, on this volcanoes journey, I was doing the same thing. I'd left my family behind once again to pursue a great dream, just like I had left Mom and Dad to pursue my career in China. Had the Seven Volcanoes Project really been necessary? I was missing out on real life, the good and the bad. Paying the bills. Commuting to work. Watching TV with Douglas in the evenings. Life wasn't just about skipping over the boring bits. It was about witnessing every last detail. To say yes to one moment, is to say yes to them all – from the mundane to the gut-wrenching.

What good was it having loved ones, when you never spent time with them? I needed to spend less time chasing impossible goals and live more in the present.

I don't want to live on the moon anymore.

I closed my eyes and fell asleep.

~

Anna woke us up a few hours later.

'It is 1.15 a.m.,' she said. 'There is a lightning storm at the summit.'

Tina and pulled on our outer layers. Anna was in the kitchen, poring over the weather charts with the other guides.

'How does it look? Can we still go up?' I asked.

'We wait an hour, see how it looks then.' Anna frowned, as if she didn't like our chances.

An hour later, the lightning was gone but the storm lingered. Tina and I stumbled about in our dark dormitory with only our head torches to see with. We pulled on our plastic boots and crampons and strapped on our balaclavas and face masks. I ran to the outhouse for one last pit stop but found there was a queue of at least three other nervous climbers. The snowcat was waiting. Climbers pulled themselves onto the back of the machine. My stomach churned in panic.

'Tina, buddy check?' My voice sounded shrill.

'Sure.' We checked each other's harnesses, down jackets and crampons. Nothing looked out of place.

I grabbed my rucksack, clambered over the snowcat's gigantic treads and flung myself into a seat. Tina and I sat side by side, facing the front. Four climbers sat facing us: people whom I had just eaten with but who were now unrecognisable in their balaclavas, goggles and hoods. Snow flew in and out of the snowcat's high beams like confetti. Otherwise, darkness enveloped us.

The snowcat's engine thrummed. There was the occasional shout in Russian. The machine lurched forward, and as it gathered steam the tall funnel spewed exhaust in our faces. We gripped to the edge of our seats as the bucking, snorting tractor carried us up the slope.

We reached the Pastukhov Rocks and jumped out. Behind us, the golden eyes of more snowcats shone through the darkness. The drivers swept the slope with searchlights. Every time the lights swept over us we looked like astronauts, intent on some sinister and lunatic night mission.

I'd thought I was acclimatised, but now I wasn't so sure. My legs shook. My chest felt tight. I took a deep breath, gripped my climbing poles more tightly, and took my first step towards the summit.

~

This summit night was different from all the others, because it felt like I was climbing in a body that was not mine. I set my legs on auto-climb and watched as the line of climbers stepped, breathed, stepped, breathed, in front of me. When the others complained, I didn't hear them. When we took a 5-minute break, I ate and drank without tasting anything. For once, I climbed with total detachment.

The plush snow creaked under our crampons. The air was dry and chilly. Dawn arrived as we reached the traverse on the slanting shelf at 16,700 feet, turning the horizon into molten orange. The sky turned pink, then turquoise. We took another break. As I sipped hot tea from my thermos, Tina and I gazed out at the Caucasus range that materialised with the sunrise. We had long passed the spot where I had given up during my last climb of Elbrus with Ivan, but there was still so much farther to go.

We reached the couloir at 17,500 feet, which traverses to the saddle between Elbrus' two peaks. On our right, we sank our ice axes into the ice and snow bank for support. To our left, the snowy ravine fell away below us. By the time we arrived at the saddle at 17,550 feet, my right arm was in pain from the constant lifting and re-planting of the ice axe, but I hardly noticed. In the saddle, the sun was warm but the wind was fierce. The wind could seriously complicate the climb by turning the slopes to ice.

When my lungs tightened up, I took a puff from my inhaler. When I felt tired, I did the rest-step. Some of the Germans were flagging, climbing more and more slowly. It was perhaps minus 20 degrees Celsius, but it didn't feel cold. Anna, Tina and I kept going. We reached the sheer mountain face to the summit plateau.

'Be very careful, it is very dangerous here,' Anna shouted from the front of the group. 'Watch your feet very carefully.' The first time I had climbed this slope, a woman had lost her footing and slid a 100 feet down the mountain, head first. She had screamed the whole way. Luckily, she wasn't hurt. Tina and I dug in our ice axes and crampons, and kept going.

The 30–35 degree slope took us up to an outcrop of rocks. We clipped ourselves into the fixed rope and teetered around towards the summit plateau, the slope to our right suddenly yawning away into the saddle below.

'Be careful!' Anna shouted again. A few minutes later, we unclipped from the fixed line and dragged ourselves over the top of the summit plateau. The summit of Elbrus was now in sight.

~

The summit of Elbrus was an unassuming snowy knoll not much higher than we were. It was only 3,000 feet away. We took a quiet break. The other climbers pulled themselves over the edge of the summit plateau. Some flopped onto the snow gasping like fish. I was breathing heavily from the exertion and the altitude, but for once I felt invigorated, as if the climb was actually giving me energy rather than draining it. Tina sat down beside me and I could tell from her silence that she was getting tired.

'How are you feeling?' I dug out some fruit juice and sugary snacks and shoved them into my mouth.

'Alright.'

'Not much farther now. We're on the home stretch.'

Tina nodded.

'Okay team, let's go!' Anna called.

As soon as we resumed climbing, my detachment evaporated. The summit grew nearer. Soon, it was only 150 feet away. The cloud bank watched us from below the edges of the plateau, pierced by rays of light. The wind rustled the hood of my anorak and all I could see was the pure white path before me, like a shining path mid-sky.

My God, it's almost over. I crossed a field of pure white, under an ocean of sky, the redeeming sun. Something shifted, and everything turned the colour of heaven. I was reduced, simplified, as if the light was shining through me to reveal all that I was: skeleton, sinew, and memories.

Fifty feet.

I couldn't stop thinking of my father. I gasped behind my face mask and marched faster, arms and legs moving in unison. Dad carrying me in his arms through the hospital doors. Dad striding up hills in the New Territories, grinning and waving me on. Dad gripping my arm as they put on the breathing mask. Dad looking up from the hospital bed with those unearthly glowing eyes. I began to cry.

Twenty feet.

We reached the point where the Earth met the sky. I stamped in my crampons and surged upwards. All of a sudden, I had wings. I had never felt stronger. A few seconds later, Tina joined me.

We had done it. This was as high as we could go. We were surrounded by pure beauty. White slopes above a blanket of cloud.

Everyone was slapping our backs, laughing, giving us bear hugs.

Dad, Dad. I'm so sorry. Forgive me for not saying goodbye.

Tina and I took a summit photo.

Dad, I miss you. I love you. I'll see you soon.

A few minutes later, we started on the miles and miles back down to Earth.

~

That night, we celebrated in Cheget village. Dozens of climbers filled the warm restaurant with chatter and excitement. The staff had set two long tables with baskets of bread and pitchers of beer, and as soon as we sat down Anna brandished a large bottle of vodka. A loud cheer went up. The staff brought out plate after plate of borsht, pelmeni and steak.

'To everyone, congratulations on climbing Mount Elbrus!' Anna shouted.

'Cheers!' the rest of the room shouted. Triumph and relief was written on the faces of the climbers, some of whom had deep shadows under their eyes and sweat-matted hair.

Anna turned to Tina and I. 'You guys were the perfect team,' she shouted over the festive din. She tipped some vodka into Tina's shot glass.

'Oh, I don't really drink—,' Tina covered the shot glass with her hand.

Anna winked at her. 'Come, Terminator, a little bit,' and filled the glass. I sniffed mine. It smelled expensive. The climbing agency had brought out the good stuff.

Anna held up her glass. 'Really, you were great,' she said. 'You had all the right equipment. You didn't ask any stupid questions. You didn't complain. Just – go.' She pumped her arms up and down like the energiser bunny.

Tina took a sip of vodka and wrinkled her nose. I smiled and lifted my glass, feeling free. Now that I had climbed the volcanoes, I had the rest of my life to get on with.

'Congratulations!' Anna shouted.

'Thank you,' I said. We clinked glasses again.

'And thank you for coming with me to Elbrus,' I said to Tina. 'It means a lot to me. I couldn't have made it without you.'

Tina smiled. 'Well, you know, if it weren't for you, I probably wouldn't have come out to Russia or gone on such adventurous climbs.'

We smiled at each other. I didn't have the heart to tell Tina about the news I'd just received. That morning, Guinness World Records had sent me an email.

Unfortunately, after thoroughly reviewing your application with members of our research team, we are afraid to say that we're unable to accept your proposal as a Guinness World Records title.

They hadn't been able to create a record category for the Seven Volcanic Summits. They couldn't confirm whether Damavand in Iran or Ka-er-daxi in China was the highest volcano in Asia.

I'd been chasing an illusion all these months. The Seven Volcanoes record didn't exist. The record was never meant to be mine. Or anybody's, for that matter. I looked around the room. Climbers were stuffing their faces with food, laughing, getting drunk. The restaurant staff watched us from behind the counter with amusement. I closed my eyes. I wanted to remember every last detail.

I wasn't going to chase the past anymore. I'd been living in this wistful, grief-stricken world for so long. I knew I would never really forgive myself for not being there for Dad. But the truth was, there was no way to repair my mistake. We only have one chance to appreciate the people we love, and I'd squandered mine. I no longer wanted to punish myself or search for long-lost memories, when there was so much to cherish in the present. Amnesia wasn't always a bad thing. Sometimes, the only way to heal is to forget.

'What are you climbing next?' Anna asked. 'Which mountain?'

'No plans,' I said. 'I'm going to take life as it comes.'

The author, Sophie Cairns, and her husband, Douglas.

INDEX

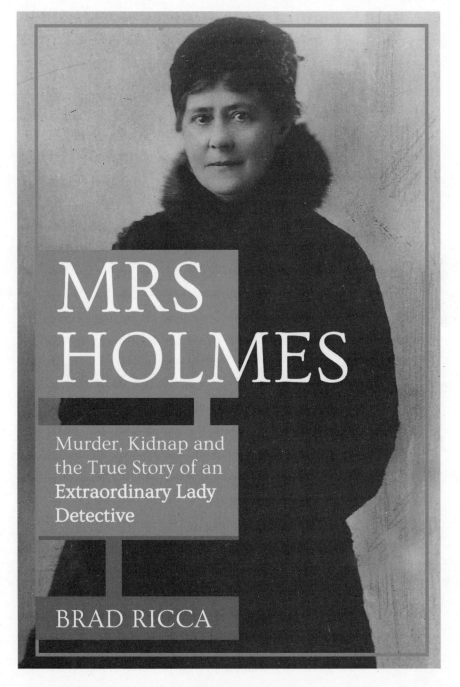